Free to Write

Free to Write

A Journalist Teaches Young Writers • Roy Peter Clark

With a Foreword by Donald M. Murray

Heinemann
Portsmouth, NH

Heinemann Educational Books, Inc.
70 Court Street   Portsmouth, NH   03801
Offices and agents throughout the world

10 9 8 7 6 5 4 3 2

The following have generously given permission to use extended quotations from copyrighted works: "The Shells of Bermuda" by Peter Meinke originally appeared in *Negative Capability* (1984) and is reprinted by permission of the author. "Uncle George and Uncle Stefan" by Peter Meinke originally appeared in *The Apalachee Quarterly*, No. 22 (1985) and is reprinted by permission of the author. Selection from Russell Baker, *Growing Up* (New York: Congdon & Weed, 1982), reprinted by permission of the publisher. Selections from Jean Shepherd, *In God We Trust: All Others Pay Cash* (New York: Doubleday/ Dolphin Books, 1972) reprinted by permission of the publisher. Material by Linda Lewis quoted by permission of the author and the publisher, *Principal* magazine. Selection from Donald Murray, *A Writer Teaches Writing*, 2d ed. (Boston: Houghton Mifflin, 1984) reprinted by permission of the author. Material from Neil Postman, *The Disappearance of Childhood*, copyright © 1982 by Neil Postman; reprinted by permission of Delacorte Press. Selection from George Orwell, "Why I Write," copyright © 1953 by Sonia Brownell Orwell; renewed 1981 by Mrs. George K. Perutz, Mrs. Miriam Gross, Dr. Michael Dickson, Executors of the Estate of Sonia Brownell Orwell; reprinted from "Why I Write" in *Such, Such Were the Joys* by George Orwell by permission of Harcourt Brace Jovanovich, Inc.

On the cover: Students from Bay Point Middle School Amy Kenyon and William Packer interview St. Petersburg paramedic John Baker. (Cover photo by Ricardo Ferro.)

Library of Congress Cataloging-in-Publication Data
Clark, Roy Peter.
  Free to write.

  Bibliography: p.
  Includes index.
  1. Creative writing (Elementary education) 2. First person narrative—Study and teaching (Elementary) 3. Journalism—Methodology. 4. Learning by discovery. 5. Group work in education. I. Title.
LB1576.C562 1986   372.6'23   86-14851
ISBN 0-435-08256-6

Designed by Maria Szmauz
Printed in the United States of America

To Alison, Emily, Lauren,
and all the children
who helped me write this book

Contents

14 **The Writer at Home** • Many good writers begin writing as children. They publish neighborhood newspapers, share their writing with friends and parents, or simply escape into the pleasure of their personal writing. The voice of the child develops early and grows with the writer. Teachers and parents can learn how to nurture young writers and reinforce their inclination to express themselves on the page. **195**

15 **Learning from Children** • Children who write every day will reveal their problems and concerns to teachers. Students may write about personal anxieties, family problems, their health, important things that affect the quality of their schoolwork. Teachers can use this knowledge to find the best way to help individual students learn. In the role of editor, the teacher supports the student as a writer. In the role of substitute parent, the teacher nurtures the student as a person. **209**

16 **Celebrate Student Writing** • Teachers of writing rarely complain about the shortcomings of students. Instead, they are inclined to celebrate children's triumphs, even the little ones. This chapter contains an anthology of student writing with an analysis of the strengths of each story. **221**

17 **Teachers at Work** • Teachers who want to grow in their craft seek out opportunities for professional development. Teachers learn best from the good work of other teachers and from writing their own stories. They also learn from direct observation of writing students. A program called Writers' Camp is described, in which teachers and young writers work together and learn from each other. **255**

Foreword

This exceptional book brings the working world of journalism together with the elementary and middle school classroom. At last students and teachers can practice what professional writers know about their craft.

Free to Write is woven from the many diverse strands in the life of the author. Dr. Roy Peter Clark, an authority on Chaucer, not only wrote scholarly articles while he was teaching literature and composition at Auburn University at Montgomery, Alabama, but also wrote journalistic essays for *The New York Times*.

This unusual practice of what he was preaching in his composition classes led to Roy's being hired to work with writers on one of the best newspapers in the country, the *St. Petersburg [Florida] Times*. From that experience as a writing coach and from research, Roy wrote an influential report on writing in American newspapers for the American Society of Newspaper Editors.

In a delightful reversal of normal career order, Roy became a writing coach, helping professionals with their writing, and then, when he was an authority on the subject, started to work in a newspaper city room to learn what he had been teaching. Nobody is more amused by this than Roy himself, who has always demonstrated the courage to commit himself, to stick his neck out, to try something worth trying.

After working in the city room, Roy knew he would not return to the world of the university. He was, however, able to remain in education. He joined The Poynter Institute, then the Modern Media Institute, the organization that owns the *St. Petersburg Times*, and inaugurated a program of seminars in writing and editing for staff members from newspapers across the country.

He continued to be a writer, producing articles for newspapers and magazines, and edited an annual collection of award-winning news stories published by The American Society of Newspaper Editors. These volumes have become texts for both practicing journalists and for university classes, partly because Roy interviewed each writer. These interviews reveal how the master writers produced their stories. The stories and the interviews have become a valuable inventory of research into how professional writers work. It was Roy who added this dimension to what would have been just another anthology of award-winning stories.

Roy is always adding something of himself to any activity in which he is involved. Those who know him well realize that Roy's family is the center of his world. Like most parents, he is intensely interested in the education his children are receiving; unlike most parents, he doesn't just grump and gripe about the schools. He volunteered to go into the classroom of his oldest daughter, Alison, and help with the students' writing.

Her teacher must have gulped, and I have heard that the Pinellas County School System in Florida did gulp. There was no legal precedent for such a thing. But it is to the credit of the system that it was worked out, and Roy began to make what he had learned from journalists and was teaching to journalists available to elementary school writers.

Roy, being Roy, didn't begin by talking at the students; he worked inductively, the way he works with professionals, listening with respect and delight to what the young writers had to say about their stories, then reading their stories with humor, enthusiasm, and understanding. He knew their problems and could draw solutions out of them. They knew more than they thought they knew! He's read my copy and listened to me talk about my writing, and I know how those students felt; they couldn't wait to write some more. A reader like Roy has to be fed.

Then Roy had a great idea. He thought that if this was such fun for him, and apparently for the students, it should be shared with other teachers. Under the sponsorship of The Poynter Institute he established a series of summer camps, where teachers and students from the county come together, write together, learn together. It is an idea that worked, and is working, and that deserves imitation.

Roy's book is valuable for teachers, not only because it has enthusiasm and good intentions, but also because it is full of practical examples of how the lessons of publishing writers can be made available to students. *Free to Write* is documented with the stories young writers have written.

And, miracle of miracles, this book on writing is well-written—with energy, grace, and humor. Again, Dr. Roy Peter Clark practices what he preaches. He is an expert reporter of his own experience and a skilled writer who makes that experience alive for the reader. It will be good for teachers—and parents—to read this book, and it will also be fun.

University of New Hampshire   DONALD M. MURRAY

Preface

This book describes the personal journey of a writing teacher. It reflects fifteen years of learning how to be a writer and how to teach the process of writing to students of all ages. I have used the techniques described in this book to teach writing both to cherubic first graders and to wizened newspaper reporters. Before I could use the techniques with confidence, I made many wrong turns and even started my journey from the wrong place. This guidebook is meant to clear the path for others.

My journey was made easier by a series of guides who helped me along the way. I became a good teacher by watching them work. Some people are blessed with a single great teacher, a guiding spirit who shapes their lives forever. I have been blessed with many.

My eighth-grade teacher, Brother Richard McCann at St. Aidan School on Long Island, asked us to write stories and read them to the class. He set us free in the public library to discover the world of adult reading. He was tough and smart and fair.

At Chaminade High School in Mineola, New York, I learned from English teachers who, in retrospect, did all the right things for me. Father Bernard Horst took my paper on *The Catcher in the Rye* and flashed it on a screen so everyone could read it. Brother Richard Geraghty read my papers aloud in front of the class because he found them amusing, if not always meaty. Brother John Kane made me rewrite and rethink and rewrite, even when I did not want to.

At Providence College in Rhode Island, Rene Fortin demanded commitment and creativity from his students, asking that we read every day and write every week. He was such a fine teacher that he made me want to be like him. In so doing, he saved me from law school.

My graduate school mentor, now my colleague and friend, was Donald K. Fry from the State University of New York at Stony Brook. Don was a taskmaster who hates the passive voice. He motivated me to write my doctoral dissertation in four months. Don read that work with a critical eye, sat me down, asked me tough questions about my style, and taught me the meaning of clear and effective prose.

I began teaching writing at the age of twenty-two at Stony Brook as a teaching assistant, or TA. The TA is the lowest creature to crawl the earth, especially one who is forced to teach

Freshman Composition when he would rather be teaching *Oedipus Rex*. So the TA teaches *Oedipus Rex* anyway.

"Why are you teaching *Oedipus* in your writing class?" asked Jack Carpenter, advisor to the TAs.

"Well," I said, off guard, "good writing comes from good reading."

"How's that?" he said.

"I don't know. By osmosis, I guess."

"You want to teach your students to write like Sophocles?"

Jack, now a dean at Kansas State University, questioned all my assumptions about teaching writing. Why was I discussing literature and not the process of writing? Why was I filling up the margins of student papers with red-penciled corrections like "AWK"?

Jack also handed me a copy of Ken Macrorie's *Uptaught*, which described another writing teacher's journey toward understanding. I took the lessons of that book with me to the Montgomery campus of Auburn University. I tried my best to apply them, to teach the process of writing to my students in Alabama. There I came under the benign influence of Guinavera Nance, who shared my enthusiasm for writing instruction, and who supported me in my efforts to develop new courses and to work with high school teachers in places like Wetumpka, Alabama.

While in Montgomery, I sent my first clumsy newspaper stories to a local editor named Ray Jenkins, who now writes editorials for the Baltimore *Evening Sun*. Ray did not know me, but he wrote encouraging words on my stories and offered advice on how to get them published.

Ray may be one of the finest journalists who ever lived, and he introduced me to another, Eugene Patterson, editor of the *St. Petersburg Times*. In 1977 Gene made me a writing coach at his newspaper. In the years since then, he and Bob Haiman, director of The Poynter Institute for Media Studies, have supported me in all my odd ideas, including the establishment of a national center for newspaper writing at The Poynter Institute. From this start grew a project using the techniques of journalism to teach writing to children.

In 1980, I charged into the office of language arts supervisor Betty Rodriguez and volunteered to teach writing to the fifth-grade class of Bay Point Elementary School in south St. Petersburg. Betty and her colleagues made my continuing adventure in the elementary and middle schools possible. Principal Bill Thompson welcomed me into his school, and Joan Collins invited me into her fifth-grade classroom. During the project I received support and encouragement from school administrators Jackie Blank, Margaret Howell, and Darian Walker, from the Pinellas County School Board, and from school superintendent Scott Rose.

I have had a chance to work with hundreds of elementary and middle school teachers through visitation and workshops. Their devotion to their students sets an example of excellence I will never forget.

Perhaps my deepest thanks should go to the hundreds of students at Bay Point Elementary School who taught me through their writing how to be a good teacher. I owe much to students like Bonnie Harris and Gillian Gaynair, who set high standards for teachers and students alike. I have enjoyed watching them grow.

I could not have written this book without the support of the parents of the more than one hundred children whose work appears in *Free to Write*. These parents gave me permission to publish and analyze their children's stories, and kept telling me I was doing important work. Their children are real children; the children's stories are real stories; and my conversations with students are real conversations, recorded in my notes and journals immediately after they occurred. I have used the real names of the children except in a few cases where their stories are very personal.

I offer special thanks to my daughters Alison, Emily, and Lauren. Alison and Emily have suffered my intrusion into their classrooms and my careful study of their own work. They have encouraged me with persistent good cheer and love beyond the call of duty. Those traits they inherited from their mother, Karen Clark.

During the middle of my journey, I met two men who changed the direction of my teaching and who have come to my rescue more than once when I was lost or confused. They are Donald Murray and Donald Graves of the University of New Hampshire. On April 9, 1982, I made a pilgrimage to New Hampshire to visit these master teachers and to seek out their advice about this book. I flew into Rhode Island and drove through Massachusetts into a horrendous snowstorm, a monster that dumped twenty-two inches on Portsmouth, New Hampshire, before it was through. I made it eleven miles short of my destination before my rental car and my courage gave out. I found refuge in a nearby hotel. Murray and Graves rescued me in the literal sense that day. The snow was too deep to park their car at the hotel, so they picked me up and drove me to a fast food restaurant in a town called Newington. The storm had broken the windows of the restaurant, so we sat huddled at a central table, gulping down hot coffee and talking about writing. They gave me an ice scraper for my car and lots of good advice. I flew back to Florida two days later, knelt down, and kissed the humidity. I figured if I could survive that storm, this book would be a snap.

Donald Murray and his work continue to inspire those who care about the teaching of writing. He has devoted his life to the study of how writers work. He is one of the few teachers whose influence extends into both the classroom and the newsroom. Readers will discover that I depend heavily upon Murray's model of the writing process in this book. I have tried to prove that the model works as well for Florida fifth graders as for reporters at *The Boston Globe*. Readers can discover Murray's important work in *A Writer Teaches Writing, Learning by Teaching, Write to Learn*, and *Writing for Your Readers.*

Murray's friend and colleague, Donald Graves, has become world famous for his work with elementary school children. His book, *Writing: Teachers and Children at Work*, will inspire generations of teachers. This gentle book speaks directly to teachers on how to "receive" the work of the youngest writers.

None of the teachers I have mentioned here ever lectured me on the rules of writing, or made me diagram sentences, or filled the margins of my papers with red ink. Instead, these teachers gave me the chance to write. They listened to what I had to say. They shared with me the tools of learning. They challenged me to new levels of excellence. They celebrated my occasional triumphs but were not disheartened by my defeats. As a group, they embody good teaching.

Under their influence, I offer this book to teachers and parents who care about children and the future of education. It comes from the perspective of someone who struggles at being a parent, writer, volunteer in the schools, and teacher of professional journalists, all at the same time. Adult writers have taught me much about their anxieties, strategies, and values. I have shared this knowledge with children, to their advantage and to mine. And my youngest students have taught me lessons on courage, honesty, and creativity I can now share with those laboring in the nation's newsrooms. I hope this book will inspire educators and journalists to collaborate on improving the state of public literacy.

From this perspective, *Free to Write* propounds what some will perceive as a new way of teaching writing to children. Readers may find some points surprising, if not controversial: that journalism holds the key to improved writing instruction in America, that children can write every day, that some children will write splendid prose if adults will just get off their backs, that writing should never be used as a form of punishment, that the best writing teachers act as both parents and editors, and that students educate teachers through their writing. I question many attitudes and strategies now dominating American classrooms. I suggest that some teachers may have to experience something of a conversion, a change of heart, to teach writing effectively.

Yet I do not mean *Free to Write* to be iconoclastic or to contribute to the current wave of criticism of American education. The teachers I work with are already doing the right things, but they are in constant search for ways to do them better. They find that the teaching of writing helps them fulfill their highest aspirations as educators, that it encompasses values as old as American education itself. The greatest of these values is the notion that teaching is a democracy's most important vocation. The teacher passes down all our important freedoms, including the freedom to write.

Chapter One

Cub Reporters

A squat, pimply frog used Shay Centanni's pretty new bookbag for a bathroom. After doing its dirty deed, Froggy hopped out and flipped toward Mrs. Collins's fifth-grade classroom at Bay Point Elementary School, a public school in St. Petersburg, Florida.

I stood in the schoolhouse door and blocked its way. "No frogs allowed!" I said as the critter propelled itself again and again against my brown shoes. "Will some *boy* please come over here and dispose of this creature?"

As if to hurl my sexist words in my face, ten-year-old Nancy McIntyre did what I could not bring myself to do. She picked up the monster, using the prescribed McIntyre forehand grip, and deposited Froggy in the high grass where it probably still lurks, waiting to violate unsuspecting bookbags.

Shay Centanni—blond hair, world-class freckles, winner of the Becky Thatcher look-alike contest—calmly cleaned things up and prepared for her first writing class. It was also my first fifth-grade writing class, late September 1980. I had taught writing at almost every other level, but I had never worked with students so young. Like so many well-meaning teachers who decide to teach writing, I was more than a little nervous about what to do on the first day. I could think of only one thing: write about the frog.

I gave each student a reporter's notebook. I interviewed Shay and Nancy about the facts of the story. The students scribbled down notes, and together we covered the first big story of the year: FROG ATTACKS STUDENT'S BOOKBAG.

It was the first of thousands of stories written in that classroom over the next three years, stories about teachers and other students, about school carnivals and spoiled Halloweens, about community events, plays, books, travel, sports, embarrassing moments and

1

frightening moments, about poets, shark fishermen, and ostrich ranchers.

During those three years, I taught fourth and fifth graders at Bay Point to take notes, describe what they observed, interview, write quickly, and edit their own work.

They published the *Cougar Chronicle*, the best fifth-grade newspaper in history, whose motto read, "If a fifth grader needs to know it, we print it." They published book-length collections of their work, typed by parents, and bound by teachers in wallpaper samples. On occasion, the best of their work appeared in the *St. Petersburg Times*.

There were a few frustrating classes, days when no one seemed to want to write, or when they were so excited about their work that enthusiasm decayed into rowdiness. I am more inclined to remember classes that were a rollicking success, a funny combination of concentration and exuberance. Students read aloud in front of the class, applauded each other's work, helped correct each other, and proudly brought their work home to their parents.

"Six weeks ago," one mother told me, "my daughter could not put two words together on paper. Now she's interviewed every member of the family." The children wrote so easily, it made me wonder why many adults suffer some form of writing neurosis, why we think of our childhood writing teachers as hooded executioners ready to chop our copy to death.

When I tell strangers on airplanes that I "teach writing," they look as if they want to hold up a cross to keep me at bay. I suspect they want to have my body jettisoned from the plane, as if I were Jonah. "Oh," they keen, "I tried to write—*once*— but I don't write anymore." Sometimes I want to counsel them: "Tell me, when did you begin to have these feelings about your writing?" My guess is that the writing neurosis can be traced to childhood. Something happened, or did not happen, in elementary school.

Writing anxiety never disappears, even for professional writers with years of experience. I know. I faced waves of anxiety trying to write this book, and I have interviewed hundreds of journalists who admit without shame that they fear the blank page. School-teachers who have taught writing for years contract the heebie-jeebies when they learn at a workshop that they too may be asked to write.

My experience in both the newsroom and the classroom taught me some strategies for helping writers to overcome their fear and insecurity. I brought these techniques with me to Bay Point Elementary School and discovered that they worked:

- Free students to write every day, far more than any teacher could grade.
- Write with them and for them.
- Help them understand writing as a process.
- Confer with them and get them talking about their writing.
- Give students support and encouragement.
- Help students rewrite to improve their work.
- Create an environment in which students can learn from each other.
- Let students discover their own writing ideas.
- Emphasize real-life writing over fiction and fantasy.

Many teachers marvel at the natural grace and simplicity of student writing, qualities too often lost with maturity. Young children intuitively understand what Donald Hall calls the "insides" of words; even their "mistakes" seem charming and effective. At the age of three, my daughter Emily called her left hand her "fooding" hand. Four-year-old Lauren referred to her dreams as "the movies." One student described snow as "swifting" through the air. Another complained that her mother was always "re-changing" her room.

Young students are storytellers and humorists. They can write prose to please themselves and communicate meaning to adults. They can write poetry, fiction, and nonfiction. I have never met a child, including some with learning disabilities, who could not write.

Yet most children do not write for one simple reason: no one asks them to.

At Bay Point we turned the classroom into a newsroom, if you will, a writing laboratory where ten-year-olds were treated like writers, and where they could confer with teachers and other students. Long before English teachers caught on, journalists understood that writing was a process even persons of modest ability could learn. Years before Donald Murray wrote about the writing process at the University of New Hampshire, he sat in a Boston newsroom getting ideas for stories, collecting information, finding a focus, writing the lead, organizing material, developing the draft, and revising and editing his work.

We taught the same processes at Bay Point. We asked the students to write every day, as journalists do. We showed them a model for the writing process and gave them the words to describe it. We offered them the building blocks of writing. Then we used brief conferences to help these young writers through each step in the process.

Because we sometimes worked with ninety students in one room, we had to develop and apply an effective routine for conferences, just as a busy city editor must develop techniques for communicating with a large and productive staff of reporters. In conferences teachers try to work quickly: a conference may be a nod of the head, a shrug of the shoulders, a pat on the back. We try to identify the major problem in the story and ignore lesser ones at first. We ask questions to get the writer talking. We make suggestions, but only after the writer has had a chance to solve the problem.

Searching for Ideas

Teachers tell students what to write about. As a result, says Donald Graves, students go on "teacher welfare" when it comes to ideas. They become passive and dependent, and fail to recognize the value of their own experience. My students receive assignments, as journalists do. But they must find many of their own writing ideas, so we brainstorm, read, and confer. Sometimes I am reduced to taking dictation.

A real conference with Kenny Jones:

"Kenny, you're not writing."

"I can't think of nothin'."

"What are you interested in?"

"Nothin'."

"What are your hobbies?"

"I don't have any."

"What do you like to read?"

"I don't know."

"What do you do after school?"

"I play soccer."

Ta da.

Gathering and Sifting

Good writers collect information before they write. So we devote many classes to gathering information and reporting stories. I read them a story, have them write down the key words, and get them to retell the story from their notes. I teach them to formulate questions for an interview and to write down the key words and phrases from the interview for use in a story. I stand in front of the classroom and have students describe my appearance in detail, or I show them slides of color photographs and ask them to describe the photographs. I send them to an event, such as a school carnival, and they write down what they see, hear, and smell. If the writing is personal (a favorite assignment is called "Welcome to My Room"), they brainstorm before they write a sentence. Sometimes a student has trouble:

"How are you doing?"

"I can't think of anything to write."

"OK. Just relax for a minute. Now imagine you're walking through the door of your room with a friend. What would be the first thing he would see?"

"The globe, I guess."

"OK. Write that down. Now, what's near the globe?"

Before you know it, the child has made a detailed inventory of his room and is now prepared to write about it.

Finding a Focus

The most important part of a newspaper story is the lead, the first few lines that catch the reader's attention and act, in the words of John McPhee, as a "flashlight" that shines down into a story.

Children become expert at this gambit. They can capture the essence of a story in a sentence. They can get to the heart of the matter. They can tease, foreshadow, and cajole, as this lead does: "One day last summer during school vacation, a boy named Billy Shannon was at the Don CeSar Beach. He was swimming in the Gulf of Mexico. He was swimming near the deep water markers and he felt something rubbery slide against his leg and saw a fin." If you want to know more about this story, you have been captured by Karin Fraser, a fourth grader.

Building Momentum

Journalists write on deadline, and so do students most of the time. They learn that there is a time to think and rehearse and a time to get your behind in the chair and your hands moving.

They learn that writing is a motor skill, an act of the hands as well as of the mind.

One way to break through writer's block is to have students write like the dickens for five or ten minutes without stopping. The result is "sloppy copy," of course, but students are astonished at how quickly they fill up a page. Then, through rewriting, they discover that they have something to say after all.

Rethinking and Correcting

Writers revise and edit their work. In the early stages of a writing project, I may encourage students to be sloppy, to cross out, or to invent spellings. But students know that as the piece gets closer to publication, they must improve and correct it. They learn editing marks, use the dictionary, and edit each other's stories. I highlight common mistakes in spelling, grammar, and usage for the class, and students begin to find and correct their own mistakes. When students edit and revise, they begin to take charge of their own education. And they begin to learn grammar in its proper context.

Reaching an Audience

Journalists see writing as a transaction between the writer and the reader. When students begin to write, they feel the urge to share what they've done with others. This exchange can happen in different ways:

- By reading the story aloud in front of the class.
- By sharing it with one or two other students.
- By sharing it in class with a teacher.
- By publishing it.

Often the structure of the class breaks down on its own, resembling a newsroom more than a classroom. Visitors see students working at different tasks and hear a hum of activity. Students share their stories with each other and then line up to show them to their teacher/editor. I always respond with an encouraging word: "That's terrific," or "You're a good writer," or even "That's a good start." But I also take the opportunity to confer:

"Susan, I like this a lot. Good stuff at the beginning. But what about the ending?"

"I was having trouble with the ending, so I just stopped."

"Can you come up with an ending? Or do you want a suggestion?"

"No, I can do it."

Susan returns to her desk, rewrites her ending, shows it to me again, and this time it's just right.

Why turn ten-year-olds into journalists? Why not let them write about unicorns, leprechauns, and Christmas elves? Why not tap into their imaginative lives in ways that creative writing teachers have for years? I will cast a vote for creativity and argue that real-life writing is no less creative than fiction or fantasy. For when students write about themselves and their worlds, they become clearer thinkers and stronger communicators. They learn values and become more independent and well-rounded. They learn a skill that serves them for a lifetime.

All of this becomes increasingly important because of the way in which the world is changing for children. Parents and teachers are worried, and for good reason. Many forces are at work within our society to complicate the lives of children, afflict them too early with the burdens of adulthood, and create obstacles to their emotional and intellectual well-being. Neil Postman argues that we face "the disappearance of childhood" as we have come to understand it.

In 1959, the year Buddy Holly died, I was a fifth grader. I had a mother and a father and they both lived at home. My mother got me out of bed each morning and waited for me to arrive home from school. I knew most of my neighbors for a square mile, and they knew me. I lived within an hour's drive of about fifty relatives. I didn't know any divorced people or unwed mothers. My only windows on the world of lust were the titles of Brigitte Bardot movies advertised in the newspaper.

Life is different for ten-year-olds today. They may change schools often. Many have suffered through one or more divorces. Their grandparents live a thousand miles away. They may have to get themselves and younger siblings off to school. When they return home, only cable television is waiting. Girls in my daughter's junior high get pregnant. Sixth graders smoke dope. I once asked fourth graders to name their favorite movies. One student said *Last Tango in Paris.* Another said *Halloween II.*

Real-life writing permits young writers to learn about themselves, about others in their community, and about the issues that affect their lives. Moreover, when they write about their lives and experiences, children teach their teachers.

Writing teachers in elementary and middle schools have at least two important roles to play. First, the teacher is a substitute parent, an enormous burden that should not be accepted lightly. Second, the teacher is an editor. As a parent, the teacher helps the student grow and mature as a person. As an editor, the teacher nurtures the student as a writer. This book explores how and where these spheres intersect.

We all accept the fact that the act of writing is more than the application of technique. You do not write a story the way you assemble a Christmas toy. Writers at any age deal with themselves as persons to make writing possible. They discover things about themselves through the act of writing and communicate their ideas and feelings to others. Through their writing, students teach their teachers about their lives, values, discoveries, fears, triumphs, and experiences.

By encouraging the student to develop as person, the teacher can help create a better writer. By coaching the student as writer, the teacher can help create a better person.

Chapter Two

Writing and Reporting

One night my daughters saw a copy of a magazine article, "The Unoriginal Sin," which I had written for the *Washington Journalism Review*. They saw my name in large letters and examined the six-page, nicely designed package.

Alison said, "Look at the story that Daddy wrote." Emily examined it, looked up at me, and announced, "You didn't write that." Since the piece was about plagiarism, I began to panic. "What do you mean?" I asked. Her reply was clear, stark, and chilling: "You don't write that good."

I wondered about the difference in their reactions. Alison accepted my work. She had seen me write in class, at home, and in the newsroom. She has written herself and seen her work published. She no longer looks at the polished, published page as a "miracle."

Emily still thinks writing is magic. She sees her dad scribbling on yellow paper, crumpling pages into crinkled balls, crossing out, thumping away on an old typewriter. It's not clean, polished, neat, or on glossy paper.

I don't write that good.

Jenny Cavins no longer thinks writing is magic. A fifth grader at Sandy Lane Elementary School in Clearwater, Florida, Jenny has learned from her teacher, Mary Osborne, that writing is a process. Jenny writes:

Sometimes when I'm at school, I can't think of anything to write about in my writing book. So I think and think and think until I think of a story to write about. When my story comes to mind, I write a rough draft and boy is it sometimes messy!

After I finish my rough draft, I show it to my teacher and she reads it and asks me questions. If there's any misspelled words, she puts little dots on the side of my paper. If there's two misspelled words on one line, she puts two dots like this ...

Then I write my story over again until I get it just right. When I get it just right, I start to edit some more. When I edit, I rewrite it nicely. I also check it over to see if there's any more misspelled words. If there are, I give them a corrected spelling. Then I'll put it in my finished folder and write on my work folder the date I finished and the title of the story I finished.

Sometimes I'll send my story to the *St. Petersburg Times* so they'll put it in the newspaper so when my mom and dad see it, they'll be proud of me.

Jenny has demystified writing for herself and, in so doing, has expressed many of the sensibilities and strategies that all writers share: the struggle for a story idea, the inadequacies of early drafts, the need for revision, the quest for publication, the hope of approval.

A hundred writers will describe the writing process in a hundred ways. I described it for myself in different ways for different stories:

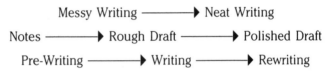

The most useful model for the writing process is one described by Donald Murray, who has been thinking and writing about the writing process for thirty years:

- DISCOVER AN IDEA—The writer finds something to write about and begins to see the world as a storehouse of story ideas.
- COLLECT INFORMATION—The writer is a reporter who collects facts, quotations, anecdotes, and descriptive details.
- REHEARSE—The writer plans and ruminates, ponders problems in the story and seeks solutions.
- FOCUS—The writer searches for the point of the story and a way to convey it in a lead.
- DEVELOP A STORY—The writer builds momentum, finds an order, and prepares a first draft.

- CLARIFY—The writer revises and edits, keeping in mind the needs of the reader.
- PUBLISH—Throughout the process, the writer thinks of an audience and finally shares the work with others.

Each part of this process will be described in detail later in this book, but no model of the process should reduce a complicated and personal act to a formula. Instead, it should help writers describe how they work and help them solve problems in their stories. Students who learn about process can begin to speak and think for the first time about their writing. They come to understand how a finished work is the product of several steps. When they face a blank page and cannot think of a thing to write, they have a process to rely on.

Most people write without a model of the writing process in their heads. Some professional writers are inarticulate about the process of writing. They just do their own thing, follow instinct and experience, and stare dumbly at anyone who asks a "how did you do that" question. Other professionals love to discuss how they work and through such discussions describe the writing tools they use habitually but unconsciously.

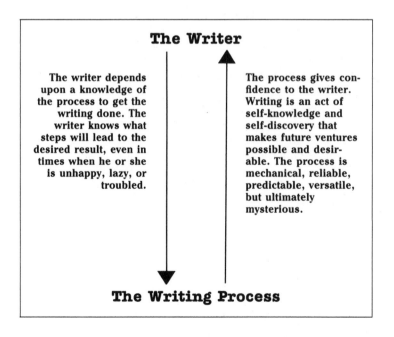

The Writer

The writer depends upon a knowledge of the process to get the writing done. The writer knows what steps will lead to the desired result, even in times when he or she is unhappy, lazy, or troubled.

The process gives confidence to the writer. Writing is an act of self-knowledge and self-discovery that makes future ventures possible and desirable. The process is mechanical, reliable, predictable, versatile, but ultimately mysterious.

The Writing Process

Journalists do not write a story by following a checklist of instructions. The process is automatic, unconscious, internalized, until it almost seems natural. When the writing goes well, the reporter may say, "The story wrote itself."

You may not think of the process of how a car works when you are cruising along Interstate 4 on the way to Disney World. But if the car breaks down, you hope someone understands a fuel-injection system well enough to find and fix the damaged part. Writers, or athletes, or mechanics must themselves identify a broken part when things start going badly. Whether it is a faulty focus, or a flying elbow, or a broken valve that slows the process, the person who understands process can mend things and get moving again.

In August 1983, distinguished newspaper columnist James Reston gave a talk at the University of Notre Dame in honor of his late colleague at *The New York Times*, Red Smith. During the talk he referred to a former teacher at Exeter, William Saltonstall, who was disappointed in the Academy's record of teaching young students to write. Saltonstall wondered whether journalism might teach students more about the process of writing than the parsing of sentences.

"We never got around to testing that question," says Reston, "but I believe the simple art of reporting may have something to contribute: if, for example, the teacher invites somebody to come into the classroom who says something, does something, and departs. And the question is put: What happened? What did this character look like, and say, and do? And then let the students write their answers and challenge one another's reports—making the practical point that whatever they do in future life, as doctors, lawyers, or garage superintendents, they must know how to make their thought clear, especially when they are writing love letters, which I hope has not gone out of style."

Journalists such as Reston understand that journalism is more than a trade or a craft, it is a way of looking at the world. Reporters see the world as a storehouse of writing ideas. The ordinary person walks down the street and sees a bar, a wig shop, a grocery store, a pharmacy, and a shoe store. The journalist sees dozens of story ideas behind the facades of those businesses. He sees people and issues. He asks himself:

- Who drinks in that bar at 9:00 in the morning?
- What kind of market is there for those huge rainbow-colored wigs in the shop window?

- Why are there small grocery stores downtown but no major supermarket?
- Is there a difference in service between the old-style pharmacies and the newer large drugstore chains?
- When so many businesses are struggling downtown, how has this shoe store managed to make it?

Such is the reporter's fate: She cannot drive home or get a haircut or go to church or go to the bathroom without discovering something to write about, or encountering something she wants to know more about.

James Reston is right. Something can happen in the classroom. Someone comes in to be interviewed. Perhaps it is a World War II hero, or a former major league umpire, or a woman who pioneered in physical therapy and helped care for President Franklin D. Roosevelt. (A reporter could find all of these, by the way, in St. Petersburg.) Students develop questions, interview, listen, take notes, observe, take more notes, find a story idea, write and edit, and publish.

Robbie Allison wrote about Jeff Klinkenberg's visit to his fifth-grade class:

Jeff Klinkenberg is a smart and a good reporter for the St. Petersburg Times. He is a nice man and he's good to children. One day he was working on a story when his friend Captain Ky Lewis called him on the telephone.

He said, "I was out catching grouper today when something ate half of the fish I was reeling in, and it was a great white shark. When I bent down to look at it, his head came out of the water." He said the shark was twenty feet long and had giant jaws and teeth.

The captain wanted to catch the shark. So he threw a big hook out in the water with thick rope attached to it and he didn't get the shark. The shark turned and charged at the boat. The captain got a rifle and shot at the shark. It turned and ran away. When he got the hook it was completely bent.

Gillian Gaynair wrote this account of a visitor to her classroom:

A Poet and his Magic Fish

Bob Oberg came to our classroom and read to us one of his stories. It was called "The Magic Fish."

Bob is twenty-three years old, he was born in Rhode Island. He and Dr. Clark went to the same college. The college they went to was called Providence College.

Students can learn to interview, take notes, and develop stories using the techniques of professional reporters. Here Ann Brown drafts a story from information she has collected in her reporter's notebook.

One night Bob dreamed of a big fish. This fish gave him the idea to write the story of "The Magic Fish." His first draft took five hours, now he is on the sixth draft. He will send out copies to publishers. Bob already has ten poems published!

Now Bob is in the process of writing "The Other Raft." This future story is about a boy who is at the beach on his raft, and then he seems to see himself on another raft.

I wish Bob Oberg all the luck in his new story, and in many more stories.

The reporting, writing, and editing of such stories integrate many of the language arts skills students need to learn: notetaking, listening, interviewing, critical thinking, close reading, and composing. The reporting process becomes a learning process, an active skill that places a burden of responsibility on the writer. The writer must acquire and communicate knowledge.

"If I got my fourth graders to write about things that were not fictional or imaginative, their stories would be boring," one teacher has said. The bias against reportage is strong. Teachers find it easier to have students sit in one place and dream up something to write, rather than to have them explore their lives, schools, and communities for story ideas. The best writers, such as Francis X. Clines of *The New York Times*, believe they can find a story if they can only get out of the office. Teachers may have to open their classrooms to visitors or free students to venture beyond the four walls of the classroom to help them see the world as their writing laboratory.

The classroom itself provides the first circle of ideas. Students brainstorm to discover their own interests and experiences. John writes about soccer. Taft about bike racing. Beth about the theater. Alison about her trip to New York. Mike about superheroes. Adam about video games. Teresa about the time she was sick. One idea breeds another.

The students soon learn that they can write about each other's lives. They begin to turn to one another for interviews. Karin writes about the day Billy thought he was being attacked by a shark. Nicole writes about Tara's birthday party. The whole class writes about Bonnie's most embarrassing moment.

And what about that strange figure seated in front of the classroom: the teacher? Most teachers feel uncomfortable sharing their personal lives and experiences with their students. But the teacher knows she is an object of curiosity, which is why children laugh when they see their teachers in the supermarket or in McDonald's. Imagine that, they say to themselves, my teacher eats Big Macs.

A teacher willing to be a bit vulnerable can take advantage of student curiosity and grant interviews. Students want to know many things, and the best interviewer may learn the most. How old is the teacher? How long has she been teaching? Does she have a family? Why did she become a teacher? Where was she educated? When did she decide that she would teach? Why does she teach Language Arts? Where are some other places she has taught? What does she like, or dislike, about teaching fifth graders?

The questions may get tougher and more complex. Has she ever had to paddle a student? Does she get depressed when she reads stories that knock teachers? Are classes too large? Does she ever feel burned out? Dozens of stories, perhaps hundreds, exist in any classroom. Through the techniques of journalism, students begin to discover them.

The second circle of ideas is the school itself. Before school and after, during breaks and assemblies and lunch hours, students can learn about the interesting folks who populate their school and about the institution that controls so much of their time. How are the policies of our new principal different from those of the old one? How long has that cafeteria lady been at the school, and what changes has she seen in the children who attend the school and the food served to them? What are the safety problems at the school and how can they be solved? Is there a problem with vandalism or graffiti? Who has been working at the school the longest? Who is the oldest living graduate of the school? When was the school built?

Buddy Snider writes:

During the last 6 years that I have been going to Bay Point Elementary, the lunches have been getting smaller and the prices have been getting bigger! I have recognized that the little mustard and ketchup containers have taken one whole space on the tray that used to be filled with a vegetable or something else.

We are also getting smaller main courses. When I get home from school I eat a lot and sometimes my mom has to tell me to stop.

Maybe it is because I'm getting older and I eat more but I think that the school lunches are getting smaller.

Through writing, students learn the value of the reflective life. The questions they ask, the observations they make, and the stories they write change their perception of the world. Students learn what James Slevin of Georgetown University calls "critical literacy" so that they can be freed rather than enslaved by information.

The next circle of ideas is the family. Consciously or not, we all consider our families to be microcosms of the problems and dilemmas of the outside world. Within the tiny world of the family, we grow, learn, suffer, and succeed.

As a journalist, I have written stories about my grandparents and my children. I am in the process of writing a story about my mother's aunt. She was born in Italy and came to America in 1898. Aunt Marietta has much to tell about her journey and the experiences of her family in a new country. My need to know about her grew from my own maturity and my journalistic instincts. After I find out about her life, I will grow in self-knowledge, and, I hope, wisdom.

We do not demand much information from members of our own family, and that is a pity. We sit across the table from these two people, mom and dad—more often it is just mom—

and we never ask the questions that would help us understand them and ourselves. As Bruce Springsteen has observed, the young think their parents are "part of the furniture" and deny them their own histories, hopes, and dreams. My guess is that most people cannot name the towns where their parents were born.

Parents, grandparents, aunts, and uncles love to tell stories about their own experiences and the development of their values. Students can learn these from interviews and share them with the world:

- How did you and dad meet?
- How did you feel when you first learned I was going to be born?
- What did you say when you saw me for the first time?
- What kind of kid was I?
- What is your earliest memory?
- What was your grandma like?

Even if the questions are not profound, they can generate experiences that become the matter of interesting stories.

Amy Kenyon took advantage of her grandparents' fiftieth wedding anniversary to write about her journey to Massachusetts and her family reunion.

Once we got to the farm, my grandpa, who is blind, came out to meet us. My grandma was inside in her wheelchair and wheeled out to see us. We had so much fun. We had more than sixty relatives on the farm. We had lobster and clams. They had a huge cake with a 50 on it. My grandma and grandpa got a T.V. and some quilts. For a joke we gave them peanuts. They were so overjoyed that they started to cry.

I find such writing more vital and interesting than poems about rainbows and butterflies. When they engage in "creative" writing, as we traditionally understand it, students can go wherever their imaginations lead them. They take no responsibility for the information in their stories.

Jason Bell, a young poet who teaches in the public schools, fights this tendency when he teaches poetry to children. In a way, he brings a journalist's sensibilities to the job. He believes that through poetic forms, students can begin to understand how their own experiences link the real and the imaginative worlds.

Imagination ◄──────── Life ────────► Real World

Jason believes that poetry is special language for special occasions and that all good poetry is rooted in real experience.

My daughter Alison wrote a poem for Jason called "The Building of My Life." Each story in the poetic building describes an early memory or event in her life: a crime, an accident, an experience, a friend, a trip, her school:

My first floor is a small motel room
where my family and I were held up with
a gun. The bad man, as I used to call him,
made us stand in the shower.

My second floor is a wet pool deck where
my friends threatened to throw me in the
water. I ran and fell because of the
slipperiness of the deck. I cut my knee and cried.

My third floor is a large abc book I try
to memorize. A is for apple, B is for ball.
I look back at that time and laugh.

My fourth floor is a house, the house of
my best friend. She and her sister are
here today. I wonder if I'll know them
forever.

My fifth floor is an airplane going to
New York. I sit in wonder trying to
think of what would happen if the engine
breaks down.

My last floor is a large cafeteria where
we have graduation to middle school. Hearing
the tune, Pomp and Circumstance, makes me
feel proud and full of joy.

Students learn from writing in different forms. The poetic sensibility brings word play, color, vigorous language, sound, and rhythm to writing. The journalistic sensibility brings interesting information, concrete detail, observation and description, and a narrative line.

Journalism also helps students develop speed, clarity, accuracy, a love for interesting information, a concern for the reader, and an interest in important issues and events.

At the end of the 1981 school year, I was ready to challenge some of my best fifth-grade writers. How would these children react to realistic newspaper-writing conditions? Could they write on deadline? Could they think up interview questions on the spot? Could they write well under pressure?

On June 8, 1981, I introduced Bonnie Harris and Gillian Gaynair to a group of journalism professors. While the professors worked in a seminar, I took the girls out to work on a story. They would have one hour to find and report a story, and one hour to write it.

In two hours Bonnie produced this story:

Mrs. Penny Burns is the manager of the Cathedral Book Store on 355 2nd Ave. North and has been working there for 2 years. The book store used to be across the street in St. Peter's Cathedral Episcopal Church where she worked for one year. The Cathedral Book Store is now 4 1/2 years old. It began very small with little bookshelves that could close in and out. This store is a profit making organization.

The Cathedral Book Store is a very religious one. "I like working in a religious book store because these books don't have to be all churchy," says Penny.

They often get alot of people in their store from off the streets that really need a lot of help. They ask Penny for money or food, but Penny can't always give them all money, so she sends them to "We Help."

The most busiest times are Christmas, Easter, and around this time because everyone like to read on vacations.

They specilize 80% in books, but they also sell things like scrapbooks, bookmarks, flowers, jewelry and games.

The books mostly come in from U.P.S. The bookstore is staffed by 12 volenteers and Penny herself is one of them in certain times of the year.

I would like to wish Penny lots of luck with her bookstore, and I hope to see her again, sometime.

Bonnie Harris's story reflects her talent as a writer. She uses many of the skills she learned at Bay Point: notetaking, interviewing, description, detail. Working under intense pressure for a ten-year-old, she produced a short feature on deadline that the college professors admired. A few mechanical mistakes resulted from the haste of writing: the spelling of *alot*, *volenteers*, and *specilize*; and the double superlative "most busiest." But the exercise proved to me that young writers can put the skills of journalism to good use.

This was confirmed for me during the summer of 1983 when I sent thirty talented young writers on an assignment to write about the Salvador Dali Museum. This complicated assignment tested the abilities of my students to the limit. They would have to:

• Tour the museum and interview a docent, listen, and take notes.

- Observe and describe the paintings.
- Collect important information from brochures.
- Verify facts and details.
- Organize the story through brainstorming and outlining.
- Write leads that invite the reader into the story.

Willie Caseber's effort was typical:

Reflections on the Dali Museum •
By Willie Caseber (Age 11)

Sitting lonely on the edge of Bayboro Harbor, is a bright new building ... the Salvador Dali Museum. The Salvador Dali museum was moved from Cleveland a year and a half ago. The museum was started in Cleveland by A. Reynolds Morse in 1942. He displayed his paintings on a floor in his office building. When that got too small, the museum was moved to St. Petersburg. It is the largest collection of paintings by Dali in the world. The collection is made up of 93 oils, 200 drawings and water-colors, and 1,000 graphics. There are 60 paintings on display. "The museum staff thought the older people wouldn't come, but they were wrong. The ones who come are mostly older people and children," stated Sunny Schurr, a worker at the museum.

Dali used cubism, impressionism, and surrealism which means above realism for his paintings. Dali also used the paranoiac critical method, which means he put himself to sleep, and he would wake up during the point between sleeping and waking and paint what he thought he saw. When he tried these methods, he mastered them all.

Dali was born May 11, 1904 in Figueras, Spain. He was named after his dead brother, who died 9 months before he was born. He kept trying to break the connection that his parents kept trying to make between him and his dead brother.

Salvador didn't fit well in school. He threw himself down the steps to get attention and was expelled from school twice.

Since his childhood, Dali had been terrified by lions and grasshoppers. This has been a big influence on his paintings, for these have appeared in many of his works.

Dali was married to Gala three times because he liked the ceremony. Dali signed many paintings Gala-Salvador Dali. Gala died last year, and Dali's health became worse. He has Parkinson's disease. Mr. and Mrs. Morse hope to see Dali before he passes away.

My favorite painting was The Hallucinogenic Toreador, painted from 1969–1970. It is an oil painting. There are many statues of Venus in this painting, and if looked at from a certain angle, they look like a toreador. Another was Oeufs Sur le Plat Sans le Plat which when translated, means eggs on a plate, without a plate. He "saw" this before he was born. There are 3 fried eggs in this painting, 2 on a plate, and one suspended from a string. There are a melting watch and a big building in the background. Another favorite was Portrait of Gala, 1932–1933. She was in an olive grove. The painting was so realistic, if you enlarged it, it would look like a photograph of Gala.

There are only 2 Dali Museums in the world. To understand the Dali Museum, take a tour!

Reading such a story reveals what a student writer can accomplish through journalism. Students suddenly take charge of their own education. The writer's tools become the keys to knowledge. Difficult assignments become interesting challenges. Through the lens of their writing, students begin to see the world as a place in which they can learn.

Chapter Three

Writing Every Day

When I taught writing in college, I never asked my students to write in class. Class time was too precious to waste on writing, I thought. That was my time to lecture, to explain the rules of writing. Students needed those lessons before they could write.

A two-year stint in the newsroom of the *St. Petersburg Times* changed my mind. Journalists never lecture each other on the rules of writing; they just write. Pick up a reporter's story file and you will be surprised by the weight of the two hundred or more stories written in a single year. My most productive month as a professional writer was July 1979. I wrote thirty-two features, columns, and reviews. I was in a groove, confident in my craft, writing every day.

Now I believe classroom time is too precious not to write. When I begin teaching a new class, whether first, fifth, or eighth grade, I write with my students within the first fifteen minutes of the first class. Thereafter, we usually write during the first fifteen minutes of each class. The most important strategy I learned as a teacher of writing was to be quiet and let the students write.

In September 1982, I met a new group of fifth graders at Bay Point Elementary. I began the class with a brief description of what the writing program would be like. I expressed my hope that we would write every day, for at least fifteen or twenty minutes. I explained that I would not grade their daily writing, nor would I mark up their papers in red ink.

I told them they would generate many of their own ideas for writing. They would receive some assignments, but they could not rely upon their teacher for story ideas. Discovering stories was a big part of their job. I explained that they would have many chances to improve their work and to publish it. If they did not finish a piece on day 1, they could finish it on day 2 and improve it, if they chose to, on day 100.

I gave them twenty minutes to write. They asked questions: Can I write a story? Can I write about animals? Can we write about a friend? Yes. Yes. Yes. I was surprised when they wrote with little hesitation, most students working quickly for at least ten minutes. A few stared off into the stratosphere, thinking of something to write, I presumed. At least they were quiet. Some appeared finished after ten minutes.

"What do you do if you're finished?"

"Read it over and see if you like it."

After twenty minutes I asked if anyone needed more time and several students said yes. Some students filled out a page with little trouble, others struggled for a few lines.

I asked if they wanted to read their stories to the class. Two bright students volunteered. I assured the class that it would be fun to share their stories. Before the first one read, I taught them the golden rule as it applies to student behavior. If they were quiet and attentive when someone read a story, they would be rewarded in kind when it was their turn to read. About twelve students read stories. Most were greeted by mild applause. Many students read too softly. Some listeners lost interest after about fifteen minutes of sharing.

A number of students corrected their work as they read it aloud. I gazed over their shoulders and watched them insert missing words and correct grammatical mistakes. One girl added a sentence to give her story a real ending. Another had written nothing on the page but stood up and recited a poem she had memorized. I told them to save everything.

A few months later I visited my daughter Emily's first-grade class. Within the first ten minutes, we were interrupted by a tornado drill, so everyone wrote about that. Some illustrated their stories with dramatic pictures of deadly twisters.

Like the fifth graders, they were asked to write about topics of their own choosing. I gave each student about fifteen minutes to write. Then we read stories aloud, discussed the writing, and revised, all in ninety minutes on the first day.

Sylvia Patterson and I were astonished at the ease with which students responded to the writing environment we created. My teaching methods were the same ones I would have used with high school students. These children were ready to write.

- Not a single first-grader thought that he or she could not write. One student could not get a complete sentence on the page, but he was eager to dictate his story and have someone else write it down.
- For fifteen minutes Emily wrote at a feverish pace and completed six full pages of a story entitled "The Sun and his Friends."
- No student was hampered by an inability to spell. The children invented spellings to suit their needs. Some inventions were so far out that the teacher thought it was "like reading a foreign language." Some students could not decipher words for which they had invented spellings. But every story was readable. A teacher or parent could easily type or rewrite these for publication, so that students could see their own words in their proper form.
- All the students wanted to illustrate their work with drawings or decorations.
- They were surprisingly articulate about their work and could easily answer questions such as, "What part did you like writing the best?" Some could respond to "What would you like to do next?"
- They wanted to see their stories in print and encouraged me to make a book out of their collective work.
- As I read through their stories, I was struck by how effectively some of these seven-year-olds wrote. I felt I could pick out the work of certain writers and predict continued success for them. It confirmed for me the need to teach writing in the earliest grades, to give children lifetime writing momentum.

Tara wrote:

A Pelican
One day it was nice out
A pelican flyid bi   it was a
Funny lookin pelican   his bekc
was red   his waks wer
geen   his ase wer red and bakc
it was a funny pelican

Tara has a real sense of the complete sentence. She opens her story with a capital letter, leaves a space between sentences, and starts some sentences on a new line. Most words are spelled correctly, and she tries her best on *beak* (bekc), *eyes* (ase) and *wings* (waks).

Natasha tells this story about Disneyland. See if you can translate the invented spellings.

I what to bieslelaed
I spaed the niegt
My kaset sloep wheth me
at bieslelaed
We waet to the haetedhous
Taen we whaet Snow Wiet
We whaet to eat

The end

Natasha makes an excellent effort to spell *Disneyland*, *cousin*, *haunted house*, and *Snow White*. She even knows that there is a *g* in the word *night*. These children will learn to spell and use mechanics effectively through the process of writing, and because they are writing, they will understand the true value of these skills.

Elementary school teachers are more open and flexible than teachers of higher grades in their willingness to develop new ways of getting writing into the curriculum. When I recommend daily writing, the elementary school teacher is likely to say, "We could do that." The middle school teacher is more likely to say, "I'd like to do that, but I don't have the time. I've got too many other things in the curriculum that I've got to accomplish. And remember, I've got 160 students in six sections." The first time I heard this complaint, I shook my head, threw up my hands, and said, "I guess you're right. It's hopeless!"

The next day I put in an emergency phone call to Donald Murray at the University of New Hampshire and explained the predicament of these teachers: "These are good teachers," I said. "They are interested in writing, but they are not sure they can make it work." Murray argued that most teachers feel comfortable with the lecture approach to teaching. In the metaphor of Paulo Freire, the students are little banks into which the teacher deposits wisdom. When the teachers were in school, they were the banks.

Many teachers believe that if you teach writing every day, some other important skill or key part of the curriculum will fall through the cracks. "What about grammar?" ask the teachers. "What about literature? What about reading?"

Bill Thompson, former principal of Bay Point Elementary, helped me solve this problem when he gave me my first chance to teach writing at his school. I told him, "I don't want to take time away from the other important things you are doing in language arts."

"Don't worry about that," he said, "we think you'll accomplish all the important things through the writing."

It may be useful for teachers and administrators to sit down together and consider the goals of an English language arts curriculum. What is it that we want children to learn? In 1960 Mauree Applegate, in her important book *Easy in English*, listed the goals for a language arts program in the elementary schools:

- To use words responsibly.
- To think clearly.
- To listen imaginatively.
- To speak effectively.
- To write creatively.
- To use mechanics powerfully.
- To regard good English respectfully.
- To acquaint children with the best.

That is a full and noble list, one to which I am tempted to add "To use adverbs sparingly." While many teachers of English subscribe in theory to Applegate's goals, in practice they limit their curriculum to the teaching of reading and grammar. I would argue that teaching the writing process is the best vehicle for reaching all of Applegate's goals.

- Writing, conferring, and revising teach students to use words in the most responsible manner. Students may be asked for the first time to ponder the implications of words and consider alternatives.
- The writing process gives students a path for clear thinking. The act of writing involves understanding the world and yourself. Young writers must think independently and respond to criticism of their work.
- Writing students learn to listen during every class. They listen to the teacher and write down key words. They conduct an interview and listen for what is most important. They listen to a teacher's question about their work or to the comments of other students. They translate

these questions into improvements in their stories. They listen to the stories of other children.

- A good writing teacher helps a student speak more effectively. The student finds her "voice" on the page and shares it with others through oral interpretation. She learns to read her words aloud to others with feeling and emphasis. She asks good questions during interviews. She responds intelligently to the questions of a teacher. Writing means speaking and sharing.
- Students who never learn to read critically are victimized and exploited by all sources of information: the news media, advertising, and propaganda. Writing forces the writer to read thoughtfully. The student discovers strengths and weaknesses in his own work and the work of others. Such discoveries result in closer reading and revision. When students read their own writing well enough to discuss how stories might be improved, they practice reading and thinking skills that will serve them over a lifetime.
- Writing demands creativity, even when the topic is not wild horses or buried treasure. The teacher who asks students to write inspires creativity. Students must discover what they know and how they feel and mine their experience for story ideas. Then they must create sentences that make meaning, sentences never before expressed or thought of in the history of writing.
- During one school year, my daughter Alison studied lists of spelling words and diagrammed dozens of sentences. During the time she studied grammar, she was required to write very little. When she wrote on her own, her sentences were longer and more complicated than those she was asked to diagram in class. I also noticed that she made mistakes in grammar and spelling even though she had supposedly mastered these skills in class. Because she learned grammar in isolation, she failed to apply it to her writing. Teaching spelling and grammar within the context of writing gives students powerful tools that free them to clarify and communicate.
- No one respects good English more than the professional writer or editor. That respect can be nurtured in the writer at an early age. For the young writer, the English language becomes a playground, a place to romp and take chances. New words are discovered like jewels

in the sand. New books inspire more experimentation and imitation. Instead of being a padlock, language becomes a key to solving mysteries and finding meaning.

- A good writing curriculum, says Donald Graves, "surrounds children with literature," the best writing and thinking in our culture. The experience of writing leads children to encounters with the work of other writers. Teachers find interesting books or passages that reveal the power of great writing to their students. And although children cannot write like Shakespeare, they can become acquainted with the best writing that children like themselves can accomplish.

I would add three goals to Applegate's list that seem especially appropriate for a language curriculum in the 1980s:

- To know yourself.
- To understand your world.
- To cultivate the best values.

Alas, in an era that emphasizes basic education, it seems as if our highest goal is to help students pass a state test. Teachers who "teach the test" inadvertently lower their expectations for all students. Good students endure boring, repetitive assignments and lose their enthusiasm for English. Weak students may squeak through the test but never learn to write a single memorable sentence.

And yet I know first graders who write pages of memorable sentences, children who learn to master complicated grammatical tools. First they write a story. Some character in the story has something to say, so the teacher shows them how to use quotation marks. They learn the great lessons through writing, lessons of language, meaning, and vision.

As Bessie Taylor Gwynn told her young student Carl T. Rowan, "If you don't read, you can't write, and if you can't write, you might as well stop dreaming." The vision made Rowan a great journalist.

Such goals and visions must seem distant to the English teacher with too many students and too little time. To write every day requires ingenuity, daring, time management, and some political savvy. The wisdom among writing teachers in Florida is that "it's easier to get forgiveness than permission."

So let us take the teacher with thirty students in a class and thirty minutes a day to work with them, a tough challenge for any teacher of writing. The goal is to get students to write for most of that period, say twenty minutes.

While students write, the teacher spends the first ten minutes walking around the classroom. As students scribble, or think, or fool around, or search through their folders, the teacher may make twenty brief stops, mini-conferences, to encourage one student, reward another, or scold another. The idea is to alleviate any initial hesitancy, to pulverize the block that appears when students begin to write. The peripatetic teacher also gains a quick overview of how the class is working and where the major problems are.

During the next fifteen minutes, the teacher conducts regularly scheduled conferences. She works with five students for three minutes each. The students know in advance that they will get to see the teacher during this special time. Other students concentrate on writing and respect conference time.

The teacher can use the last five minutes of the class to teach a brief lesson based on problems in students' papers, to share one or two stories with the whole class, to answer questions, to conduct more brief conferences, or to plan the next day.

The teacher could follow such a schedule for the first three days of the week: Monday, Tuesday, and Wednesday. At this rate, it would take two weeks to conduct a regular conference with each student. Since many students go through their academic careers without talking to any teacher about their writing, teachers should not be demoralized by the prospect of conducting only eighteen conferences with a student each year. Smaller classes or longer periods make things easier.

Each student tries to finish a draft of the story in three days. The goal is to have a rough draft ready to share with others. On Thursday the class breaks up into critique groups of no more than five students. Students get a chance to share their papers with others in the group. Other students listen and must respond in two ways: tell the writer the part they liked best and ask the writer a question that will evoke more information about the subject. For example, "The part I liked best was when the kitten ate the kitty litter. That was funny, but what was the kitten's name?" The student must make note of these questions and respond with what he plans to do next.

The teacher moves from group to group to make sure things are going well. She may want to share some of the more interesting papers with the entire class. In thirty minutes, each student and his story get at least five minutes of attention.

Friday becomes rewrite day, a day of major revisions, conferences, more revisions, and consultation of the dictionary. All the students should have changes to make in their stories. The teacher can sit at her desk while the children are rewriting. Students sign up for conferences as they need them. The teacher can collect the stories to read and review over the weekend, not to grade but simply to identify the most important problem in each story. The teacher can then be prepared for additional conferences and revisions in the following week. Perhaps after two weeks, students and teacher may be interested in publishing the stories.

Teachers can adjust this hypothetical schedule to meet their curriculum goals and to suit their own teaching styles. Teachers may find, for example, that their regular activities—lessons, worksheets, homework assignments—are greatly enhanced by a schedule that includes daily writing. The teacher can select student sentences to correct or diagram, study whether lessons in grammar and spelling carry over into student writing, and keep track of the skills the student has mastered in a notebook or on the student's folder.

A teacher of six sections may not want to teach writing to 150 students a day, fearing burnout. I have never experienced such a feeling because I find the conference approach so challenging and exhilarating, even if a class is going badly. The teacher is vulnerable. He must respond to the surprising writing of the student and find a way to communicate a new technique or plan for revision. This is hard work, the pedagogical equivalent of gardening, and good exercise.

But a middle school teacher may decide to break up the school year into modules to provide a variety of experiences for herself and her students. The schedule might look like this:

> Ten weeks of writing.
> Ten weeks of grammar.
> Ten weeks of literature.
> Ten weeks of writing.

Or better yet:

> Ten weeks of writing.
> Ten weeks of writing and grammar.
> Ten weeks of writing and literature.
> Ten weeks of writing.

Ten weeks of writing can teach a student a skill forever. Daily writing helps her understand a process, one she can turn to again and again. Taking ten weeks off to teach literature may not be the most desirable way to advance writing skills, but the teacher may find ways to remind students of how the study of literature leads to writing or relates to it. Novelist Erica Jong says that when she reads a good book or poem, she is moved to write a good book or poem herself. She is not inspired to write *about* the book, necessarily, the way literary critics do, but is moved to the act of writing itself.

Teachers whose students write every day must be prepared for the unpredictable. Students will come up with five writing ideas one day and none the next. They will write for thirty minutes without stopping one day and will lack concentration the next. In October they will write wonderful stories. In February they will regress. On some days they will be well behaved, on others they will seem too noisy and excited to work effectively.

Teachers should realize that these are the normal results of a year of daily writing. Writers all experience their ups and downs. I learned while writing this book that on some days I could write twenty pages without stopping but on other days I thought of a thousand excuses not to. Because the writer can be victimized by these vicissitudes, the teacher must create a classroom environment that helps the writer progress in his work.

What environment works best for writing class? I suggest the structure of the writer/painter's studio, the workshop, or the newsroom. Almost any classroom organization works if students are free to write, confer, and rewrite. But the traditional structure puts emphasis on the lecture. When I stand before a class of smiling faces, I am tempted to talk for an hour. If I sit at a table or walk in and out of circles of desks, I am more inclined to confer.

Imagine a group of painters working around a model in a quiet but productive environment in which teacher and student can confer. The teacher walks from canvas to canvas, giving a bit of advice here and there to suit the special needs of each aspiring artist.

Imagine the newsroom, a hive of writers and editors. Productive work goes on in spite of an energetic hum of activity. Writers collect information on the phone, flip through their notes, brainstorm a lead, or fire out a draft on a computer terminal.

Editors confer with writers, read and correct copy, or coordinate the activities of the staff.

- A healthy environment for writing is one in which students have enough quiet to concentrate, to write without distraction.
- Students can sit side by side with teachers to confer about their work.
- Students are able to find a comfortable place. If a student says, "Can I sit in the corner, or at a table?" the environment should tolerate some eccentricity. When the writing is not going well for a professional, he sometimes changes his location or writing environment. I see no reason why a productive student should not be permitted to do the same.
- The class structure encourages teamwork, collaboration, the sharing of stories, editing, and "instant publication."
- The workshop environment permits students to spread out and allows teachers to move around like bees pollinating flowers. Sometimes the environment seems like controlled chaos. A pleasant buzz of activity fills the room. Sometimes a lot of noise should be tolerated.

Writing classes, when they are going well, generate their own excitement. Students who concentrate and write diligently have the urge to share their work with others. Because writing is an intense personal act, the writer needs to blow off a little steam. After long periods of writing, I enjoy sports or physical labor. Students need outlets too.

But students must also learn the lessons of Ecclesiastes. There is a time to every purpose. Writing time is a silent, intense period of thought and concentration, sometimes fifteen minutes, sometimes longer. It is a time when the teacher may be writing with the students. Distractions are unwelcome. Students should not be sharpening pencils, or asking someone to spell a word, or going to the bathroom. The teacher should enforce the silence. Students should not interrupt teachers conferring with other students but work quietly on their own until it is their turn to confer.

At other times, noise is acceptable and even desirable. Students may confer with each other, look up words in a dictionary, ask important questions, and read their work out loud. Many students learn to write in such an environment. But students who are downright noisy or disruptive must be brought under control so that they do not destroy the workshop atmosphere. You do not usually hear raucous laughter in a newsroom or an art studio.

In my years of teaching children, I have found serious disruptions of the classroom rare. I have never had to yell at a student or send one to the office, although on many occasions I have had to quiet down a noisy and busy group. One of the wonderful side effects of writing every day is that students have too much to do to get themselves into trouble.

Chapter Four

Talking Writing

The most serious obstacle to daily writing is the teacher's desire to mark and grade every student paper. Let's say Mrs. Collins teaches language arts to 120 students a day and has them write each day of the school year. Let's say that Mrs. Collins, a dedicated teacher, spends five minutes correcting each paper. To accomplish this, Mrs. Collins would have to spend eighty-three days, without eating or sleeping, grading papers.

Some teachers feel that if they don't correct all the mistakes on a student's paper, they are shirking their responsibilities. Marking papers takes time and frustrates the teacher, who discovers that students learn little from her corrections and that she must note the same mistakes time and again. The endless and fruitless drudgery may influence her not to ask students to write at all.

The alternative is to conduct writing conferences, and that means getting students to talk about their own writing. To do that, teachers must begin to ask students questions, but not in the Socratic style in which teachers lead students to some predetermined conclusion. The questions I am thinking of demand much of the student and even more of the teacher.

I once taught a workshop in which a high school student, Andrew Benjamin, wrote a short feature story about a beautiful Episcopal Cathedral in downtown St. Petersburg. Andy read his story to a group of journalism professors and editors gathered together for a week's discussion of the writing process.

I asked the group if anyone could help Andy improve his work in one minute. A fine editor used his minute to make perceptive observations about the story, and offered specific suggestions on how it could be reorganized and improved.

Then it was my turn:

"Andy, what do you think of the story?"

"It's OK, I guess. It's only a first draft, so I know it needs some work."

"What did you have in mind?"

"Maybe I should work on the lead."

"What part of the story do you like the best?"

"I guess the part near the end when I describe the stained glass windows."

"That's my favorite part too. What would happen if you move that up higher in the story?"

"I don't know."

We asked Andy, who went on to Yale, which approach he preferred: the editor's directions or my questions. He said he much preferred specific helpful directions for improving the story. "You're the teacher. You're the expert. I want to know what you think so that I can make the story better."

The incident is revealing. Andy found it difficult to talk about his writing, to take full control of it, and to articulate the values that shaped it. He much preferred to have an expert do it for him.

But what is the point of that? The editor will not always be there to provide Andy with a specific list of helpful revisions. Andy needs to make some of the same revisions on his own. He needs to struggle with tough questions about his work and to perceive in those questions the solutions to various problems in his writing.

A writer will ask himself a hundred questions during the process of writing a story: Is this any good? How should I begin? Where is this thing going? Do I need to do more reporting? Why am I feeling so uneasy about this passage? Will someone be offended if I phrase it that way? What will I do next?

The good city editor has mastered the art of the two-minute writing conference. He has no choice since he must work with a large group of writers under frustrating time constraints in a crowded and sometimes chaotic environment.

- He knows he must work quickly with the writer. He has no time for psychiatric consultation.
- He asks questions to see how the writer feels about a story and what a writer knows.
- He figures out where the writer is in the process and what is the most important problem the writer faces.
- He gives something to the writer, information or advice or encouragement.

- He turns responsibility for perfecting the story back to the writer.
- Through his questions, he provides a model of the type of questions the reporter should be asking himself.
- His responses are predictable and reliable. The reporter knows what he's in for when he hands the editor his story.

City editors learn these techniques or die. Imagine the difficulty in dealing with twenty or thirty reporters at once, trying to give assignments, edit stories, and answer questions at the same time in a busy city room. The editor may have less than a minute to help the writer.

"Whatja get, Roy?"

"The story on the new postal rate increase."

"What did you find?"

"The guy in charge at the main post office quoted Shakespeare. He says he and his coworkers get the blame when people have to pay more to mail letters."

The editor laughs. "Is that your lead?"

"Yeah."

"How long will the story be?"

"I think sixty or seventy lines."

"We've got the room. Go to it."

That encounter took thirty seconds and was most helpful to me as a writer. Mike Foley offered me no advice whatsoever. He asked good questions and responded in a way that I found encouraging. The smile on his face and the tone of his voice were as important as anything he said.

Mike Foley and his brethren share some of the same traits as my first-grade teacher, Sister Mary Leone. Her classroom at St. Aidan School on Long Island was crowded. We shared desks, stuffed our clothes into lockers, and connected our galoshes with clothespins. We were always sick, and the teacher assumed that she would have the desks of sick students to use for others. (This was, of course, in the era of mumps and measles.) We had as many as seventy-two students in a single classroom. One teacher.

Yet I never remember feeling neglected or overlooked. Discipline was part of it. Yet I now marvel at my teacher's ability, under those trying conditions, to give praise or criticism with a glance. To shake or nod her head. To smile or scowl. To lay a hand on your shoulder.

That is what a writing conference can be. I walk around a classroom, ask a question, move on, move back, grunt, make a suggestion, pat a head, say "Right on," or "Holy cow!"

Mostly, I ask questions, but not the questions that some teachers ask: "Why do you keep making the same mistakes?" or "Why can't you be neater in your work?"

Donald Murray and Donald Graves taught me the following questions for writers, and I now realize they are the questions I always ask myself at the typewriter: "What surprised you most about what you wrote? What part was the most interesting for you to write? What do you plan to do next?" These questions permit the writer to make the key decisions about a story. They permit the student to think like a writer.

The questions themselves became a model of the writing process. A degree of predictability and repetition helps the writer, so I ask the same questions over and over, especially during the early classes. The questions sound simple, and they are, even if the answers are not.

I begin to ask these questions during the first week of class so that everyone can hear them:

"How's it going?"

"How do you feel about the story so far?"

"What part do you like the least?"

"What will you do next?"

"What works?"

"What needs work?"

When a teacher asks these questions for about a month, something interesting happens. A teacher may hear two students conferring with each other, following her model.

"What part do you like the best?"

"What part do you like the least?"

"What will you do next?"

When I teach this way, I hope that each writer will internalize the process and in the absence of a teacher begin to ask herself the same questions during revision.

As a student grows in practice and in confidence, she gains a vocabulary to speak about her work. Questions and answers become more specific and more challenging. Each conference seeks to solve a major problem in the story.

During the most effective conferences, teachers and students sit side by side. Here Pat Stanton creates a relaxed, nurturing environment in which Shannon Tierney can feel free to share her story.

"What's the focus of this story, Amy?"

"What it was like to be stung by a jellyfish."

"Is that what you're trying to say in your lead?"

"I guess not. Maybe I can change the lead to show the reader that something dangerous is going to happen."

"I'd like to see how you work that out."

To get students talking about writing, I like to write with them, especially on the first day. I ask my students to write on any topic for fifteen minutes. I tell them this work will not be graded and not to worry about their spelling. Just get something down on paper.

As they write, I write, sometimes on the blackboard. Then I share my writing with them. They are required to tell me which part of the story they liked the best and then ask me a question about what I wrote.

During the summer of 1983, I shared my writing with a class of thirty students, ages nine to thirteen. I wrote a piece in about twenty minutes on the birth of my first daughter, Alison, who happened to be a student in the class.

First Born

I remember the day my first child was born. The day was December 19, 1972. The baby wasn't due for four or five days, and we figured it might arrive on Christmas Day.

But I woke up in the middle of the night and heard Karen doing her breathing exercises on the couch. The couch would squeak each time she took a breath. Breath, squeak, breath, squeak.

She was in labor, all right, which meant our baby would be born the next day. I did what any faithful husband would do on such an occasion. I rolled over and went back to sleep. After all, I would need my rest.

At six in the morning, Karen was breathing faster and could barely walk. I ate a big bowl of Rice Krispies and made two tuna sandwiches for myself. I figured we were in for a long day.

"First babies take a long time coming," said our doctor when we called and woke him up. "Stay home and relax. Call me later."

So we waited as the labor contractions came faster and faster. Ten minutes apart. Eight minutes apart. Five minutes apart. Each time a contraction came, Karen would tense up, breathe rapidly until it passed, and then straighten up.

I figured it was time to get to the hospital. I helped her into the car, drove around the corner, and stopped at a delicatessen. More snacks for me of course, and some lollipops for her. We had been to childbirth classes, after all, and we knew everything about having babies.

Or did we?

By the time we got to the hospital, Karen couldn't walk; contractions were one minute apart and a receptionist rushed her to the labor room.

I went to a locker room to change into doctor clothes. I got to wear a medical robe, what looked like a shower cap, and one of those funky little masks. I met the doctor there and we were talking about the weather.

Suddenly a nurse rushed in.

"If you want to see this baby come into the world, you two better hurry," she said.

I couldn't believe it. I expected eight, maybe 12, hours of labor. I expected to be here all day, to eat my tuna sandwiches.

No way. Karen was ready. She wanted to push and the doctor told her "Go ahead." I helped her up and she gritted her teeth and grunted. She did this two or three times. One more time: up, push, grunt. POP!

Out came a squirmy, wet, wrinkled bundle of squirmy, wet wrinkles. We could see right away she was a girl. We were smart.

They washed her off, tied the umbilical cord and handed her to Karen who looked as if she had just run a mile.

The baby had blond hair, and we named her Alison. It was so much fun, we had two more daughters.

I held up the paper for them. They saw how sloppy it was and how many changes I had made, even in twenty minutes.

Students were specific about what they liked in the story. They liked the vividness of the description and the humorous nature of the piece. They quoted specific lines which appealed to them: "Out came a squirmy, wet, wrinkled bundle of squirmy, wet, wrinkles." But they wanted to know more: "How did you feel when the baby was born?" "Were you happy it was a girl, or were you hoping for a son?" "How did your wife feel about all this?" I recognized that each question could lead to some improvements in the story.

When they saw me, the vulnerable, egotistical writer, offering up my work to their questions, it gave them an incentive to do the same. It seemed like a harmless process, even fun. By the end of an hour, about a dozen students had shared their work and answered questions about it.

When I conduct an in-service day with teachers, I always try to have some students there. I ask everyone to write, and I write myself for a few minutes. Sometimes the writing goes well for me. Sometimes not. Then we talk about the writing process and confer. Usually, students are more eager to share their work than are teachers. Many teachers tremble at the prospect of sharing their writing with peers.

"I don't mind sharing my work with my students," said one teacher. "But the prospect of sharing it with other teachers frightens me."

There are many reasons for this. Teachers may not write often or at all. They lack confidence. They want their work to be perfect and know in their hearts that teachers who wield red pencils may call attention to the imperfections in their work. They are concerned about the negative consequences of sharing. And so are many students.

One of the saddest sights is that of a student, usually one who does not know me, throwing her body across her paper to hide it from my inspection. Other students see me coming and stick their papers in their desks so I can't get at them. These students lack confidence and know from experience that the only result of sharing your writing is a feeling of humiliation and failure. In such cases, I try to reconstruct the egos of these writers with praise and encouragement, and by finding specific strengths in the story. I ignore all weaknesses at first.

I was once teaching at a writing conference for high school journalists and walked up to a girl who was writing her first news story. I had never worked with her, and I didn't know her name.

"How are you doing?" I asked.

She was almost in tears. "It's a mess," she said. "I want you to know that I'm not feeling well. I've never done this before, and I don't think I can."

She looked so threatened that I backed off. I simply explained to her that news writing was not easy and that she should not feel discouraged, especially since she had managed to get some good information into the story. I pointed to a couple of paragraphs.

I was shocked, but delighted, when she approached me minutes later with a new version of the story that gave greater emphasis to the sections I had underlined. When I demonstrated to her that no evil consequences resulted from sharing her work with me, she was anxious to try me out again.

This works in the newsroom through a process known as "editor shopping." A writer knows that if he gives his work to one editor, the result may be grief and anxiety. Sports writers tell stories about a famous editor known as "the knife" who would always cut the writer's favorite passages out of a story. To avoid this, writers funnel their work to a more friendly or compassionate editor, or one who will not tamper with the story.

In an essay called "Why I Write," George Orwell says that the first reason is ego. Joan Didion, in an essay with the same title, finds the answer in the vowel sounds of the title: I, I, I.

Writing is a risky business. The act of writing, like the act of making love, involves the whole person. Writing makes the writer both vulnerable and insufferable. The wrong kind of criticism can be damaging.

Students develop defense mechanisms to protect themselves against invasion by teachers. "This is stupid," says a student, referring to a paper she handed in for consideration. I hear that response in every class. At first I thought it reflected a lack of ego, but I have changed my mind. A student who says "This is stupid" may mean: "I don't really think this is stupid, but I want you to tell me," or "In case this really is stupid, I don't want you to think that I don't know it."

Although Jeff Klinkenberg of the *St. Petersburg Times* is considered by some to be among the best writers in American journalism, he was seventeen years old before he received any praise or encouragement in his writing. He says of himself that he was "not a good student," although he did write for his own pleasure.

One of Jeff's most important and highly praised stories, written in 1983, concerned the life and death of his father. Jeff wrote: "He teaches me how to bait my hook and how to unhook a snapper without being pricked by the fins. He unhooks the catfish, which have venomous spines, and he does not complain when my line snags on the bottom. We bring home long stringers of tiny snapper for Mom to admire. She still has the photograph, yellowed with age." It was not the first time Jeff wrote about his dad. When he was about fifteen, Jeff wrote a paper for school entitled "My Father":

When I was four years old I thought of my Father much differently then I do today. Then he was like a God. At mealtimes in order to get me to eat, my mother would say, "If you want to be big and strong like daddy eat your dinner." Just the thought of that prompted me to eat my dinner. To me, he also was the man who brought things home to me and brought me places.

At seven, he was the man who brought me places, and also was the person who spanked me when I did wrongdoings. At home every night I would sit by the window with my nose on the glass and shout gleefully, "I see daddy!"

Now at fifteen, I see my father the way he is. He is a man. He is the man who married my mother, raised a family, and supports it. He is the one who takes me, my brother, and my mother places. He is the one who buys us food. He buys us (pertaining to my family) food and clothing. He pays the bills. He pays the taxes. He is the one who "cracks the whip" when it is needed. When I am an adult I hope I can be like him.

The teacher who asked Jeff to write this story was doing him a favor and contributing to his development as a writer. But she did not know what to do after the piece was handed in. Many good things stand out in the story, but the teacher's corrections ignore them. The piece has a good focus, putting all the attention on Jeff's maturing perception of his father. The lead sentence reflects that. The story has a decent structure and smooth transitions. And I especially like the image of a young Jeff with his nose pressed against the glass.

All that Jeff receives for this effort are four red marks on the page to correct spelling and punctuation. Two grades at the top say: Content B, Mechanics C. The teacher adds this sentence at the bottom (in red, of course): "Could be a little longer!"

I am not out to criticize a hard-working and well-meaning teacher, but I am struck with the futility of her grading exercise, not because she is too tough on Jeff but because she is not tough enough.

If Jeff is weak in mechanics, hand the paper back to him and let him try to find and correct his own mistakes. If the teacher thinks it should be longer, why not confer with Jeff to evoke more interesting and important information about his relationship with his dad? A simple question from the teacher such as, "What do you and your dad like to do together?" would probably have inspired Jeff to write about their fishing adventures.

What we have here is a fascinating first draft with numerous strengths and flaws. When we teach the old way, we never ask a student to get beyond this. We simply correct his mistakes for him.

As I write this, I realize something for the first time: through eighteen years of education, kindergarten through graduate school, I was almost never asked to rewrite a paper. Don Fry, my dissertation director, demanded important changes in my style. But most of the requests for rewriting and revision have come since I began writing for newspapers.

Although I wrote a great deal as a student, I never had what I would call a real writing conference. Teachers would write good things or bad things on my papers. I would smile if they were good, or get disgusted if they were bad and do my best to figure out what would please the teacher next time around.

Some English teachers behave as if they hold some great secret to the mystery of writing, some key that would unlock doors for the student. But they rarely give the key to the student. "I would work very hard and try to figure out what the path to success was," said one frustrated college student. "He would smoke his pipe, smile, write a few words on our papers. We never felt that we had a chance to learn." This professor assumed that you could just show some students a John Updike short story or a Hemingway novel and they would be able to write by transference or osmosis.

I was asked to write very little in elementary school. In high school I wrote much more. And in college I was writing at least an essay a week. Graduate school brought more writing, and I was cruising through my dissertation on Chaucer before my advisor, Don Fry, sat me down.

Don, a Beowulf scholar, asked me one question that turned

my writing around. "Roy, do you know what the active voice is?"

Of course, I learned about voice in the fifth grade, but I never did understand its application to my writing. As I looked at page after page of my work, I discovered how fat and flabby my verbs had become, especially when the article was a "scholarly" one. I suddenly began to rewrite, and the revisions made my work tighter and clearer.

I should have learned the lesson long before. Verbs mean everything to a sentence. The verb creates meaning, generates action, and makes clarity possible. Weak verbs, passive verbs, the verb "to be," create weak sentences, sentences without backbone or flair.

We should not wait until a student is twenty-six to communicate this. The fifth graders I know are ready to hear it. Many of them write with interesting, active verbs. Many others could do so through conferences and revision.

Chapter Five

Growing Writers

Earlier, I described a conference with a student named Kenny, who on the first day of class could think of "nothing" to write, but who finally revealed that he played soccer after school. I took dictation from him that day because he was so blocked in his writing. I conferred with him the next day: "Could you tell me about a time when you played soccer?" That question inspired a story which was eventually published in our class book:

Soccer on My Birthday
I like soccer. I play in a field with my friend. One time we lost our soccer ball and that night we went out with flash lights. At 11:30 we found the ball.
    I said that I was tired. When I went in the house everybody yelled "surprise." I said "What?" Someone said, "It's your birthday."
    I got Mr. Mouth, a checker board, and a new bike, then I fainted.

This story represented a dramatic improvement in his work. Through our conversations, he was able to discover something to write about, an interesting little story with a humorous ending.
    I tried the same technique with first grader Ryan, who had written this story:

I wit fisce [I went fishing]
I cot to fis [I caught two fish]
tin I cot a macrl [then I caught a mackerel]
tin tib [the end]

Although he struggled to write this much, I was determined to confer with him, to challenge him to improve the story.

A student and teacher confer about a story. The teacher begins with a question: "How can I help you?" Often the student already knows where the problem is and what needs to be done. Through more questioning, the teacher challenges the student to take responsibility for improving a story.

"I like the story, Ryan. It must have been exciting to catch fish."

He smiles and nods.

"How big was the biggest one?"

"About six inches."

"I think people would like to know that. Could you write it on the back of your paper and then decide where in the story it should go?"

Ryan went back to his desk for five minutes and returned. He had written "tin fsi wose 6 icis" (the fish was 6 inches) and drew an arrow back to the word "macrl." The conference had worked.

Donald Graves emphasizes the importance of using conferences to inspire revision and to improve the content of the story. Too often, I go after spelling, grammar, handwriting, and punctuation, rather than helping the writer find something to say. I am forever intimidated by the student's question: "Do I have to copy it again?" I want her to make substantive revisions, yet I am afraid they will slow her down and frustrate her.

Graves thinks this has something to do with "who has control of the story." If a student feels she is in control, the student will rewrite six times or more. Making students confront substantive changes in their work is an act of courage. It means facing some sour faces at first. But at some point students will commit themselves to revision.

Conferences excite and challenge both students and teachers. They test a teacher's energy and ingenuity. Each student and each story present a new problem to be solved, a new opportunity to teach.

• • •

Today Tiffany refuses to write. The assignment was to write a letter to someone you know. Tiffany writes one sentence and then stops. She does anything she can to avoid writing.

"I don't have anything to write about."

"Who are you writing to?"

"Teresa" (another student).

"How about a relative? Maybe you could tell her about school and things."

"My grandmother."

"OK. Write 'Dear Grandmother.' "

"I don't have anything to tell her. I spoke with her on the telephone."

After four or five tries, I get really frustrated with her. I threaten to take dictation. She resists.

"Did something happen to you that she doesn't know about?" I ask, hoping to inspire a narrative.

"My brother tried to choke me."

"Great!" I am almost beside myself with joy.

She writes one sentence. Then nothing. I know not what to do.

• • •

Eric cannot organize himself well enough to get any writing done at all. His work habits are atrocious. His desk looks like a war zone. He keeps a compost heap of papers and books growing in and on top of his desk. Things decay and get lost. (I've had to give him three notebooks.) And when he writes, he sticks a crumpled piece of paper on top of the heap. I've heard of rough drafts, but this is ridiculous.

"Eric, where's your writing folder?"

"I can't find it."

"It's over there in the file box. When you are not working on it, you should keep it there. Do you have any clean paper?"

"Sure."

"Let's keep it in the file. That way you can be more organized."

"OK."

"You must be a little uncomfortable trying to write with all that stuff on your desk."

"I could put it on the floor."

"All right. Or maybe you will be more comfortable working on that table."

First things first.

• • •

Elonda shows me a story describing her two friends. It is only three sentences long, and she says only that she likes them and that they play together.

"So you play together?"

"Yeah. Games and stuff."

"Can you tell me a story about a time you played together?"

• • •

There is a God! Tiffany, the most difficult of last week's students, is off and running on a book entitled "The Dangerous Stories of Tiffany," all generated by last week's conference. She wrote a story about how her brother tried to choke her. Now she has a dozen stories to tell about broken arms and bloody noses.

• • •

Anna Blackwood has written a long story about her dog.

"What happened next?" I ask.

The question produces another page of narrative.

• • •

Elonda has written three short paragraphs on three different subjects. I ask her which one she likes the best. She says "Games," and I ask if she could write more about that. She returns to her desk and writes.

• • •

Jimmy misspells many words and acts as if writing is not a cool thing to do. I want him to deal with mechanics, but not until he has something to say. I tell him to leave a space for each word he does not know how to spell. I tell him it is OK to invent spellings, as long as he tries to correct them in the final stages. He looks relieved.

• • •

Raymond writes a story about the battles of World War II. He is interested in the topic and enthusiastically writes several pages. They read like a history lesson.

"This is neat stuff, Raymond. It must have been exciting and scary to fight in the war. Do you know anyone who fought over there?"

"One of my neighbors did. He told me about it."

"Maybe you could write what he told you, or if you have a chance, maybe you could interview him for the story, or for another story."

• • •

Donna writes but does not want to rewrite.

"How do you like this, Donna?"

"Fine. It's finished. It's completely finished."

"What part do you like the best?"

"I like it all."

"What part do you think needs work?"

"None of it, it's finished."

"What are you going to do next?"

"Start a new story."

Oh, well.

• • •

Today Anna writes a great dream story. I ask her what she likes best about the story. After saying, "Uhhh, I don't know," she describes how she created suspense by delaying the humorous climax. She is exactly right. I am surprised when children can articulate what makes their stories work. If I only remember to ask them.

• • •

Lorna has been handing in stories filled with mechanical errors. I have ignored these to concentrate on content. Today she hands me a fourth draft of the story. It is mechanically perfect, although we have not discussed mechanics at all. She is more willing to work on the mechanics of the story if she has some investment in it.

• • •

"I've done this story on Mrs. Driver," says Wendy, who wants ten conferences a day.

Teachers who confer with students create a vocabulary for talking about writing. Students catch on right away. They begin to share their stories with each other, imitating the conference strategies they have learned from teachers.

"It looks good."

"But I've had to leave these blanks. I didn't get the name of her daughter. What should I do?"

"Do what reporters do. Do a follow-up interview. Collect the information you need."

• • •

Today I conduct conferences in groups of three. I let other students make suggestions about changes in the story. Alison suggests an exclamation point at the end of Eric's story, and he likes the idea.

• • •

Before school this morning, Michelle comes up and tells me that her mom's car caught on fire. "That would make a good story to write," says John. Nice conference.

• • •

Jenny writes a story about Jeff Klinkenberg's visit to class.

Her first draft is filled with mechanical problems. She leaves out his name and does not include the most interesting part of his visit, a description of a great white shark. She has taken a few scattered notes, and the information in her story is limited to what she had in her notebook, and in that order.

"What was the best part of his visit?" I ask.

"The part about the shark."

"Can you put that in the story?"

I praise her excellent description of Jeff and mention that she has forgotten to name him. She works on the draft, making two major changes: 1) names him in the margin and draws an arrow to where it should go; 2) writes about the shark and changes a transition to make it work. Her second draft is markedly improved. She corrects several mistakes on her own.

● ● ●

"I've checked all the spelling words," says Lydia. "I'm completely done."

"Looks good, Lydia, but I see a problem in line five and in line nine. See if you can find those on your own."

● ● ●

"What have you got, Anna?"

"I've added a new part, and I think I'm finished."

"This is going to be a great story. But it's one long paragraph. Why don't you mark off where the paragraph breaks should be and bring it back up to me."

● ● ●

I love to teach this way. I can teach a lesson when the writer is ready to learn it. If the student is ready to learn about leads or endings or semicolons, I can teach it to him and he can apply the knowledge immediately.

It also permits me to work with students at different stages of the writing process. One day I kept a record of the conferences that I conducted during a half-hour period.

Zaneta: clarify, prepare for publication

Wendy: find new story idea

Cesar: add new information to story

Lydia: break into paragraphs

Sherie: collect more information

Wendy: work on the lead

Gillian: the lead

Emily: prepare for publication

Robbie: brainstorm a title

Kelly: make a list

Dalia: collect information

Sherie: begin work on final draft

Dale: figure out how to shorten a very long story

Each of these students approached my desk and signed up for a conference. They returned to their own desks to work on the story until I was ready for them.

At the very end of class, I conducted nine more conferences in a process I call "the assembly line." It does not always work, but it can be an effective tool for communicating in conferences that last less than a minute.

Students line up in rows of five or ten. Then I crank it up. I must concentrate and take advantage of our limited time. The students on line can reread their stories or have conferences, so that the fifth person in line has the benefit of four overheard conferences, like a golfer going to school on someone else's putt.

"John, what have you got?"

"My lead and my middle, but I can't think of the ending."

"What are you thinking about?"

"About sort of going back to the beginning."

"You mean echo the beginning at the end? Sounds like a good idea."

● ● ●

As students assume more control of their writing, they save the teacher lots of work. Teachers discover they do not even have to read the story to help the student. The students know the story and the subject matter better than the teacher. So in a crunch, the teacher can still ask questions, like the wise city editor, and help students discover what they need to do next.

"How's it coming?"

"Great. Almost finished."

"What are you working on?"

"Just working more on my lead."

"Got a problem?"

"No, just changing the words around."

"Great, go to it."

● ● ●

Darold is a student with a learning disability. He is an affable young man about twice the size of most other children in the fifth grade. He is sometimes ridiculed because of his low level of achievement. What impresses me about him is his willingness to write. He is capable of dictating his stories to another student. We have published his dictated stories, and he seems to gain satisfaction from this.

I often face this criticism from teachers: "The techniques you talk about may work in an honors class or with a group of advanced students, but how do you keep mediocre or poor students 'on task' and interested?"

I expect students of every academic level to write. All students can learn from writing. Not every student will produce a piece worthy of publication in the *St. Petersburg Times*, but forced to make meaning, forced to communicate, a student may be able, after great struggle, to write a paragraph instead of a sentence, or a sentence instead of nothing. And that is education.

It is easier to confer with weak students than with strong writers. The weak student may write a sentence or nothing at all. The strong student may write a five-hundred-word essay. A conference with a weak student may inspire him to collect more information or simply to continue writing. It requires a more sophisticated understanding of the writing process to diagnose a good story and discover ways to make it better.

The weak student may be open to criticism because he hears it so often. When the response to his writing turns out to be helpful and friendly, he may be excited by the prospect of taking control, perhaps for the first time, of his own work. The strong student, conditioned by unqualified praise, may be unwilling to revise and rewrite. She may see the conference as a challenge to her perfection. "If he wants me to change it, there must be something wrong with it." Teachers must work hard to move these students to higher levels of excellence.

Chapter Six

Making a Mess

By the end of the first week of class, I ask students to revise their work. Writing is rewriting, they learn, even though no one has asked them to rewrite a story before. I ask them how they could improve a story. They suggest:

1. Add things.
2. Change words.
3. Correct spellings.
4. Change punctuation.
5. Make things clearer.
6. Take things out.

Students in one class lacked enthusiasm for this stage of the process. Two students wanted to write new stories. One girl said that making changes was "too hard." I told the class to cross out words rather than erase them. I taught them editing marks for inserting new material. I showed them how to mark the margins to indicate change.

While they worked, I conducted about fifteen conferences in a half hour.

"What do you think about this story, Michael?"

"I like the story the way it is," he said. "I don't want to make any changes."

(I noticed two misspelled words but ignored them.)

The story, about his sick grandmother, was eventually published in the *St. Petersburg Times*.

"Did you visit your grandma in the hospital?"

He nodded.

"Write about that at the bottom of the page."

Five minutes later he approached me with what he had written.

"Now where in your story could these sentences go?" I asked.

He drew an arrow showing where he wanted to insert the new information. I suggested to him that he begin another draft of the story. He completed it quickly. I discovered misspellings. I ignored these for the time being and praised him for doing the revision.

During this class, I introduced the strategy of the Messy Draft and the Neat Draft. This technique is one of the most important I teach because by the time students reach the fifth grade, they are conditioned to the idea that "neatness counts."

My daughter Emily once brought home a handwriting exercise in which the teacher instructed her "not to erase or cross out." As a result of such exercises, students come to confuse writing with handwriting. Using my own work as an example, I argue that messiness is a necessary step toward neatness. I scribble, I cross out, I draw arrows, I fill the margins with notes. I begin in disorder and through the process of writing achieve some order. Messiness becomes neatness.

To prove my point I show students *Authors at Work*, a wonderful book displaying large photographic reproductions of the manuscript pages of famous writers: Pope, Boswell, Shelley, Balzac, and many others. It is gratifying to see the splendid confusion, disarray, and messiness of these pages, each a map of the writer's mind.

Students ooh and aah when they see these pages. They begin to understand the creative importance of formlessness in the early stages of a work. "The sculptor doesn't begin with a finished statue," I tell them, "but with a lump of clay."

Donald Graves argues that when a student stops erasing and begins crossing out, he achieves an important step toward writing maturity. A cross-out indicates: "I know this is imperfect, but I'm trying to make it better. By making it sloppy now I'm moving closer to neatness and perfection."

The more students cross out and revise, the more they come to know that imperfection is inevitable. Some literature teachers never become good writing teachers because they study, assign, and explicate only the greatest, most polished works. Imperfection

Writers, young and old, think of writing as magic because they often study the product rather than the process of writing. Teachers can demystify this process for students by sharing with them the early drafts of famous writers. This page reveals the handwritten manuscript of *A Christmas Carol* by Charles Dickens. Notice the messy markings and extensive revisions.

with permission from
The Pierpont Morgan Library

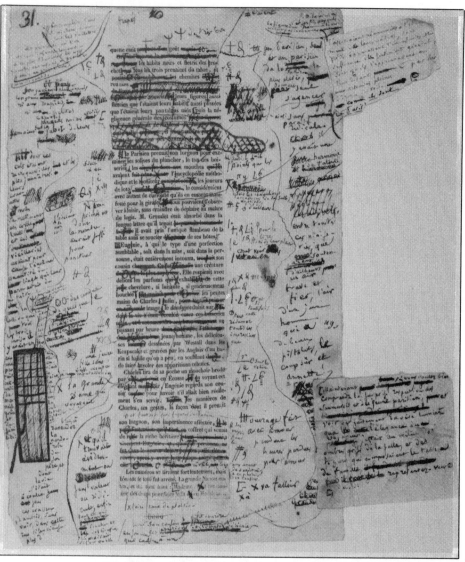

Has there ever been a page with more messy and extensive revisions than this one? It is the work of French author Honoré de Balzac, a corrected galley proof of *Eugenie Grandet* (1833). If you want to teach children that good writers revise, this page usually does the trick.

with permission from
The Pierpont Morgan Library

makes them anxious, and they pass on their anxieties to students. When a student erases a mistake rather than crossing it out, he is saying: "God, something bad slipped in here. I hope I can eliminate all traces of it before somebody sees it and makes me write this paper again."

A teacher at a private school said that her students were weak writers. A parent told me that the students at the school were required to write their stories in italic print. If I had to write everything in italic print, I would go crazy. Worrying about the neatness of handwriting in the early stages of the writing process can frustrate and immobilize the writer.

So while some teachers tell their students to slow down and be neat, I tell them to speed up and be sloppy—*in the early stages.* As students have more and more time and energy invested in a story, as they undertake several revisions, they come to understand that the story should be clearer, neater, and better.

Publication also helps students write with a purpose. We improve a story while striving to reach an audience. Eventually, we want it neat and error-free so that our meaning is clear and readers can enjoy it.

This process puts both handwriting and grammar in context. They need not be boring school tasks, although most children think of them that way. Handwriting and grammar are the tools of clarity. I tried to get one student to improve her handwriting so I could read her papers with greater ease. The lesson did not sink in until the day she shared her story with a friend who read a few words, pointed at some scribbles, and said, "I can't read that."

Many students, especially girls, receive praise for the neatness of their handwriting and their ability to create a story that pleases the eye and avoids errors. This is understandable. Some student papers are so sloppy and error-riddled that the sight of them demoralizes a teacher. So when a teacher finds a story that reflects care and concentration, he rightly praises it.

Even neat, bright, concerned students must be taught the value of planned messiness. Doreen, a fifth grader, always handed in excellent work. She received awards and recognition for her writing. Her penmanship was beautiful, and if she made any mistakes, she would erase them into oblivion. When she handed in a piece, it was always with the same confidence: "I'm finished," or even, "I'm completely finished."

Doreen was confused and put off by our early conferences.

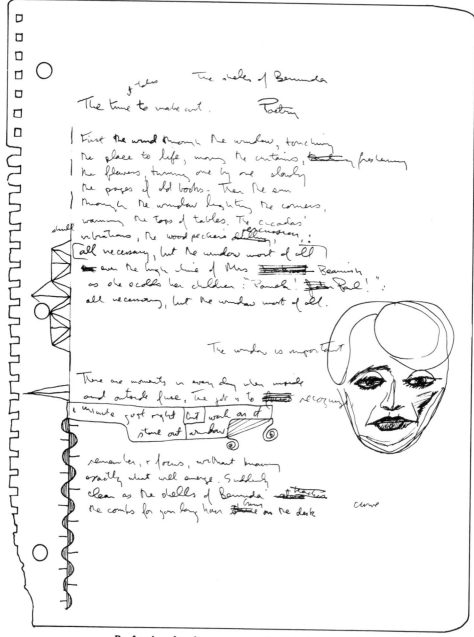

Professional writers are not afraid to be messy in the early stages of writing. Here is a handwritten draft of a poem by Peter Meinke, one of Florida's best and most versatile writers. Notice the doodling and

THE SHELLS OF BERMUDA

First the wind through the window, lifting

this room with breath, tugging the curtains, waking

the flowers, turning one by one slowly

the pages of old books. Then the sun

through the window glinting in corners,

warming the tops of tables. The cicadas'

shrill vibrations, the woodpecker's percussion,

even the high whine of Mrs. Reinhold

as she scolds her children--"Pamela! Paul!":

all necessary; but the window most of all.

There are moments in every day

when a hunger seizes and the hands

tremble and a wall turns transparent

or a cup speaks. Suddenly

bright as the shells of Bermuda

the combs for your long hair blaze on the desk.

revision. The first two lines read: "First the wind through the window, touching / the place to life, moving the curtains, freshening. . . ." Contrast these lines with the published version of the poem above.

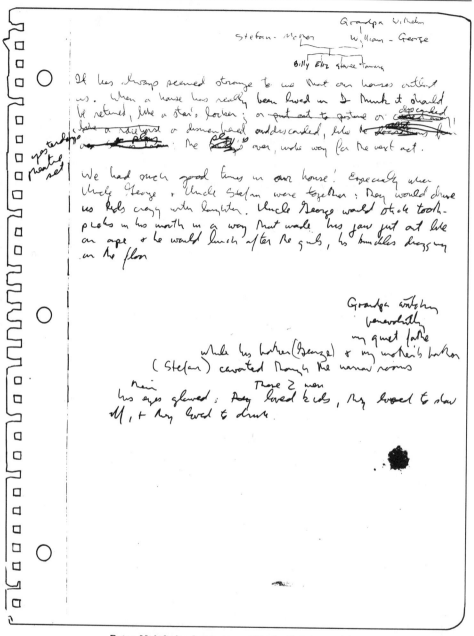

Peter Meinke's short story, "Uncle George and Uncle Stefan," was selected for inclusion in *Prize Stories 1986: The O. Henry Awards*. The story began, humbly and messily, with Meinke's handwritten draft. Notice the mysterious stain in the lower right-hand corner of the page. The neat final draft is reproduced on the next page.

UNCLE GEORGE AND UNCLE STEFAN

It has always seemed strange to me that our houses outlive us. When a house has really been lived in it should be retired, like a star's locker; or dismantled and discarded like yesterday's theatre set: the play's over, make way for the new.

We had such good times in our house! Especially when Uncle George and Uncle Stefan were together: they would drive us kids crazy with laughter.

"Tamara!" Uncle Stefan would frown at me across the dinner table. "Eat every carrot and pea on your plate!"

"Yes sir," I would say, while the others whooped and hollered. I was a slow learner, and my older sister Elizabeth would shake her head in disgust at my gullibility.

Neither Uncle Stefan nor Uncle George was a mean man: their eyes bulged with high spirits. They loved us kids (more than our parents did, we thought), they loved to show off, and they loved to drink. At some point during most parties, Uncle George would stick toothpicks into his mouth in a way that made his jaw jut out like an ape's and would lurch after us, his knuckles dragging across the floor; until Uncle Stefan, using the fireplace poker as a rifle, would leap in front of the roaring creature and shoot him through the heart. George would collapse in a moaning heap, whereupon we children would leap on him like gnats on a bull: Uncle George was <u>big.</u> One time, in an excess of fearsome invention, he jumped on our wooden cocktail table, which exploded into splinters so quickly that there was a minute of confusion while everyone tried

-page 1-

Students are sometimes afraid to revise because they have been conditioned to believe that neatness is always important. With daily writing, they come to understand the importance of editing their own work. Eventually, they become proud of the revisions that improve a story. Here Karen Wright shows off her early draft of a story on visitors from the People's Republic of China.

She wondered why I would not shower her with praise, or why I wanted to know more information, or why I would want her to try another draft. She saw my efforts as an implied condemnation of her work. Doreen assumed that she could "get it right" the first time. What was she to make of this teacher who always wanted to "talk with her" and always wanted her to make ugly marks on her perfect page?

I understood her feelings. My handwriting was always terrible, but when I handed in a piece of writing, I expected to receive praise. I did not want anyone telling me how to make my work better. I wanted them to tell me that my writing was . . . well, perfect.

In those days I most hated someone looking over my shoulder as I wrote. I was like the student who throws his body over his paper to hide it from the teacher's view. If someone saw my paper before it was perfect, that person would see all the "bad" writing. I notice that teachers, too, will only share the best of their writing with me or other teachers. Anything less would be a sign of weakness, ignorance, or imperfection.

The more I write and the more I understand the process of writing, the less neurotic I become. Now I share my writing at every and all stages with anyone who wants to see it. Want to look at my notes? My outline? My early drafts? My crumpled pages? Want to look over my shoulder as I struggle to think of a word and then pick a stupid one? Fine. Go ahead. No one judges the race by examining the warm-up exercises or criticizes the statue by examining the shapeless lump of clay. As Peter Elbow argues, a writer may have to find the wrong words to say the wrong things before he discovers the right words to say the right things.

My students quickly learn that lesson. Students such as Doreen, once unwilling to cross out a word, now proudly offer for my inspection papers decorated with arrows, additions, cross-outs, and second thoughts. They know they will always have a chance to write it again. Teachers who only give students one shot at writing a story, one chance to get it right, do not understand how writers work.

To break through the natural block that stands between the writer and the page is no easy task. Students cannot say important things when we teachers act like masons, piling stone after stone on top of the block. If our standards are too high during the early stages of work, students become paralyzed in the face of them.

As I wrote the early drafts of this book, I often ignored spelling, style, and even accuracy of information because I knew I could deal with these problems later. (At the end of the process, I devoted two months of work to fact-checking alone.) When I begin to draft a story, I struggle to get something on paper. Taking poet William Stafford's advice, I lower my standards to build momentum, but only to raise them with each successive draft. I never expect perfection. When I summon the courage to read this book for the first time, I will find many words I wish I had not written. I will, on occasion, read a sentence and slap my forehead in disbelief.

One night I received a phone call at home. The young voice on the line said, "Hello, Dr. Clark, this is Jennifer." Since my daughters have at least ten friends named Jennifer, I thought it was one of them. Not so. "This is Jennifer Stiles," she said again, "from the *Cougar Chronicle*."

Jennifer wanted to interview me for her fifth-grade newspaper. She had prepared a list of questions, and we talked for about twenty minutes. The story she produced was entitled "This writing teacher flunked kindergarten":

Dr. Roy Peter Clark has been coming to our fifth grade and we have had a good time. Here is some information about this very funny man. He went to kindergarten twice. For high school he went to Long Island and for college, it was Providence College and for graduate college, Stony Brook.

He decided to write with the newspaper while he was a teacher in Alabama, and was interested in the South because he always lived in the North, so he wrote stories to newspapers and the manager of the *St. Petersburg Times* asked him to work there. He seriously started writing in 6th grade and wrote a Christmas poem and different stories and enjoyed it.

During high school he had many odd jobs like being a paperboy. He was also a soda jerk, which is a person who makes soda, but got fired because the ice cream kept on floating to the bottom. He worked in a supermarket and played the piano with a rock group. He had lived in New York, Rhode Island, Alabama and then moved to Florida. He also spent a summer in England.

He also now works with other writers at the Poynter Institute. He has been to 30 different states. He was invited to go to Hawaii and Alaska but has been too busy. He has worked full-time at the *St. Petersburg Times* only but has written freelance to 10 different newspapers.

He has interviewed many people. His most famous were Farrah Fawcett Majors, Carol Burnett, James Garner, Glenda Jackson and Lauren Bacall and has met Jody Powell. He also said and I quote, "Bay Point 5th graders are very hard workers and I enjoy working with them."

Students who read Jenny's story were impressed with the quality and quantity of information she derived from interviewing and careful notetaking. They also loved the delicious irony of the "failed" teacher, the expert who flunked kindergarten and whose ice cream sodas flopped.

Jenny explained to the class how she wrote this story. She described our telephone conversation, how she sat on the floor of her parents' bedroom, the phone tucked between her shoulder and her ear, and scribbled notes on what I said. "I went through my notes to pick out what was the most important," she said. "Then I wrote the lead and then a rough draft of the story. Then I went through it to find as many mistakes as I could. Then I rewrote it neatly."

Jenny's description of her writing process reminds me of my own. The story is not projected neatly from the writer's mind onto the page. Sometimes the writer starts scribbling notes while sitting on the floor. First comes the messy draft. Then the writer improves it and makes it neater.

Lydia Abrams was a fourth grader who wrote well and enjoyed praise for her work. At first she resisted the notion that she should revise her work, but after several conferences she learned the techniques that would help her improve her story. In a piece entitled "That Sad Night," Lydia marks up her first draft and creates the opportunity for significant revision:

~~I have a neighbor named Bernie Paul.~~ She has a husband named Bernie ~~a / we call her Bobbie.~~ Bobbie's mother, Kerry, lives with them. One day ~~they~~ *the three* went on a trip for about 2 weeks.

On ~~about~~ Tuesday or Wednesday it was 9:00. Bed time for me. My father was putting my 4 year old sister to bed. My mom was watching T.V. We heard bells ringing. I thought it was just the T.V. I went to get some water and a lady I know, who lives on my block, was at the front door. She did not look happy at all. She wanted dad, ~~so~~ I got him. Dad talked with her out side. When he came *back* in he didn't look happy either. He said to me, "Bobbie died from a heart attack in the car." *[For a long time]*

Only two tears came from my my eyes. ~~Then~~ I went to get some water and started to cry alot. Dad put me to bed that night. I laid down and started to cry loud and long. Dad sat on my bed and calmed me down. The next morning I forgot all about it. *[about Bobbie.]* *Until* ~~Then~~ my mom told my brother & sister. I didn't get *I started crying some more.* over it. Finelly I did.

The End

Every day that week I keep saying to myself or to another person, "There will never be another person like that special like Bobbie." I also say "Bobbie is so wonderful and nice."

Print makes this draft seem neater than it was. Lydia's two pages were messy enough for her to undertake a number of important revisions in the story:

1. The beginning: Rather than introducing all the characters at the top, Lydia considers eliminating her first four lines and beginning the story with the narrative.
2. The ending: Lydia changes her mind about the ending, rejecting a conclusion that puts undue attention on herself for one that makes us remember how special Bobbie was. She also crosses out a final sentence, recognizing that one statement about Bobbie would be better than two.
3. Paragraphs: Lydia has a good sense of where her story shifts gears. She marks off paragraphs as a function of revision.
4. Clarifying information: Lydia recognizes some passages that may confuse the reader. So she adds new information to help make things clearer.
5. Unnecessary words: By crossing out "about" and "then," Lydia attempts to eliminate clutter from the writing.
6. Mechanics: Lydia corrects "alot," but she must deal with other spelling and grammar problems in subsequent drafts.

She constantly seeks to improve her work through revision. Two weeks earlier she would have handed in a neatly written draft of her work and said, "Here. I think it's perfect." Now she knows differently.

During the summer of 1983, eleven-year-old Nancy Taylor wrote a first draft of a story about an embarrassing moment. Here is her draft with some revision marks she made after a conference:

The embarrassing moment

In 5th grade when I used to go to a private school we had to wear a uniform, a skirt ~~with a shirt or~~ a blouse ~~with a crest on it with~~ shorts underneath.

It was time for P.E. and we ~~have to slip off~~ our skirts ~~and go~~ outside. ~~Naturally under the skirts we had shorts on.~~

Well that morning when I was getting dressed for school I forgot to put the shorts on under my skirt. ~~So when p.e. came around~~ I slipped of my skirt and everyone started laughing like crazy.

I couldn't figure out why but my legs were cold and (I had put my skirt away already) and I looked down and thats when I discovered I was in my underwear and my blouse!

Two of my friends (which were guys) were on the floor dying of laughter.

I pulled down my blouse (which was seethrough) and stood there for ~~about 5 minutes~~. Then the teacher had someone get my skirt and we went out to P.E.

From then on whenever we had P.E. I was ^very^ careful to check underneath my skirt before I took it off.

Also the next day when I took my skirt off everybody stared and when they saw I had shorts on they started clapping.

~~Now that is what I call Embarresing. But at least~~ I laughed along with them. ~~Because it was so funny I really liked the laugh but I would't like it to happen again besides the fact it was humorous.~~

Nancy made most of her revisions after a slightly argumentative conference during which we discussed the ending of the story.

"Why did you decide to end it there?"

"I wanted to show that I was laughing with them."

"I like the spirit of that. It shows you're a good sport. But I also like the scene where they clap because you have your shorts on. It might be a good place to end."

"But then it would just stop."

Students who learn "In conclusion"-type endings may fail to recognize a story's natural conclusion. Even professionals are prone to carry their stories one paragraph too far. Nancy resisted this change at first, but when she began to consider other changes in her story, she came to agree that she should revise her ending. Nancy makes many sophisticated revisions in this next draft:

The Embarrassing Moment

In 5th grade when I used to go to a private school we had to wear a uniform, which consisted of a skirt with a blouse and shorts underneath.

One morning when I was getting ready for school, I forgot to put shorts underneath my skirt.

It was time for P.E. and I slipped off my skirt and put it away and everyone started laughing at me like crazy.

I couldnt figure out why but my legs were getting cold and clammy. I looked down and that's when I discovered I was in my blouse and underwear!

Two of my friends (who were guys) were on the floor clutching their sides dying of laughter. I have to admit it was funny so I laughed along with them.

I was so embarrassed I pulled down my blouse (which was see-through) and stood there for a couple of minutes just standing there looking stupid. When our teacher stopped laughing and calmed down enough to talk she told somebody to go and get my skirt. I put it on and we went out to P.E.

From then on whenever we had P.E. I was very careful to check underneath my skirt before I took it off.

Also the next day when I took my skirt off everybody stared and when they saw I had shorts on they started clapping.

Consider the variety of revisions that transform Nancy's messy draft into a neat one:

Messy Draft	Neat Draft
The embarrassing moment	The Embarrassing Moment
with a crest on it	deleted
paragraphs 2 and 3	order reversed to establish clearer chronology
. . . my legs were cold . . .	. . . my legs were getting cold and clammy. (Gives the word *clammy* emphasis by placing it at the end of sentence.)
. . . I was in my underwear and my blouse!	. . . I was in my blouse and underwear!
I had put my skirt away already	moves it higher to help chronology
see through	see-through
about 5 minutes	a more modest "couple of minutes"
. . . the teacher had someone get my skirt . . .	Teacher has a fuller role, laughing along with everyone else.
they started clapping	becomes the ending (Nancy deletes most of her original ending.)
I laughed along with them	She retains this but moves it higher in the story.

Notice that Nancy also rejects some of her first revisions.

The strategy of the Messy Draft and the Neat Draft should not lure students into thinking they need rewrite a story only once. A single revision can accomplish a great deal, as Nancy Taylor has illustrated. The student who understands the need for revision, not just of mechanics but of content, will be willing to undertake four, five, or six messy drafts before she is satisfied with her neat one.

My Cats   Laura Daly
                                                     Sept. 10, 1985
                                                     Writing

I've lived ~~with~~ cats all my ~~life. The~~ life. The
~~only cats that~~ my family has had ~~that I~~ don't remember
~~we Benpie & Christopher.~~
~~Arthur is the first cat we had that I can~~
~~remember~~

got Arthur is the first cat that ~~I com~~ ever
calico remeber having. ~~I~~ He was a calico cat
and Than my family ~~we~~ got Gwen for a Valentine's present
for my mom. When Arthur ~~saw~~ met Gwen, he ran
away. Gwen is a calico too. We ~~got~~ had her
spaided so she couldn't have babies. ~~We we~~
~~still tow~~ have Gwen

About a year after we ~~got~~ got ~~Gwen~~ ~~Gwen~~.
Gwen our neibor's cat had kittens and we
took ~~two~~ 2. We named them ~~to~~ Fred &
Goerge. Fred was all black. And Goerge was
yellow. We had Fred and Goerge for a while,
but then Fred got ran over by a car. A couple
of months later Goerge ran away.

And then we got Rio & Tia. They were sisters.
Rio was gray & white, and Tia was black. One day
my dad left some weed poisoning outside and ~~then~~
Tia got into it and died. ~~One night a dog~~
~~cts~~. A couple of months later a dog attacked Rio and

Fifth-grader Laura Daly has learned how to mark up and revise her early drafts in productive ways.

~~Then one day we got it she died.~~

found a
pregnant cat
that was
going to have
kittens in
our yard.
We took her
inside and
called her
Peggy. About
an hour later
she started
to have kittens
we named
them Waddles
and
Lizzy. Then
we found a
home for
all of them.

A couple of
months later
Rio got
attacked by
a dog that
lives across
the street,

she was the
best ~~~~
she

^Then when I was in 3rd grade ~~we c~~ my sister ~~brought~~ brought home 2 kittens from ~~her teacher~~ school. We named them Cindy & Sally. Cindy had light yellow + white striped fur, and Sally had dark yellow + white striped fur. Cindy was always fat but Sally was always skinny. ~~He~~ Cindy always liked to sit in the middle of the road. And then one night she got hit by a car and we had to put her asleep because she had a broken leg. ~~And last And last~~ Christmas ~~we~~ our friend gave us a cat that thier nieghbor (abandoned). We named her Shadow. She's all gray. ~~Then Sally had~~ Then Sally then had 4 ~~kittt~~ kittens. We named them Tommy, Matilda, Snow paws, and Joanyy. We found homes for all of them but Tommy.

2½ weeks after Sally had her kittens, Shadow had 4 kittens. We named them Rowdie, Fluff, Samatha, and Stripe. The best one in that group was Fluff. ~~Fluff~~ was all gray, had really long fur, and looked exactly like a Persian, but she wasn't.

3   And then Saturday, Sept. 7, 1985, Shadow had babies. They have long fur and are very fluffy and cute. Their names are Puff, Cocoa Puff, Wombo.

Chapter Seven

Exploring

On August 16, 1984, a group of student writers had a visit from Rabbi Arthur Baseman of Temple B'nai Israel in Clearwater, Florida. The students had been studying writing and journalism for three weeks, and on this day I issued a special challenge. During a twenty-minute period, I would interview Rabbi Baseman while they listened, observed, took notes, and planned to write a profile. Following the interview, the students would have forty minutes to make sense of their notes, draft a story, revise, and proofread.

Karen Witham, about to enter the eighth grade, took this set of notes:

Dalia's father
Rabbi Arthur Baseman
Temple Bnai Israel
Rabbie—true pron. in Hebrew
my teacher
teaches anyone who
    will listen
being a Rabbi is a
    full time job
day begins with a task (hosp. visits, correspondence)
meeting with people
teens—mitsvahs
adults—troubles
preach
prepare sermons
pastor (counsel)
Priest (blessing, wedding, funeral, naming)
Pusher (gets things done)
1964—ordained
15 yrs. Temple B.Is.
Always want to be a rabbi? loved his religion,
not 'till senior in college did realize wanted to be
a rabbi
Temple
3 major functions
1 House of Prayer

2 House of Assembly
3 House of Study
synagouge or temple
sanctuary—worship
place—light is always burning
eternal—man & god
chooses words so carefully for sermon
"people are the key"
but are frustrating

That clear, crisp set of notes, which puts my system of notetaking to shame, produced the following draft:

What It Means to Be a Rabbi

Rabbi. Pronounced Rab-e in Hebrew, it means "my teacher." Today Rabbi Arthur Baseman from Temple Bnai Israel taught us a few things about what it means to be a rabbi.

First, I learned that all rabbis (or Jewish men, for that matter) are not solemn looking men with long grey beards, black robes, and little black hats on their heads. Rabbi Baseman has black hair, no beard, and wore normal, everyday clothes. He was very nice and a great speaker.

Rabbi Baseman told us there are five "p" words that best describe a rabbi and what he does. They are:

1. Preach
2. Prepare Sermons
3. Pastor (counsels all kinds of people with their problems)
4. Priest (performs various ceremonies of life stages like namings, bar mitzvahs, weddings, & funerals)
5. Pusher (he pushes people to get things done—but in a nice way)

Ordained in 1964, Dr. Baseman is now celebrating his 20th anniversary as a rabbi. Fifteen of those years were spent at Temple Bnai Israel. He has always loved his religion, but he didn't know for sure until he was a senior in college that he wanted to be a rabbi.

I then learned that the temple (or synagogue) has 3 major functions; a House of Prayer, Assembly and Study. The sanctuary is the room of Prayer. A light is always burning in this room to symbolize the eternal relationship of men/women & their God.

Dr. Baseman's sermons must be an incredible experience, for not only is he a good public speaker, but he chooses his words with care, knowing they might influence a life.

When asked what was the most frustrating for him, he quickly replied, "people." But he went on to say that "people are the key."

After he led us in a moving prayer, he left. And I realized that this was a man that loved people, loved his work, and loved his God.

In this story, Karen displays an impressive array of writing skills. Her story contains interesting information, quotations, explanation, description, and opinion. She creates a remarkably concise and interesting picture of the rabbi, not through flourishes of style, although her style is smooth and effective, but through the efficient collection and processing of information: notetaking, interviewing, listening, observing, and rehearsal. She is not weaving stories out of thin air or playing rhetorical tricks that call attention to her language rather than her subject. Instead, she writes with concern for her reader and with the sensibilities and strategies of a young journalist.

To improve students' writing we must make them efficient collectors of information. This takes hard work. Students are used to being passive receivers of information, what one teacher calls "the dirty sponge." They listen to what the teacher says, soak it in, wring it out for exams, and forget it. The sponge is dry.

Students sit passively in class and passively in front of their television sets. They receive stimuli in bright bursts that shorten their attention span. They tune out teachers who lecture on the rules of writing and grammar without requiring them to turn that talk into action.

As a student, I did my best to reject passivity. I could soak it in as well as the next student and wring it out better. But I was interested in the classroom dynamic, in the exchange of ideas, and in the struggle to learn. I might ask impertinent questions to engender an outraged response from the teacher, but at least I was asking questions. I felt it was my responsibility, not just the teacher's, to make an hour of class interesting and productive.

I was not so courageous or determined in my writing. I remember a time during the 1960s when students received writing assignments on contemporary issues: "Is pollution threatening our environment?" or "Is priestly celibacy a good thing?" We received these assignments in the name of relevance, and they might have resulted in some interesting stories.

They never did, though, for one important reason. We never had the chance to develop these stories outside our limited classroom experience. We would sit in a classroom or at our desks, stare into space, and say to ourselves, "Well, I suppose I should have something to say about the environment." The result was always a snow job: "Everyone should be concerned about the dangers of industrial pollution to our environment. If we want to preserve clean air and clean water for future generations. . . ." Such writing results from the "spider syndrome," the notion that the web of writing can be spun from our own juices without contact with the world outside ourselves.

Journalists learn the lesson early: "You can't write writing," or "Write with your legs." Writers need information, quotations, anecdotes, details, and human characters to bring a story to life. All this comes from reporting. We were asked to write about pollution without ever visiting a polluted pond or interviewing an environmentalist. We were asked to write about priestly celibacy without ever interviewing a priest or a married minister.

Young writers can become collectors of information in many ways. Through the process of reporting they can bring together the raw material of their stories and use the tools of the professional writer: notetaking, listening, interviewing, observing, brainstorming, journal writing, and research.

Notetaking

One day, somewhere in their schooling, children will be told they are expected to take notes. Notetaking is a lifelong educational skill, a way of collecting, organizing, and synthesizing information. Yet, except in some journalism classes, students receive little or no instruction on how to perform this difficult task. Students can learn to take efficient notes with some direction and practice. They come to see notetaking as both a physical expression of thinking and a step in the process of writing.

Here is some of the advice I share with young notetakers:

1. Listen and concentrate.
2. Write quickly, but clearly.
3. Write down key words.
4. Invent spellings. Develop a shorthand.
5. If someone is talking quickly, don't be afraid to ask the person to slow down.
6. Read your notes while your memory is fresh.
7. Fill them in from memory.
8. Consider copying them over and filling them out.
9. Use the notes to write a story.
10. Do not be a slave to your notes. Do not write a story about your notebook.

11. Do not be afraid to go back and collect more
information.

When Bonnie Harris, age thirteen, took a guided tour of
the Salvador Dali Museum, she took her reporter's notebook
with her. Here is the first page of her notes:

Salvador Dali Museum
been a little over a year. used
be Cleveland, came here.
over 1,400 works of Dali. Very famous
eccentric Spanish Painter, old,
now ill. Surrealism. Docent =
latin: Teach. 45 min. Tour.
Janelle Barlas—Docent
20th century. 1942 M/M Morse started
collecting 93 major oils
200 draw. water over 1,000
graphics. 5,000 books
not open to public yet.
Mr. & Mrs. Morses
60 pictures on desplay in
chronological order.

On her forty-five-minute tour Bonnie collected more than ten
pages of notes, dense with information. Not only was she able
to use this information to create an interesting story, but she
learned more by taking notes than by letting the docent's information wash over her.

Bonnie reached her level of proficiency after two years of
practice that included a variety of writing experiences under my
direction. When she was in the fifth grade at Bay Point Elementary,
she received her first reporter's notebook, got the feel of filling
its slender pages, and began to manipulate the holy objects that
make up the ritual of writing.

I often ask a class to take notes while I read to them. Then
I read as fast as I can to teach them, in a half-minute, that they
cannot record every word I say. They must concentrate on the
key words. I then read some short sentences to them slowly
and ask them to identify the key words. We write these on the
board. "Animal abuse in America in the 1980s is a national
tragedy" becomes "an abuse 1980 tragedy" in their notes.

I then read an Aesop's fable to them, such as "The Ants
and the Grasshopper." After reading it once, I read it again more
slowly and ask them to take notes so they can retell the story

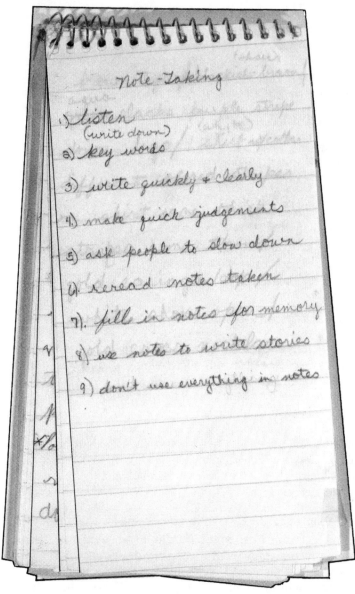

A reporter's notebook is slim and handy. Children can carry it around in their pockets for spontaneous writing and reporting opportunities. They can also fill up the pages quickly. This gives them a sense of momentum and accomplishment. Here is a page from Ann Kenyon's notebook.

in their own words. The class repeats variations of these exercises throughout the school year until children grow in their skills.

The early results are always mixed. Some students, such as Bonnie, catch on quickly and fill notebook pages with information. Others are frustrated by their inability to get down every word, give up, or start to cry. Some students take good notes but cannot process them into an interesting story. Some students need to be cajoled into writing a single word in the notebook.

Notetaking is generally unpopular with most of my students. They often ask, "Do we have to take notes on this? Can't we just enjoy it?" This is because taking notes requires concentration and labor. We have promised them that writing is hard work and fun. Taking notes is the hard work part.

With a little practice, students gain confidence, and notetaking becomes less a chore and more a necessary step in the process of creating a story. Even young children, like fourth grader Regina McGrew, can become proficient. Writing a story on her visit to the *St. Petersburg Times* newsroom, she collected these detailed impressions in a page of notes:

On one of the
desks in the newsroom
there is a Michael
Jackson Album,
a phone book,
telephone, the A
section of a
newspaper.
Most of the
desks in the
news room
are very junky.

Listening and Interviewing

Armed with their new reporting notebooks, students prepare to learn another new skill, one that all reporters learn but only the best master: the art of listening.

How many teachers have been frustrated by even an intelligent student's failure to listen? At times, students seem to receive information from the teacher as if they were watching television. But children *watch* television, not *listen* to it. In the same way, they often hear their teachers but fail to listen to them.

Professional writers sharpen their listening powers. They pick out the important words or themes from an interview so that they can record these in a notebook for later use in a story. They strive to detect nuance and subtext, what is really being said, and they relate this to body language and context.

Teachers rarely challenge students to accept the same kind of responsibility. Perhaps students never learn to listen because we line them up in a classroom like pumpkins on a fence and talk at them until their eyes glaze over. When we teach them how to listen, we give them some responsibility for their own education and show them how to be active acquirers of information and knowledge. One way to encourage listening is to create a serious environment in which listening is possible. Another is to practice it.

We start with straight dictation. I read students a paragraph from a story: "One December day in 1938, a fisherman in South Africa caught a strange fish. The fisherman had fished all his life, but he had never seen a fish like this one. The fish was almost five feet long. It was a beautiful deep blue and was covered with large scales. The strangest parts of the fish were its fins. They did not lie flat the way most fins do, but sprouted out of its body like paddles."

I repeat the paragraph slowly and spell the difficult words for the students. I tell students to listen carefully, concentrate, and write what they hear. A few students can complete this exercise with perfect scores. They spell words correctly, their punctuation is exact, and they avoid common errors of grammar and usage (*it's* for *its*).

Other students make dozens of mistakes of all kinds, fall behind in their transcription, and panic. They lack control over mechanics and cannot process information through their ears and onto the page correctly. If I use the words *ask* or *rural,* they may come out "aks" or "rual," reflecting the way the children pronounce these words in their dialect.

This and similar exercises, while laborious, can be effective diagnostic tools for teachers who want to identify skills mastered by students over the course of the school year. The tedium of such exercises can be relieved by the more interesting and creative activity of interviewing. Reporters learn to listen and transcribe with care so that when they interview interesting and important people, they can write down what they say.

Parents and teachers know that children ask lots of questions. Why is the sky blue? Where do babies come from? Can I go to the bathroom? Why can't I have a phone in my room? That is our typical perception, and anyone who has faced a battery of questions from an inquisitive child understands that it is partially true.

Too often, we ignore this untapped reservoir of curiosity, sit it in rows in a classroom, and preach at it. Students are the banks, as Paulo Freire has described it, and we teachers are the depositors of wisdom. But we fail to inform them that there is a significant penalty for early withdrawal and that a lot of our talking will whip by them like the wind in the night. The alternative is to offer students learning skills that last a lifetime. One of these is the ability to ask a series of intelligent questions to evoke interesting and important responses.

● ● ●

Wendy Witham writes: "We also got to interview a photographer named Ric Ferro. He told us that his job is fun because you get to take all sorts of pictures, from sport pictures, animals, to beautiful girls in bikini bathing suits."

● ● ●

Raymond Melton writes: "Grover Cleveland Hackney, a 92 year old resident of South St. Petersburg, Florida, is the last survivor of the 27-man team that mapped the route across Florida from Fort Myers to Miami. This route is now known as the Tamiami Trail."

● ● ●

Alison Clark writes: "When Jack was 22 he had a tragic accident. He was waterskiing. Jack was being pulled over a ramp and let go of the rope in the air and fell flat on his back and broke his neck. This caused him to be a quadraplegic. That means both his legs and arms are paralyzed. Jack has overcome his handicap very well. He really is fascinating."

● ● ●

Wendy Witham, again, writes: "My next door neighbor's name is Webb V. Turner. He is a retired Marine. He was born in North Carolina in 1908. He was raised on a farm, and is one of fourteen children."

● ● ●

Katrina Clark writes: "Denis chose to come to the United States because 'Someone said to me that the United States was a good country and I should visit it sometime.' The parents of tall, dark-haired, 18 year old Denis sent him with the group of 40 French exchange students because he did very well on an exam in school."

• • •

These paragraphs come from students who have practiced the craft of interviewing as a key part of the writing process. Like professional journalists, they encounter events and people with openness and curiosity and a desire to share what they learn with a larger audience.

Journalists understand the importance of the craft. They conduct interviews almost every day, but the process never becomes routine because each interview with each person is a new adventure and a new challenge. One politician answers your questions in a rambling stream of consciousness, another responds in monosyllables and looks for any chance to hang up on you or chase you from her office.

The reporter prepares for the interview in advance, rehearses an order for the questions, tends to save the hardest questions for last, tries to conduct the interview like a conversation, and listens carefully for nuance, contradiction, or subtext. Fifth graders are capable of learning the basic skills of interviewing, of growing in knowledge from those experiences, and of writing stories based on the results.

After I had offered students a brief introduction to the craft of interviewing, I was surprised one morning by Kathryn Miniter and Bridget Pacuch. The previous night, they had brought a tape recorder to the school Halloween Carnival. Without supervision, and dressed in their Halloween costumes, they had conducted an interview with Elaine Bailey, a parent working one of the carnival booths. The girls collaborated on a list of questions and wrote a story. Here is a transcript of the interview:

Q. Are you in PTA?
A. Yes I am.
Q. Do you enjoy the PTA?
A. I enjoy the PTA very much.
Q. Do you like to help out with the carnival?
A. I sure do. I've enjoyed working with this carnival extremely well.
Q. Why?
A. Because I get to see all the pretty costumes the mothers have taken time to make and how the children just enjoy being here.

Q. Have you seen any favorite costumes that you like? Do you remember what they were?

A. Favorite costumes? You know, it was really hard. I can't say I've seen a favorite one. They all were so nice.

Q. How much money do you make here?

A. We haven't had time—we've been so busy we haven't been able to count our profits. But we're doing really good.

Q. What things do you sell?

A. A little bit of everything. We have plants, shoes, baby clothes, toys, books, you name it, we have it here at the White Elephant Sale.

Q. Why do you call it the White Elephant?

A. That was the name one of the mothers gave it. One of the parents named it the White Elephant.

Q. Do you get paid for doing this?

A. No, this is all volunteer, and I enjoy doing it.

Q. Did you get to pick? Do you want to do the White Elephant, do you want to do the Sponge Toss? Did you get to pick out of that?

A. No. I believe how it worked, the mothers were assigned certain things to do and they got other mothers to help them. So there was a mother assigned to do this, and I volunteered to work with her.

Q. How many people do you get here?

A. You mean working here with me or coming to purchase items?

Q. Coming to purchase items.

A. Oh I would say we must have had ... gosh, maybe 60 to 75 people stop by.

Q. Have you bought anything that you like?

A. I sure have. I bought my little boy a football game.

Q. What are the ages you get here? What are the most ages?

A. The most ages so far have been the young women, I'd say maybe between 21 to 26.

Q. When you got picked out to do it, were you happy with it or did you have something else planned to do?

A. No, at the time I didn't have anything planned to do because I really wanted to come to this carnival to see all the GOBLINS AND WITCHES [says this in scary voice].

Q. How long has the carnival been going on?

A. OK. It started at five o'clock, and I'd say it has been going on for a good three and a half hours now.

Q. I mean years.

A. Oh, sweetheart, this is my first year working with the carnival.

Q. OK, thank you, I think that's about enough questions.

This transcript fails to communicate the tone of the interview, which was businesslike, yet friendly and conversational. Bridget and Kathryn were not afraid to ask follow-up questions to clarify information or to help each other out. They had a list of questions of their own but let Mrs. Bailey help set the agenda.

After the interview, the two girls collaborated on this brief story, one of a series written by the class on the carnival:

Elaine Bailey from the White Elephant tells us how she likes her job at the carnival.

Elaine is in PTA for the first year and enjoys it. When we asked her what was her favorite costume at the carnival, she said that she liked them all and that she couldn't decide.

You can buy almost anything you want at the White Elephant sale: toys, shoes, baby clothes, plants, shawls. You name it and the White Elephant has it.

At the White Elephant, Elaine thinks that 60 to 70 people bought things that night.

After we interviewed her she went back to work.

A conference would help the girls make better use of the information they collected in the interview. But this is a strong first draft based on a solid interview.

In conducting an interview, students learn to be open, to be organized, and to work hard. When they ask, "Do we have to take notes? Can't we just go and enjoy it?" they must be told that listening, interviewing, and taking notes help you fully understand and enjoy a person or event. It may be easier to sit back and relax, but why not try to understand a person's feelings, experiences, motivations, and values? That is part of intellectual growth.

Some students are shy, introverted, or unwilling to take chances. They dislike approaching neighbors or adults or teachers or figures in authority to ask them questions. Other students are relentless and courageous, and willing to ask a principal how she feels about the use of corporal punishment in the schools.

Practice in the art of interviewing gives shy students a chance to break free of the chains imposed on them by their personalities. In fact, some shy children are gifted interviewers because their quiet tone forces the person interviewed to rush in and fill the void. When Cindy, a tiny fourth grader who never spoke above a whisper, interviewed her neighbor Mike Foley, managing editor of the *St. Petersburg Times*, she so intimidated him with her

Visitors to class often inspire students to collect information and write stories. Here a group of students and teachers gets a chance to interview young politicians from the People's Republic of China. One Chinese visitor teaches the group how to represent his name in Chinese writing.

quiet demeanor that he blurted out all sorts of interesting things, which helped Cindy write a terrific profile.

I taught a college student one year, a candidate for a Rhodes Scholarship and a talented thinker and writer, who was so shy that she would have fits of anxiety before an interview. After six weeks she came to me and said, "I now understand that journalism is morally good for me. It has forced me to deal with the world in a new way. I can't sit in my chair and observe from a comfortable distance. I have to ask questions, understand, and communicate."

The fun part of learning to interview is to have interesting people from your community visit your classroom. St. Petersburg is filled with working and retired experts, professional journalists and writers, and visitors from the nation and abroad. Many are thrilled to have the opportunity to visit schoolchildren, and the children, in turn, enjoy the experience of a special event.

One day I introduced Jeff Klinkenberg to a large class of fifth graders. I wrote specific information about him on the board:

Jeff Klinkenberg
Outdoors writer
St. Petersburg Times

Students enjoy feeling a kinship, inspired by visits from professionals, with the larger community of writers. Visitors also provide students with a reason to write. Students begin to connect their writing to the outside world. They recognize that people's lives and activities can be the subjects for interesting stories.

I tacked up a story that Jeff had written on the board. I wanted the children to see the writer and the published work. I also wanted him to tell them some stories, to answer some questions, to talk to them as a fellow writer, and to describe the process of writing a story, all of which he accomplished in a quiet, friendly manner.

While they took notes and listened, Jeff told them the story of a fishing boat captain who had a close encounter with a great white shark. Jeff even brought in a large metal hook, which the mammoth creature had bent straight in getting away. The students were entranced, grossed out, and delighted.

He told them about a dog that digs for clams, a story he was writing for the next day. They had dozens of questions to ask. "What was the dog's name?" "Does the dog have to go under water?" "What was the breed of the dog?" "Was it a boy or a girl dog?"

The students also expressed interest in how Jeff writes. Amy Seibert asked him how many times he rewrites a story. When Jeff said eleven or twelve, she seemed relieved and sympathetic. She realized they were members of the same guild.

On another occasion I brought in Gordon Jackson, a journalism student and teacher, whose native country is South Africa. Gordon has the looks of an Oxford librarian and a lyrical accent, and the children seemed fascinated by his voice and demeanor. He gave them a lesson in geography and politics, explaining South Africa's strategic location and its racist policies. He explained how different, and better, things were in the United States. To be honest, the students seemed a little bored with the serious talk, but came alive when Gordon began to share with them his experience as an ostrich rancher.

They asked lots of questions, which evoked interesting answers they could use in their stories. Gordon talked about the size of an ostrich egg, that it could feed as many people as twenty-four chicken eggs, that a human could stand on it and an ostrich sit on it without breaking it. He explained the value of ostrich feathers, that you could saddle up and ride an ostrich, which moves very quickly (even though it can't fly), and that ostriches do not stick their heads in the sand.

"What would you do if you stuck your head in the sand?" asked Gordon.

"Suffocate," said one student.

"So would the ostrich!" The presentation convinced the students of how interesting the lives and experiences of others could be. At such moments, students are ready to write.

Observation

Elonda was having trouble writing stories until I told her it was all right to write down what she observed in her classes. Then she produced this paragraph:

Ms. Kisten is a very nice teacher. She's pretty and very kind. She wears nice clothes. She's very funny too. She is my second period teacher. I like to work on Social Studies. Ms. Kisten helps me when I need help. Ms. Kisten has brown hair and she's so pretty and very kind. She also wears jewelry. She is always helpful and very intelligent. She always checks over our work. She's always saying "hohoho!"

The reader learns much about Ms. Kisten from this brief portrait, written by a student who has trouble with most of her schoolwork. For Elonda, observation was the key to writing.

I feel humble when I teach observation because I am so bad at it myself. I can be in a room for an hour with the world's most beautiful woman and not be able to tell you the color of her eyes or what she is wearing. I come out with a general impression of beauty and nothing more. Maybe all those hours of watching television, until my eyes were black holes, has atrophied my observation muscles. So I force myself to undertake the kind of observation that leads to interesting details in my writing.

My best friend is my notebook. When I hold it in my hand, it reminds me to collect details through observation and to write them down. If I use all my senses and channel stimuli to my hand and into my notebook, the writing will come alive. Here is a story I wrote for my class in about twenty minutes after a tour and interview at Bayboro Books:

One year ago, four women worked a month to sweep 35 years of sawdust out of a building that housed a woodworker named Jonathan Jones. Now that building houses Bayboro Books, a modern, cozy little book shop nestled on the St. Petersburg campus of the University of South Florida.

Sally Wallace is one of the four women, whom she describes as "book people." "We love to read," she says, "and we know what books to order."

At the age of 53, Sally looks young and thin. She has short, blondish hair, and wears a neat white polo shirt and tan slacks. She is an energetic woman who splits her time between running the book store and being a member of City Council.

She conducts a brief tour of the book shop, pointing out cases full of classics, textbooks, contemporary authors, humor, business, and children's books. Handsome displays show off a wide variety of titles, from *Babar Saves the Day* to *Oriental Rug Primer* to *Arthurian Romance* to *The Baked Bean Supper Murders*.

The shop also sells cards, student supplies, and bookbags.

Opening such a shop is risky business, according to Mrs. Wallace. The university has its own bookstore, but the owners of Bayboro Books feel they can do a better job in some areas. They feel they are in the right place. "We think our location is ideal," says Mrs. Wallace.

She and her partners, Marianne Rucker, Marty Wallace, and Marion Ballard, have created a pleasant atmosphere in which to shop. Art posters decorate the walls. A table holds books in a picnic basket next to a bowl of real fruit. An antique student desk, with inkwell and quill pen, suggests a scholarly tradition. And a new microfiche reader, which helps in ordering books, represents the new technology.

But, most of all, Sally Wallace says Bayboro Books represents service to students, teachers and book lovers. They will order any book that is not in stock. "The most satisfying thing," says Sally Wallace, "is having the right book when the right person comes along."

None of the descriptive details in the story—Sally Wallace's clothes, the book titles, or the list of furnishings—would have been possible if I had not reminded myself to write them in my notebook. This simple act permits the writer to create a sense of person and a sense of place.

I will never forget putting on my first pair of glasses at the age of ten and walking out the front door of my house to the school bus stop. I could once again see details that had been blurred by myopia. The great journalists see the world as their writing laboratory. They notice the shine on shoes, the shades of gray in hair, the configuration of clouds in the sky. Students can share this attitude toward the world through experience and practice.

Even young children are good at observing a person and writing down as many physical characteristics as possible. I often pick a student to be the subject of a writing exercise. I look for someone wearing something interesting and distinctive, a strange T-shirt or multicolored blouse. Students have one minute to compile a list of descriptive details about the person. Here seventh-grader Bonnie Harris describes her friend Gillian Gaynair in her notes:

turquois blue slacks with
red stripe down sides
loop gold earrings
white shirt, striped w/
blue, green, pink & yellow
stripes, diffrent sizes for
diffrent colors
white sandles
cross necklace; gold.
Braces   small heels on shoes

Students then compare lists to see who has come up with the most interesting and revealing details. This exercise builds their confidence because the subject cannot move away or avoid their observation. Students learn to take into account body language, facial expressions, and idiosyncrasies. They love to do this exercise with teachers. I have cheerfully endured, for the sake of good writing, those children who dutifully record my bald spot, big ears, long nose, yellow teeth, and bad posture.

This exercise can be taken a step further through the use of colorful posters or slides. I project on a screen a photo of children with a clown at the circus, a group of old people watching a parade, a hot air balloon against a sunset. Children begin to see patterns, details, and structures: that the children and the clown are wearing the same colors, that all the men have their hands over their hearts, that the balloon in the photo looks higher than the sun. The photos pique their curiosity, and they ask questions that lead to more detailed notes and better description.

Students begin by observing and rehearsing. They simply look and remember. After they have seen a few slides filled with scenes and faces, their vision improves along with their insight. Then they record a list of descriptive details. Finally, they write a paragraph of description.

The slides are static, of course, moments frozen in time. This is not the way reporters view people or events. A third exercise adds the dynamic dimension. I take the class into a library or out onto a playing field or into an auditorium or cafeteria. Students view the scene, observe and listen, take notes, and write description.

One day we went to the top floor of a library to view the lovely Bayboro Harbor in St. Petersburg. Students took in the scene and had five minutes to record their impressions and fifteen to write a description.

Ann Kenyon produced this list of notes:

St. Petersburg Harbor
Dali by water
Crane
Sailboats
Water   Fishing Nets
Palm Trees/Park   green grass
Fishing Boats/bl.wh.
lots of lines & cables
blue covering of sails
docks   sailboat in middle of harbor
Factories
tall & short building
Red Barge

and turned it into this story:

As I looked out over the Bayboro Harbor it reminded me of a still painting. But as small fish jumped out of the water, this painting was interrupted.

On the far side of the harbor stood fishing boats docked side by side. All of them are of black, white, or grey.

To the right, a white crane waits until called to pull the stacked sailboats on land.

Factories line the harbor. Broken windows are a common sight on the old factories and smoke filled chimneys in the new.

The Dali Museum is a new site on the harbor. It has a beautiful green landscape, full of shrubs, trees and flowers.

It was bizarre, the harbor was so quiet. I guess everyone has gone home, but I know there will be noise tomorrow.

Ann does not use every detail in her notes, nor is she afraid to include details she did not record in her notebook. She writes her story from her notes, not about them. They help her memory and provide a framework for her description and narration.

Teachers can learn much from the different ways in which students see the same scene. We were interested in how the description written by the girls differed from that of the boys. Most of the girls described how sunlight played off the water in the harbor, or how colors and shapes blended together, or how a bird flew gracefully overhead. Many of the boys ignored all that and concentrated on what framed the harbor, a construction crane, big buildings, and a Coast Guard station. The world of beauty versus the world of work. As her story shows, Ann Kenyon can appreciate both. Part of education is freeing the girls to see the construction crane and freeing the boys to appreciate the beauty of the seabird.

Students use observation and description to enrich and enhance their stories. April Piterski writes: "Everyone went to sleep except me. I listened to the owls, and the wind rustling through the trees and against our tent. I saw the moon and heard many eerie sounds. Finally, I fell asleep, and before I knew it, it was morning."

● ● ●

Joshua Dreller writes: "The Batmobile is about eight to ten feet long and about six feet wide. It is blue and has two compartments in the front. The trunk is about four feet of the length of the car. The two compartments have glass over them. They can be taken out, too. There is a hole in the back the size of a pan pizza that shoots out fire to make it go faster. The headlights are rectangular. The trunk is so big because there is stuff in there like oil, grease and nails to help it get away faster."

● ● ●

Leah McRae writes: "They couldn't control the direction they were sailing. Their sail was blowing like a leaf on a chilly morn."

Dawn Piscitelli writes: "It began September 17, 1979, and it was awful! Devastating, you might say. The wind was howling. The rain beat upon the windows like grasshoppers."

• • •

Raymond Melton writes: "As I talk to him in his home he sits calmly as he goes back through his childhood. He sits comfortably on his couch in a blue shirt with blue checkered pants."

These children have encountered the world in a special way. Through their writing they find meaning in experience and communicate it to others. Through observation and description they share what they have learned with their readers.

Brainstorming

I love to brainstorm. I love the word and so do my students. A storm in the brain. I want my storms to be great lightning storms, crackling with sound and excitement and even a bit of danger. The brainstorm permits me to consider risky or unusual ideas which I can hold up for inspection but then return to a safe place in the back of my mind. Or, I may brainstorm to get mind and memory working to collect for a story the various threads of my experience and feelings.

Students can brainstorm on their own or, even better, with others. One child's idea gives birth to another. Collaboration becomes the key, since it takes others to help you remember what you know.

One day after we had compiled a list of story ideas on the board, I wrote a personal brainstorming list for my students:

spaghetti—why spaghetti is a funny food.

dreams—I always dream that I'm on my way to a class I have never attended before, and that I've forgotten something important.

last night a barking dog kept us awake.

having babies—I've witnessed the birth of all three of my daughters.

Star Wars—why is it so popular.

my first day of school—what do I remember about it.

the day I was born—how did my parents feel.

TV—does TV turn kids' brains to mush.

I can't tell you how I got from spaghetti to *Star Wars* to kids' brains. The mind works in mysterious ways, and sometimes we must let it do its work by free association to free ourselves from logic and reason, at least for a time.

Students who swear they have nothing to write may generate a dozen good story ideas during a brainstorming session. Looking for story ideas is a little like prayer; you have to ask to get an answer. A student or a class or a newspaper staff that consciously seeks out interesting ideas, that pushes the storm button, that puts on the thinking cap, will be rewarded.

Here is the student list that inspired mine:

something funny
dreams
animals—pets
food
our class
trips
movies
adventure
outer space
favorite performers
teachers
school
people
favorite things
collections
hobbies
family members
changes
pain
books
old friends
summer
interviews
the future

Some underlying logic helped construct this list: "outer space" flows from "adventure," and "collections" from "favorite things." But other connections are more subtle, such as "changes" and "pain." Other topics stand alone.

As I review my own list, I realize that "spaghetti" comes from "something funny," and my dream also derives from a suggestion on the board. Such collaboration is fun and rewarding. It inspires thought and participation. The next step requires students to choose among many story ideas to find the best one, and to continue the process of brainstorming to collect information that will support it.

Journalists learn quickly that there are two kinds of people: those who get ideas and those who get assignments.

Journal Writing

Writing this book was possible because I kept a journal or daybook. I did not write in it every day, as I had promised myself I would. But after every class I taught, I rushed back to my office, picked up the journal, and wrote. Sometimes I would only jot down a line or two to remind me of some insight or anecdote. At other times, I would write quickly for fifteen to twenty minutes, never more than that.

The first draft of this book came from typed transcriptions and elaborations of journal entries. As I typed them, I marveled at the facts, observations, and examples I had forgotten I knew. I was surprised at how those twenty-minute exercises grew into more than two hundred pages of typed text. The secret of journal writing is that no one expects entries to be particularly well written. They are, after all, written in haste, often without careful regard for mechanics. This casual lowering of standards permits the writer to overcome writer's block and to find in the journal a friendly, noncritical receiver of information. If the passage has little meaning or relevance, no one cares. If it contains the seed of a good idea, the writer can expand it, improve it, and correct it in a different context.

The journal, I explain to my students, is not a diary ("Jeff passed me in the hallway today and smiled. I think he, likes me"). Don Murray prefers to call it a "daybook," the Anglo-Saxon form of *journal* from the French *jour* meaning "day," which is also the root of "journalism."

As the bumper sticker proclaims, professional reporters "do it every day." They may not be very good at it, but even hacks can bang out copy daily. Journalists keep their writing muscles in shape. They can match their skills to an assignment, including some seemingly impossible ones.

Students should learn their craft through daily writing, but they may only have the chance to write once a week, or in nine-week units, or once in a while, or not at all. Responsible teachers may feel that they must grade or correct everything a student writes. Writing every day seems to create an unworkable system, generating too much copy for the teacher to consider.

The journal is one solution to this problem. When students keep a journal, they understand that the teacher may not read every entry. In fact, days will go by when no one reads it at all. The journal is a companion, an amanuensis, an outlet for students who want to write, a lap dog that should be fed every day.

Students know they can write anything in any form in their journals. They do not have to worry about handwriting or spelling, but they often do because they care very much about the quality of their work.

The journal may contain:

- Free writing.
- Observations, funny or outrageous scenes.
- Experiences.
- Feelings.
- Brainstorming lists.
- Reminders.
- Story ideas.
- Reactions to things read.
- New words, interesting images, word play.

We permit such freedom in the journal because the practice keeps the writer in shape, and because the journal is a starting point, not a destination.

Ten-year-old Jenny Seelig kept a wonderful journal during the fifth grade and filled it with story ideas, notes, and brainstorming lists. The first entry is seven lines of writing under the title "A picnic at the beach." The story goes nowhere, so Jenny scribbles over it. No harm done.

The next entry is a promising two-page draft of a story called "Gymnastics and Me." This is followed by a brainstorming list of twenty-four story ideas, including dreams, holidays, vacations, summers, pets. This list gives her an idea for the next entry, a story entitled "My New Pet."

A nifty story, "The Hurricane Room," follows:

Going to the Museum of Scince and Industry was a real treat.
The thing I enjoyed most was the hurricane room. I sat in the
first seat next to the huge pipe that blew up to 74 mile an hour

winds. The strange googles protected me from anything that might fly out of the other 74 peoples hands.

When I came out of the huge monster all my hair was to one side from the fast winds witch the hurricane room blew. I want to go back real soon! LIKE NOW!

More stories follow, and then a page with a description of the writing process: "IDEA, COLLECT (information), REHEARSE (think), FOCUS (main thing), DEVELOP (1st draft), CLARIFY (edit)."

A poem is next: "Oh, four leaf clover, / That I'm looking over. / Cast your spell, / Bring me luck, / For I sure need an extra buck."

The next entry is an aborted effort, one of those days when the writing has not gone well, but who cares? Her title is "My Future," and it reads "When I grow up I would like to be an . . . . so on."

What follows is the masterpiece of the journal, four chapters of a work entitled "Crazy Camp," which begins with this inviting passage: "I went to camp this summer. It wasn't so great but I did get used to the snakes, rats, bats, moles, chickens, turkeys, fish, scorpions, alligators, ants, frogs, roaches, mosquitos, and not to mention the spiders in the bathrooms."

More stories follow, and Jenny's journal concludes with several pages listing the spelling and grammar mistakes she commonly makes in her stories. Her teacher has asked her to record these in a special place in the journal so she can avoid these mistakes in future stories.

Students like Jenny take their most interesting journal entries and turn them into stories, expanding, revising, and correcting. That is the way I use my journal, and I should not expect anything else from my students.

The hardest part is developing the daily writing habit. Spending five minutes at the beginning or end of class to help students develop a daily writing schedule may reap many rewards. Teachers should check the journals periodically, praise faithful students, and encourage others to do better.

Research

Two fifth-grade girls read a children's version of Shakespeare's plays and write a report for their classmates, introducing the life and work of the great English playwright to their friends.

Another student goes to the library and collects books and

articles on the dangers to young people of drug use. He writes information in his notebook for use in his story, which he will publish for the class.

After a trip to Egypt with her family, a seventh-grade girl studies Egyptian mythology and writes a long fictional account of the death of young King Tut and his descent into the Egyptian underworld. Katrina Clark's father remarks, "If I ever wanted to teach anyone about the Egyptian gods, the best thing I could do is let them read Katrina's story."

The kind of fiction writing I like best is work that springs from both deep interest and supporting research. When children combine research and their imaginations, the result can be enlightening and charming, as is the case with Phillip Adamski's "Gart: A Day in a Garter Snake's Life."

It begins at dawn when life starts. The birds begin singing as Gart awakes. Gart is a two foot blue-striped garter snake. He crawls out of his den in search of fish, his main meal.

As his tongue flickers, he crawls down to the bank. He slithers through the marsh grass and there he sees his prey. There, in front of him, sits a giant minnow! He approaches it quietly, sneakily, silently, and then with no warning, strikes! No more minnow.

After his meal, which usually lasts him a couple of days, he goes to his favorite log for a few hours of basking because it helps in digestion.

Then, he hears, through his super sensitive organs in his stomach, footsteps. It is a hungry, wild dog. Gart tries to get away, but fails. He's cornered! As he coils up to strike, he sees a crack in the wall. He strikes! It's a hit! While the dog is busy with his aching nose, Gart snakes away into the crack. Finally, the dog leaves puzzled by where Gart went. In about five minutes, when Gart sees everything's all right, he goes back to his log with no further trouble.

At twilight, when it gets cooler, his snake instinct guides him back to his den for an evening of rest.

The richness of detail, derived from research and observation and enhanced by imagination, moves the narrative forward and entertains and instructs the reader. Through research, Phillip takes responsibility for the quality of the information in his story.

Teachers encounter frustration when they assign research papers to students because, too often, the result is plagiarized from the *World Book* encyclopedia, *National Geographic*, or the dust jacket of the book they were supposed to report on. Students learn to undertake responsible research when the teacher concentrates on process rather than product. A teacher can lead a class step by step through the process of writing a book report in order to reveal to students how information collected during research can lead to effective writing.

The teacher may ask students, for example, to record in their journals or notebooks different kinds of information about the book they are reading:

- Write down ten different sentences from this book you think are interesting or important. Be sure to put these in quotation marks.
- In a single paragraph, tell another reader what this book was "about."
- What is the most important chapter in this book and why?
- Who is the author and why do you think he or she wrote the book?
- Which part was the least successful and why?

By asking such questions, both formally and in conference, teachers challenge students to read carefully and critically. To answer them effectively, students must concentrate and comprehend. The result of the process is pages of notes that can become the stuff of a well-written and original book report. Armed with interesting and important information, students can turn to the next step in the process, the search for the heart of the story.

Chapter Eight

Focusing In

Journalists think of themselves as most creative when they write their leads. The lead, the first few lines of a story, captures the news and offers readers a reason to keep reading. The lead entices, cajoles, entertains, and informs the reader. It may offer a promise of things to come or illuminate the essence of the story. It may answer the reader's most important question, "Why am I reading this?" Or it may simply ease the reader into a difficult or complicated subject.

Some writers spend half their composing time working on the first paragraph. They may be unable to write another word if the lead is not "perfect." Others spend most of their reporting time "searching" for the peg on which they can hang a plumb line of narrative or exposition. Writers are known to attempt dozens of leads before they find one that satisfies them. As Joan Didion says, "What's so hard about the first sentence is that you're stuck with it. Everything else is going to flow out of that first sentence. And by the time you've laid down the first two sentences, your options are all gone."

Leads can be simple: "The first war dead from Europe came home yesterday."

Or scenic: "The shells were falling closer by the time the man called Abu Ammar finally appeared, poking his bearded face from the side window of a dirty blue Chevrolet."

Or explanatory: "Boeing loses millions of dollars on every new 757 it sells."

Or newsy: "An Air Florida Jetliner taking off from National Airport in a snowstorm crashed into a crowded bridge this afternoon and broke as it plunged into the Potomac River, leaving at least 10 persons dead and more than 40 missing, according to unofficial police estimates."

Or sensational: "Richard Hornbuckle, auto dealer, golfer, Baptist, came within two feet Friday of driving his yellow Buick Skylark off the Sunshine Skyway Bridge into Tampa Bay."

Or argumentative: "Jewelry work in Rhode Island is life at the bottom of industrial America."

Students who discover interesting story ideas and collect pages of information to support them are ready to learn the skill of lead writing. Even first graders find writing leads fun and helpful, as evidenced by a student of Donald Graves who wrote: "A jaguar would make a sports car look like a turtle."

Students find lead writing a wonderful alternative to the dreaded "topic sentence." Rather than laboring over the first sentence in each paragraph, which clogs the process like cholesterol, students can craft an opening passage that suggests an order for the rest of the story.

Children write excellent leads once they understand the concept behind the skill. They enjoy the challenge of finding something interesting and important. When they discover the lead, it makes writing the rest of the story easier. Yet, in many cases, they will write their lead last, during revision, after they come to understand the focus of the story.

Journalists recognize that different types of leads are appropriate for different types of stories, and students learn this quickly. They also learn that they can write several beginnings before deciding on one that works best.

Without attention to lead writing, the beginnings of student stories come out flat and predictable: "The Dali Museum is an interesting place to visit," or "A man named Gordon Jackson came to our class today."

Gordon Jackson happened to work on an African ostrich ranch, so it was easy for students to come up with interesting leads from information he shared with them:

"An ostrich doesn't hide its head in the sand."

"An ostrich can run 50 miles per hour."

"You could feed breakfast to a family of 12 with one ostrich egg."

"A fat man can stand on an ostrich egg without breaking it."

After a tour of the Salvador Dali Museum, I challenged my students to write two good leads in five minutes, during which time I would try to write five. I came up with:

- Walking into the Salvador Dali Museum is like stepping into the dreams of a mad but brilliant artist.

- Melting watches, a fried egg hanging from a string, a statue of Venus that turns into the head of a bullfighter. These are a few of the strange images that can be found in the recesses of the Salvador Dali Museum.
- The Salvador Dali Museum contains more eerie images than Disney World's Haunted House.
- Salvador Dali looks like an image from one of his paintings, bizarre, outrageous, shocking, larger than life.

The students answered my challenge with leads such as:

- When we went to the Dali Museum, we saw paintings with such colors you'd think they would reach out and grab you.
- The Dali Museum is a bizarre painting gallery where there are paintings worth over millions of dollars and masterworks over twelve feet high.

We discussed which beginnings worked best and why, and we conferred about the type of lead that would be best for their stories. No longer were students willing to settle for the first phrase that popped into their minds, the thing that "completes the assignment in a satisfactory manner." Writing leads proves to young writers that they can take control of their own work and find the heart of the story.

● ● ●

Each of the following children found the focus of a story and related it to readers in a carefully crafted lead:

Joshua Dreller: "My mother dragged me through the studio saying she had a surprise for me. We went through a long hallway with many doors. A guy came to my mother and said to go through the door on the right. We went in. My mother sat down with a lady and I saw the Batmobile!" (Joshua begins with compelling action, "My mother dragged me . . ." and wisely ends with the most important word and point of focus, the Batmobile.)

Christa Roberts: "Was the floor moving down or was the ceiling moving up? Thoughts were running through my mind: 'Let me out of here. What's happening to me and my claustrophobic self?'" (Christa invites the reader immediately into the action of the story, which we soon discover is about the Haunted House at Disney World.)

Frank Witsil: "I didn't feel it at first, but after I saw the blood streaming down my arm I ran to the bathroom in pain.

Bright red blood was dripping off my elbow in small drops and falling to the floor, hitting it with a splat." (Frank uses description to allow his reader to experience vicariously the day he was cut by broken bottles. He lets us see the bright red blood and hear it splattering on the floor.)

Jennifer Ulsberger: "Once my whole family was on a local talk show because my sister and brother, who are now six, are the largest twins ever born in the state of Florida. My sister, Jacki, weighed 9 lbs. 6-1/2 ozs. My brother, Jason, weighed 8 lbs. 2 ozs." (Jennifer attracts readers with interesting information. First we learn that the twins were the largest born in the state of Florida. Then we are ready for the numbers, which total more than 17 pounds of babies!)

Kristin Klinkenberg: "This summer I went to Pennsylvania. While I was there, I visited my relatives including two very special cousins, Matthew who is eight and Michael who is five. Both of them are handicapped." (By placing the word *handicapped* at the end of her lead, Kristin supports her characterization of her cousins as "very special.")

Alison Clark: "Sore feet, blisters, sweat, and the unfortunate loss of not finishing your homework because of a dance class, the practice, the recitals, and the fame, are all part of becoming a dancer." (Concrete details enliven this lead. The rhythm and balance of the sentence give special emphasis to the word *dancer.*)

Sandra Virtue: "The smoke rose, the lights flashed, and the Jacksons came up from beneath the stage. What a start of a concert!" (What a start for a story filled with color, sound, and action.)

Clark Blomquist: "It was that dreaded kind of day. A hot, boring, T.V. day. *Gilligan's Island*, *The Flintstones*, and *The Price is Right* comforted me, but I knew what would be asked of me sooner or later—most likely sooner. I was right. My mom casually walked over to the sofa I so comfortably sat upon and said those immortal words, 'Mow the lawn.'" (This lead has voice, the illusion that this eleven-year-old boy is speaking directly to the reader. He creates a bit of suspense by delaying his mother's command, but in so doing turns a typical kid's experience into something funny and universal.)

With a sharp focus and a good lead, each student will write a story with a tight organization and coherent structure. The story will not drift to the right or left. It will flow in a single,

Limiting the Topic

A simple strategy for helping students write with more information and a clearer focus.

Students receive a topic for an essay contest during American Education Week: "A strong nation needs strong schools." Most students write obvious, platitudinous pap, full of generalities, without bite, insight, color, or concrete detail.

There is another way. Teachers can encourage students to find and interview and write about a single person who exemplifies the topic. This limits the topic, facilitates the collection of information, and leads to a sharp focus: "When Gene Patterson was sitting in a country schoolhouse in Adel, Georgia, he never dreamed he would grow up to become one of the most important editors in American journalism."

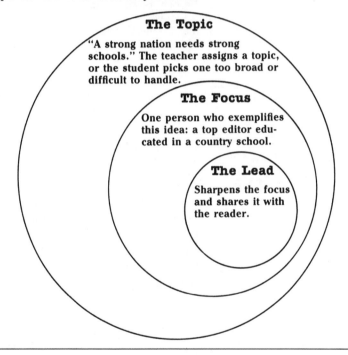

The Topic

"A strong nation needs strong schools." The teacher assigns a topic, or the student picks one too broad or difficult to handle.

The Focus

One person who exemplifies this idea: a top editor educated in a country school.

The Lead

Sharpens the focus and shares it with the reader.

unobstructed stream of information that carries the reader from beginning to end.

My Mother's Broom •
By Nancy Taylor

When you think of your mother's old treasures you would probably think of an apron or an old class ring. When I think of something my mother treasured, I think about her broom.

Her broom is special because of the many things she did with it. The broom was brown and was made with real straw.

I remember the time she was burning trash and a spark landed on the ground and caught fire. She ran inside for water and her broom. By the time she got outside the fire was too big so she called the Fire Department.

Another time, her close friend, Mr. Oberheim saw a snake on our basement steps and my mom handed him the broom and he beat it to death. He bent down to pick it up and then he saw it was only a strand of straw.

The last encounter I remember was with some kind of spider in the corner of the ceiling in my sister's room and sure enough that was the end of the spider.

These are some of the many stories of her broom. The broom is gone because it was old and falling apart and is replaced with a new broom whose handle falls off every time you sweep.

This six-paragraph story has a sharp focus and a unified structure. The unity derives from a good title, a strong lead that ends with the key word *broom*, illustrative anecdotes, and a wonderfully ironic ending that tolls the death of the golden age: they just don't make brooms the way they used to.

When teachers confer with students about their leads, they inspire them to consider the structure of the whole story. Stories have beginnings, students learn, and also middles and endings. A good lead results in specific examples and an ending that gives the piece development and closure.

Jaws! •
By Karin Fraser

One day last summer during school vacation, a boy named Billy Shannon was at the Don CeSar Beach. He was swimming in the Gulf of Mexico. He was swimming near the deep water markers and he felt something rubbery slide against his leg and saw a fin.

He called "Help!" about 4 or 5 times. A few people went out of the water. The movie Jaws flashed through his mind. The lifeguard went to him in a jet-ski. He pointed out that they were dolphins.

Billy swam back to shore. He went to the pool where his parents were. He was quite embarrassed. He told them the story and they thought it was funny. His brother made fun of him and he punched him in the jaw.

The repetition of the word *jaw*, in the title, in the body of the story, and at the very end, punctuates the fine and funny focus of Karin's story. Her lead leaves out enough information to keep the reader intrigued.

When I try to write a lead, I often go through a process that some teachers of writing call "rehearsal." Rehearsal is a fancy word for writing in your head, and that is what I find myself doing. I have returned from reporting a story, perhaps with pages and pages of information. Before I can begin a draft, I sit back and stare out the window, or get something to eat, or go to the bathroom, or walk my dog.

Writers can solve some of their problems in their heads. They begin to imagine what the story will look like. Or they mentally compose a lead, a transition, or an ending. One of the paradoxes of writing is that this delay makes writing quickly possible.

On January 3, 1979, I was sent to review a performance of the circus. The show ended about 11 P.M., so I had to leave a few minutes early to make a tight deadline. To save time, I wrote the body of the story during breaks in the performance. When I returned to the office, I would have twenty minutes to write the lead, revise, and proofread the story. Moments before I left the performance hall, an accident during an animal act knocked over a flaming bar. A pillar of fire shot up in the middle of the center ring, causing a brief panic until attendants were able to extinguish the blaze.

I took furious notes and sized up the danger of the situation. During my five-minute drive to the office, I composed the lead in my head and rehearsed a new structure for the story that would include the fire but also deal with the rest of the performance. Adrenalin gave me this top for the story:

A brief, frightening but uneventful fire in the center ring marred an otherwise outstanding performance of the Ringling Bros. and Barnum & Bailey Circus Tuesday night at the Bayfront Center.

Near the end of the three-hour circus performance, Anna and her Dobermans were in the exciting conclusion of their act when something unexpected happened. One of the dogs tripped over a flaming bar and upset it, sending flames shooting up in a brief circle near the center ring.

As the flames grew, about a hundred spectators sitting toward the front rose to their feet in a moment's panic before a vigilant crew put the fire out with heavy pads and a fire extinguisher. The blaze generated some confusion as the circus crew sought out a missing Doberman.

Students may not rush back to the office to make a deadline, but they can learn the value of rehearsal. I do not mind if their hands are not moving and they stare into space, but I may ask a question to transform blank staring into planning and rehearsal. "That must have been an exciting trip you took to Sea World," I say, "but what was the best part?"

Similar questions encourage students to find a lead and plan the next stage of the story:

- "What is most important?"
- "What is the story really about?"
- "Did anything surprise you?"
- "What will make readers want to read more?"
- "What will readers learn from this story?"
- "Where will you begin?"
- "What is your title going to be?"
- "Where do you plan to end this story?"

I may send students home, after a busy day of reporting, with some of these questions in mind. Students can then prepare for the next day's writing. With rehearsal as a tool, students can solve some problems in their heads or even in their sleep. They return to class with a good lead or some other strategy for developing a story.

Too many teachers and writers fail to include rehearsal—that time when our hands are still—in their models of the writing process. We wrongly conclude that we are writing only when we scrape a pencil across a page or bang the keys of a typewriter or word processor.

Researchers studying the behavior of writers have found that as much as 80 percent of the time they spend working on a story involves mental preparation and rehearsal. At the idea stage, during collection, searching for a lead and structure, and during revision and clarification, much of the work goes on in the head. Some writers, who say they only write a story once, are conscientious rehearsers. They think, play, tinker, and rethink until the sentence is in final form in their heads. They then commit it to the page.

Students, like professionals, experience writer's block. They can learn how to plan and rehearse stories, both on paper and in their heads. A student like Benji Sutcliffe may be writing even though his hand is not moving.

I prefer to execute most of my revisions on paper and so do most children I know. But I have come to understand the value of using all my available time to think, rehearse, and plan. The frustrating alternative is to perceive oneself as procrastinating, as not writing.

As a college student, I would often receive a writing assignment with a two-week deadline. I would usually read the work in question, *Hamlet* perhaps, put it down and wait. And wait, and wait, and wait. With three days left I would wait some more. With a day left I would wait until after dinner. Then, when my roommates were asleep, I would sit in semidarkness, a halo of light above my desk, and bleed it out. I would chastise myself for my inability to organize my time and get to the writing earlier. I was blocked. I could not write when I had to. I would procrastinate.

Now I embrace the "Lamaze method" of writing. In childbirth classes, women learn that labor pains are muscle contractions they can measure and control. In their minds, women transform agonizing discomfort into useful work. In the same way, I have transformed procrastination into rehearsal. Instead of berating myself for not moving my hand, for not writing, I write in my head, or plan to write, or at least hope to plan to write. Such preparation now seems a necessary step in making the writing go quickly and well once my backside finally hits the chair.

I advise students, "Always look for your lead," which is another invitation to rehearsal. Look for the one thing, the one scene, the one place that lends a story its focus.

At times, this becomes a matter of limiting the topic. How does a writer begin to manage a topic as large as "the American bureaucracy" or "the effects of recession on American business," or "the future of downtown redevelopment." Professionals learn that they write more effectively and collect more interesting information when they limit their topics. They do this by selecting one corner of the American government, or one representative business, or one building downtown, which becomes a microcosm for their larger concerns.

A high school student wanted to write an essay about "the problems of vandalism in the Pinellas County Schools." When I heard the topic, I knew immediately that the writer lacked a focus. Through a conference, I tried to help the student limit the topic and prepare for the reporting and writing.

"Does your school have problems with vandalism?"

"You bet."

"What kinds?"

"Different kinds."

"What place in your school is most often vandalized?"

"The boys' room on the second floor."

"What kind of vandalism?"

"Everything from graffiti carved on walls, to ripped out dispensers, to toilets being intentionally clogged."

When I heard his answer, a light went on in my brain. I saw a possible focus, a microcosm for the problem of vandalism in the school. Next came a set of questions that gave the student reporter lots of work to do:

- "Who is responsible for maintaining the room and repairing the damage?"
- "Have security measures been taken?"
- "How much does repair and prevention cost?"
- "Where does the money come from?"
- "What is the impact on the entire student body?"
- "Why this particular room?"
- "Do other schools have similar problems?"
- "What do students, workers, teachers, and administrators have to say about this?"

Another paradox of the writing process is that a narrow topic provides the writer with more opportunities to collect information efficiently. Most students believe they can write more about "pollution in Florida" than "why it smells in Bayboro Harbor." Information on the harbor is easier to acquire and organize. It is likely to be more specific, descriptive, concrete, and anecdotal.

For example, a student might decide to write a story about "what it means to grow up," and write abstractly about maturity, responsibility, putting away childish things, growing independent, and making decisions. The topic can grow in dozens of directions unless the writer can narrow the topic and find a focus.

Annie •

By Bonnie Harris

When I was born I received many gifts from relatives, but my mom bought me something that I later grew to love more than anything else.

It was a Raggedy Ann doll and I remember exactly how she looked. She had on a blue and white flowered dress with a white apron. Her feet were covered with black shoes and her stockings were red and white striped.

Around when I was one, I started carrying the red-headed doll everywhere. I'd drag her by the foot and yank her hair out until she went bald. When I learned how to talk, "Annie" was one of my first words. She was like my best friend in the whole world. She'd listen when I talked and I knew she understood.

Then one year we went to my grandma's for Christmas and I left Annie there. When we got home, I discovered she wasn't with me and I cried for days. Grandma said she'd mail it, but in the meantime, my mom bought me a new one.

I did not like the new Annie. She wasn't dirty, she wasn't nearly bald, and she didn't listen when I talked.

Years later, my mom brought out the doll and showed her to me. What a mess she was! We put her up in my closet where she sits now. No matter what, Annie will always be there for me.

Through a sharply focused narrative, Bonnie develops the delicate tension between changing perceptions of maturity ("What a mess she was!") and the clinging to childlike innocence ("Annie will always be there for me").

Books for professional journalists are full of advice on how to write leads and develop the focus of a story. The advice boils down to a few good tips, habits experienced writers have followed for decades. Students can learn them, appreciate their value, and put them into practice:

- Keep leads short. Even a long story can flow from one carefully crafted sentence.
- Never forget the news. The lead should tell the reader what the story is about.
- Include elements that dramatize, foreshadow, create a sense of foreboding or anticipated surprise.
- Do not be afraid to write more than one lead until you find the focus you want.
- If you cannot find a good lead, try to write the rest of the story, and then try the lead again.
- A lead does not have to be a sledgehammer. You can ease a reader into a story.
- The beginning and ending of your lead are positions of special emphasis. Interesting or important words work well there. ("Friday, August 12, it was a warm and humid night, but not too hot for a *burglary*."—Laurie Doerr)
- Don't always swing for the fences. Settle for a clean single to center. On bad days, bunt. Throw yourself in front of a pitch. Anything to get on base.
- If you find a good lead that violates any or all of these rules, use it.

Writers who know how to limit their topics, who rehearse and plan and brainstorm leads, have mastered important learning and organizational skills. They are exploring the nucleus of the writing process, searching for the core, the nut, the heart of the story. "If I had to construct my own model for the process," says Donald Fry, "I would write one word in the middle of the page in large letters: FOCUS."

Chapter Nine

Getting Organized

If you could see me writing at this moment, you would understand how dependent I am upon the sacramentals of writing, those holy helpers that make up my daily liturgy of writing this book. These objects include a gray Royal standard typewriter with green keys and white letters. It rests on a tan blotter, which covers a sixty-year-old desk that once belonged to an elementary school teacher.

In one corner of the desk sits a ream of white typing paper. In the other corner is a manila folder filled with about 250 pages of typed manuscript, second draft. I also have a stack of newspaper clippings and children's stories nearby, some notebooks, and journal entries.

In a double drawer near my right hand I keep file folders that represent chapter headings. These contain notes, first draft material in disorder, and more student stories. On the front of each folder is an index card which lists, in no special order, the contents of each file. A large file contains about 300 pages of gray newspaper copy paper on which I furiously typed my first draft, or what Peter Drucker might refer to as the "zero draft" of this book.

In another right-hand drawer I keep No. 2 pencils, tape, and paper clips. In the central drawer, which is difficult to open if you don't know the trick, I keep tape cassettes and correction tape. I know where everything is. On good days I feel like a church organist with all the stops at his command, and I get uncomfortable, and at times cannot write, if the altar is not set and decorated as it should be. Sometimes, if the writing is not going well, I might pay attention to the organization of my desk, or the order of my files, or the sharpness of my pencils to build the physical momentum I need to compose.

Tools of Momentum

My students come to share in this writing priesthood and rely on their tools and their sense of a workplace to get their writing accomplished. Most of my students work with a journal, a reporter's notebook, a "work file," and a "finished file." The journal contains free writing, ungraded work, brainstorming, and occasional writing exercises. The reporter's notebook is for notetaking, recording interviews, and collecting information. The work file, a simple manila folder, contains drafts of works in progress. On the outside of this file is a list of story ideas and on the inside, my brief notations on conferences with the student and new skills acquired. The finished folder contains stories that have survived numerous drafts, final editing, and proofreading. Some will be published in a class book or newspaper. Over time, these physical tools become symbols of momentum and achievement. Students can flip through their files or run their fingers down lists of story ideas or skills learned, and gain a sense of accomplishment. Teachers, parents, and administrators have tangible evidence of the child's work and progress.

On the first day of class, my gift to the children is the reporter's notebook. I think enough of them to give them a professional's tool, and they know it. But the notebook is empty, and they understand we are about to begin an adventure together that will fill it.

One of the best ways to build confidence in a writer is to create the sense, sometimes the illusion, of momentum. Writers have many techniques for convincing themselves that they are getting somewhere. One of the simplest is to forget quality and emphasize quantity.

When Donald Murray is into his daily writing schedule and someone asks, "How's the writing going?" he may respond, "Great! I wrote ninety words today." Never mind the quality, just count those words.

Or, if production is way down, the writer can stress quality: "I wrote a terrific sentence today," or even the wonderfully vague, "I'm working on a great idea." Such are the little confidence builders that keep the writer sane.

Less can be more. When students write on standard loose-leaf paper, their three or four sentences, engulfed by the whiteness of the page, look like a piddling achievement. Yet those four sentences might fill a page in a reporter's notebook. Students' faces light up with accomplishment when they turn one notebook page and begin work on the next. One of the great honors in the class is to receive a new notebook because you have filled the first one. At such moments the new notebook is bestowed on the writer like the Order of the Garter.

The One-Page Barrier

After six weeks of daily writing, most students enjoy discovering their own story ideas, collecting information, and writing leads, but they will not make progress in a steady upward curve of achievement. Some days they will falter, unable to write at all. The school year will show peaks of success and valleys of frustration. By the end of the year, the peaks should be higher and the valleys not so low.

Progress may manifest itself in dozens of little ways. After a month, Jimmy, who would never write more than two sentences, can now regularly generate half a page. But most students seem limited in the development of their stories to the length of a single page of loose-leaf paper, the One-Page Barrier. For a while, whatever the topic, the students seem unwilling or incapable of penetrating this psychological boundary. Stories end magically once the writer nears the bottom of the page. Only the best students generate enough steam to burst the barrier.

To overcome the One-Page Barrier, I give students a chance to write a single story over several class periods. Students may write the beginning one day, the middle the next, and the ending the day after. They may have several more days to reorganize and revise their story. They may think they are finished and then weeks later find more information to add to it.

Story Forms

Length and story development are also determined by the writer's choice of subject and form. Personal narrative and chronological order generate longer stories without artificial limits. The stories tend to justify their length. When Elonda writes "My Friend," the story is a brief, affectionate description. But "A Strange Adventure with My Friend" leads to something longer and more fully developed.

When Regina Hoyt writes "The Tornado," her story develops its own compelling chronology and momentum: "One day I was taking a nap when all of a sudden my mother woke me up and told me to put my slippers on and go into the basement. I couldn't figure out what was going on so I asked my mom and she said there was a tornado warning. After I heard that, I ran into my room, got my old bunny, and ran downstairs. I didn't like going down the ladder so I threw my bunny and then carefully climbed down."

The force of narrative gives this story a strong organization. It is easy to write and fun to read. It moves in a straight line. Later in the story, we learn that a tornado touches down nearby. "My sister was still riding in her car. Once she rode it right under a window and the glass came smashing in right over her head. I just couldn't get over how no one got hurt! Our house was okay except for some glass nick-nacks and windows. We were all safe but I was still shaken up a bit. My sister was still playing. My bunny was okay, too."

The inertia of narrative can have an undesirable effect on some young writers. Andy constructed long personal narratives in strict chronological order that contained dozens of trivial and boring details. It was never enough to arrive at camp to undertake a new adventure. We also had to wake up, eat breakfast, get in the car, start the car, turn left, turn right, and hear conversation that did not move the story along an inch. A student whose narrative is too long can learn to select the best material to make the story shorter and more appealing to readers.

A conference might go this way:

"Toni, this must have been a terrific vacation. You've got so many details here. What part of the trip did you like the best?"

"When we went to Virginia."

"What was interesting about Virginia?"

"My cute little cousin."

Toni now has a focus and an opportunity to reorganize: "Sammy is 7 months old. He has brownish hair and greenish-brown eyes. He is chubby and is a big boy. He doesn't crawl but uses a walker. He gets in a corner and slides down the floor in his walker. He can do this because one end of the house has settled."

The Dreaded Topic Sentence

Without the help of chronology, students find it hard to produce a story with unity, coherence, and development. Their description follows no meaningful order. Their argument zigzags across the borders of logic. Even their narrative may violate the order of time. In short, they need some direction, some structure, to help them organize their thoughts.

My previous paragraph has a topic sentence, three illustrative examples, and a conclusion. I used that structure because it reflects one of the oldest strategies for teaching students order and development.

Teachers tell students that a paragraph should have a topic sentence that tells what the paragraph is about, three supporting sentences, and a concluding sentence to wrap it up. The five-sentence paragraph gets students to think about organization for the first time. Students in some schools have to pass a "paragraph" test to prove they have learned this form. Unfortunately, many teachers teach the test so that a tool for making students orderly becomes an end in itself. What results are paragraphs like this: "I really like cars. I like red cars. I like black cars. I like fast cars. As you can see, I really like cars." We may be creating a generation of students who cannot think of more than three examples on any topic.

Students gain confidence and momentum when teachers pay attention to the entire process of writing. By the time the student is ready to write a first draft, she needs both information and purpose. A well-organized assignment can help children build momentum. Consider one such assignment entitled, "Welcome to My Room."

Most children have special feelings, good or bad, to express about their own rooms. They may love the room because it is equipped with games and toys. They may hate it because they have to share it with brothers and sisters. Teachers can discover much about the affluence, family lives, values, and anxieties of children from reading what they write about their rooms.

When you tell a class, "We're all going to write about our rooms, the place where we sleep," children look up in disappointment because they fail to see anything of value or interest to the reader. But they change their minds after simple brainstorming.

We begin by compiling lists of things that strangers could see, hear, feel, smell, and taste in the room. We use all the senses, but some of the details are still general and uninteresting: "bed, desk, closet, walls, floor, ceiling." Brief conferences evoke more details: "What's on the walls, in the closet, under the bed?"

"A poster of Michael Jackson is on the wall, video games are in the closet, and dirty socks are under the bed." Suddenly, a picture of the child's life begins to emerge as she produces a full list of details, such as this one (in the original spelling):

brass head bords	chair
(two) beds	bary dolls
anteck desk	candy
wordrob (closets)	hairspray
bathroom	gum
ballons	jell beans
telavishion	
stufed animals	
dressor	
shower	
books	
mirror	
chiars	
ribbon box	
shoes	

At this point we share lists with each other so that students can ask questions that evoke additional details:

- "What color is your desk?"
- "How many Barbie dolls do you have?"
- "What is your favorite kind of jelly beans?"

Students add more details, and other students are reminded of details they have left off their lists.

We then move to the world of feelings and begin to associate the room with experiences of joy, sadness, or frustration. Under the heading "feelings," Meg writes:

wonderfull
great
tarible
scarry
terrifying
do homework
fight over sterio

One student reveals that her mother sends her to her room for punishment, but she doesn't mind because she likes it there.

Another student confesses frustration because her mother insists on "rechanging" her room. A familiar complaint is that they must share the room with a "yucky brother" or "gross sister." Once again, we exchange lists, ask questions, share experiences, and collect more information. We write leads, and then students devote ten minutes to writing as quickly as possible, stopping only to check their lists. Results vary, of course, but most students are surprised by the quantity they have written in ten minutes. They have a first draft they can now alter, manipulate, or correct. They have not been asked to write a story without direction or information. The teacher has helped them through the process, building and focusing, so that their momentum increases and the draft comes with a certain ease. Here is an example:

My Room •
By Wendy Witham

My room is a very special place to me. If something goes wrong in my family or I don't feel good, I go in there and spend time alone.

In my room I have a little white closet that I keep my shoes, some of my clothes, skates, games, and other important things that would get in my way.

In my room you can hear my radio, stereo, tape recorder, and sometimes if my window is open you can hear the cars go by.

When I go to bed at night I can feel my soft white and blue bed-spred.

Sometimes I will bring food into my room and eat it at night. Mmmm—boy does it taste good!

If you are doing something in the evening and my Mom is cooking dinner you can smell it. Mmmmm—does it ever smell good! Boy do I ever enjoy having a room to myself to spend time alone in or if I have to do homework or something else I go in there and do it.

This is a capable first draft that actually spills a line over the One-Page Barrier. It was written in about ten minutes and contains clear and detailed information, honest feelings, and a recognizable voice. It appeals to all of our senses. Now that Wendy has written it, she can confer with her teacher to sharpen her focus, develop a better order for the information, and work on paragraph structure and mechanics. These techniques would be meaningless if Wendy had not discovered something to say. Now they are the means for polishing and sharpening her thoughts and language.

Assignments That Create Order

Teachers can help students organize their writing by assigning topics that offer freedom but demand order. Children enjoy writing about their scariest, funniest, or most embarrassing moments. They learn the forms quickly, generating personal narratives and interesting anecdotes that provide models for other students to emulate.

Lloyd Chalker writes about his mother: "One day at Coquina Key soccer field the moms' team was practicing for the soccer picnic. Cindy Chalker was playing center forward when she fell over the goalie while trying to score a goal. She went head first into the ground. She hurt her nose and got a black eye. This all happened in March. Her coach said that she gets the position because she was aggressive."

Karen Higel writes: "On their wedding night as they were leaving the wedding reception, Mr. and Mrs. Higel were backing out their car and hit a pole. They started driving down the road. They thought they had a flat tire. Someone let the air out of the tire for a joke. They drove into a gas station and asked if they could use the air gauge to check their tire. All the time the attendant stood there with his mouth open. He thought they were nuts standing there in their wedding clothes at 2:00 A.M. They were very embarrassed."

Both students enjoyed reading these stories aloud in class. The readings met with laughter and applause and inspired other students to think of funny moments they could develop into stories.

Students gain confidence when they find a structure for their writing, and good assignments can give structure. Writers should depend upon themselves, not their teachers, for most of their story ideas. But I see value in giving students some specific assignments to help them create stories with structure. These assignments will not handcuff the writer; rather, they will help him select material and channel energy.

Vicky had trouble writing more than a few lines on any topic. After a lesson on parody, however, she wrote a hilarious four-hundred-word modern version of "Goldilocks and the Three Bears." She knew the structure of the story and played off it, making Goldilocks a teenage vandal and the bears respectful citizens.

One Christmas, Mrs. Collins taught point of view to her class. The lesson resulted in stories written from the point of view of a Christmas object or ornament: the star who is proud to be atop the tree, or the angel who is uncomfortable with the tree branch up her back, or the ornament that gets nosed by the curious dog, or the tiniest package under the tree. The story was one page long, glued into a folder. On the back of the folder, children drew pictures of their Christmas object. The fifth graders then visited second-grade classes and read the stories aloud. The children could see the picture on the back of the folder while they listened to the story.

One student wrote:

I'm a sheet of red wrapping paper. I've been sitting in the Christmas bag for many years now.

Each Christmas somebody will go to the closet and get the Christmas bag out and some wrapping paper out to wrap presents. Every Christmas when somebody does that they always choose wrapping paper with pretty Christmas designs.

One Christmas a little girl went to the closet and got out the Christmas bag. She was looking through it to find some nice wrapping paper. Suddenly she ran into me. The little girl thought I was the neatest wrapping she had ever seen. So she took me out and put me over a present. Boy was I thrilled! She put a bow on me and put me under the Christmas tree. All of the Christmas lights were shining bright. It was so pretty. I was glad I was put under there.

As the days passed soon Christmas time came. The whole family woke up and went to the Christmas tree to open presents.

The present that the little girl wrapped was for her mother. Her mother was very happy.

After they all opened their presents, they had some breakfast. Then everybody looked and showed each other their presents. They really enjoyed all of their presents and breakfast (because they were starving).

They gathered up all the gift wrapping and threw it away. Except the little girl's red wrapping paper because she liked it so much. So they folded it up and put it in the Christmas bag, to wait for next year.

This turned out to be one of the most successful assignments of the year. All the children participated. Through model stories by the best writers in the class, the other children learned the structure. They responded to the simple structure of the assignment, which made the work orderly and manageable.

Journalists rely upon a range of story types to help them organize their thoughts and material. Like most adult writers, reporters must apply their writing skills to specific assignments and find the most useful form for the resulting story. Writers prefer to discover their own story ideas, but they understand that their job is to work on stories that editors think are important.

Students are moving into a world where responding to assignment is important. During high school and college, students will receive dozens, perhaps hundreds of assignments that require them to write. On the job, they will be assigned to write memos, reports, and letters. Their ability to do so will in large measure determine their professional status. No employer wants a great mind or creative genius who cannot get his or her thoughts across.

Creating Class Experts

Giving students assignments and story forms such as "the embarrassing moment" does not contradict the need for children to discover their own ideas. Over a period of time, writing every day, students learn different forms and develop their own favorite ones. They also develop areas of expertise that generate story after story. The result is a series of stories on the same subject, which the children publish in class books.

In one class, during a single week, Amy produces several individual stories that are published together in a booklet entitled "My Friends." Alison writes several chapters of a fictional work, "The Girl and the Sunflower." Tiffany publishes eighteen stories under the title "The Dangerous Stories of Tiffany." The story titles tell the tale:

- When My Arm Went Through a Window.
- How I Got The Cut In My Ear.
- When I Was Hit With a Hammer.
- My Poor Foot.
- My Head.
- My Head Again.
- My Eye.
- My Leg.
- My Hand.
- When I Had Pink Eye.
- When I Had Mono.
- At P.E.
- My Friend Who Popped My Blister.

Each story runs about a half-page in length and follows a similar structure but with different details and anecdotes. She has discovered a form that gives her enough momentum to write a booklet. Michael likes Tiffany's stories so much, he borrows her form to recount several personal disasters that have befallen him. Michelle decides to write her autobiography, using each chapter to tell an incident in her life. Chris Pyhel's expertise is fishing. The result is "The Young Angler," a twenty-chapter booklet on his first love. Chris writes an introduction on why he likes fishing ("I like pulling in fish and casting") and devotes a chapter to each of his favorite fish and favorite types of fishing.

The Problem of Order

A poll of newspaper editors and writing coaches revealed that the most important writing problem for reporters is poor story organization. Writing a lead is easier and more manageable than finding just the right order for the various types of information reporters bring to a story. Newspaper writers always struggle with questions such as "Where should the background information go?" or "At what point should I describe him?" or "Should that quotation go early in the story, or should I save it for the end?" Students can learn to ask the same kinds of questions. They can then undertake revisions that result in a more organized and meaningful structure.

Fifth grader Niffer Rey was having trouble organizing a story about her trip to Jacksonville to see Michael Jackson in concert. She assembled information about the trip itself, about the reaction of the crowd, about people in the audience, about the songs, about costumes and special effects. But her first draft mixed these elements in a confusing order. In my conference with her, I introduced her to "chronological order" and asked her to number sentences and paragraphs in the order she experienced them. The result was a more coherent second draft:

The Concert •
By Niffer Rey

I was dreaming of going to Michael Jackson's concert, so when he went on tour I begged my mom to go get tickets. She got tickets to the concert. The trip was great from Clearwater to Jacksonville. We stayed at a motel for that afternoon. At last it was time to go to the concert.

While I was there I saw a juggler who opened the concert. Then a guy came out and said Lionel Richie was there. He also said Elijah Mims was there and that he was 111 years old. We had to wait fifteen minutes before the show started. The fifteen minutes were over and the Jacksons came on. Michael wore a red suit. He also wore his glove and a white shirt with black pants when he sang "Billie Jean." One of the songs he sang was "She's Out of My Life." When he sang that song, he sat at the edge of the stage.

The first song they sang as a group was "Wanna Be Startin' Somethin'." Randi and Marlon threw their shirts into the audience. Randi played the piano for "She's Out of My Life." Jermaine sang his song called "Let's Get Serious." He also sang "Tell Me I'm Not Dreamin'" with Michael. Their last song was "Let's Dance, Let's Shout." The audience was singing and clapping through the whole concert.

They had special effects which were great! There were laser lights in all different colors. They showed different colored laser lights for different songs. Another special effect was a hand-like thing which came from the top of the stage. They had stick-like figures with lights on them. They were above Michael and they were coming down on him. He was screaming into the microphone. There were a lot of special effects other than these. After the show, they had fireworks that were great, too! The last song they sang was very a nice song because it got everybody groovin'. Well, for me, it was great. I stood the whole time, which was for two hours.

People at the concert were asking me where I came from. I said "Clearwater." We stayed at the motel for Monday night and left Tuesday morning for home. I enjoyed the trip and the concert was "Great."

Although Niffer's story is not in strict chronological order, she does create a time line that helps her and her readers keep things straight. Even when she moves off the time line to describe the special effects, for example, it feels right, and the special effects paragraph has a chronology of its own. Only the last two sentences of paragraph 3, where she describes the last song and the audience reaction, seem out of place. Another conference might lead her to find a more logical place for that information, perhaps at the end of paragraph 4. The key is that the strategy of chronological order helped her make sense and communicate her experience.

Fifth grader Laurie Doerr struggled through several drafts of a story on her friend Kelly Klasek. It was a difficult story, one with many facets, and it was hard to keep things in order. Finally, she had a lead and a first page she was happy with:

Liver donors are needed almost once or twice a month. My

friend Kelly is special that way. She was fortunate enough to get one.

My friend Kelly Klasek is very special to me, my family, her family and many other people. Kelly Kay Klasek is the second longest living liver transplant patient in the world.

When Kelly was born her liver wasn't strong. So that made Kelly weak also. They waited for a liver for two years. When her family and friends were celebrating her third birthday on Valentine's Day, the phone rang. Bringgg. Bringgg. "Hello?" "Yes, this is the Klasek's residence." "Oh thank you! Oh my gosh!" "Are there any instructions to do?" "Sure, anything. Thank you, thank you!" Click, hangup. "They found a liver donor. We have to fly to Denver, Colorado, tomorrow!"

The party was over. The Klaseks started to pack. Kelly was operated on by Dr. Thomas Starzel. He is still living and is one of the best surgeons in the world.

At this point, Laurie loses control of the story. She is dissatisfied with the order of the information on her second page and marks it up with arrows, brackets, and circled numbers in order to regain control. The page looked something like this:

Then after the operation and many tests, Kelly's

① family moved to Florida. This was not the end of tragic happenings. Two years ago they discovered that Mr. Klasek has MS (multiple sclerosis).

Kelly has one brother and two sisters. All three

③ of them have children ages 7 mon.—13 years. *help out* Mrs. Klasek is an attractive and strong lady.

Kelly is thirteen years old. She is unable to do many things such as ride a bike, go to heavily crowded areas and play rough sports and games be-

② cause of infection. Kelly was also unable to go to school. She had a home-bound until last year. Now she attends St. John's Private School in St. Petersburg Beach. Kelly has to take medicine and a couple of pills each day that stunt her growth. Very few people make fun of her that way. Kelly has succeeded and plans to go on!

Sunday, May 8, 1983, a tragic thing happened.

Saturday night, Kelly's dad didn't feel well. He

④ had sharp pains. Mrs. Klasek was scared and wanted to take him to the hospital.

Laurie continues to move things around until she finds a structure that works and that leads her to a meaningful conclusion. Here is a revised version of her second page:

Then after the operation, Kelly's family moved to Florida. Kelly has one brother and two sisters. All three of them are older and have children ages 7 months to 13 years. Mrs. Klasek is an attractive and strong lady.

Kelly is thirteen years young. She is unable to do many things such as ride a bike, go to heavily crowded areas and play rough sports and games because of infection. Kelly was also unable to go to school (she had a homebound) until last year. Now she attends St. John's Private School in St. Petersburg Beach. She has succeeded and plans to go on!

Sunday, May 8, 1983, a tragic thing happened.

Saturday night, Kelly's dad didn't feel well. He had sharp pains. Mrs. Klasek wanted to take him to the hospital. He said no and he'd be all right. Mrs. Klasek didn't like the idea but said OK. Sunday morning he didn't feel good and couldn't go to church. When they came back he had died.

In June, Kelly and her mother went to Pittsburgh, Pennsylvania for a reunion. Most of the liver transplant patients were there. They stayed at a motel. They played games, ate cake and just plain had fun. They had a great time.

In a conference, Laurie and I discussed whether the information on Mr. Klasek should be included in a story essentially about Kelly's liver transplant. She thought it would show what a courageous family the Klaseks were and how much they had suffered. Her revised structure has more chronological momentum than her earlier versions. She has continued to move things around, and has even become dissatisfied with her lead sentence, so that "Liver donors are needed almost once or twice a month," now reads, "In the news, a few times every month, there are stories about the need for liver donors." Laurie is really writing now. She has taken command of the content and structure of a story that is changing and shifting with each revision. Her revisions extend to the subtle, textual level so that "thirteen years old" becomes "thirteen years young."

Laurie is ready to learn many of the sophisticated strategies that professional journalists use to develop and organize their stories.

1. *Write fast without notes:* Even when students collect good notes from an interview, it may be easier for them to build up some momentum by writing without their notes. When they write directly from their notes, they

sometimes write a story about their notebook instead of their subject. They tell the story in notebook order. If they write a first draft without notes, they can go back and include important information from the notes in a second draft.

2. *Copy your notes:* Some reporters return from assignments and immediately sit down to type out their notes on paper or in a computer terminal. To some this practice seems like a waste of time or a duplication of effort, but for those who practice it, the method has distinct advantages: a) The writer, who probably takes notes stenographically, can learn the information in the notebook. b) He does not copy the notes slavishly. He fills things in and leaves things out, beginning the process of selection. c) He gets his hands moving and works toward a first draft.

3. *Use an outline:* Writers such as John McPhee grew up writing from outlines and depend upon the technique in their professional work. Many teachers teach outline writing, and many children benefit from the practice. Alas, I was not one of them. I found the outline too deterministic, too reductive. It forced me to make decisions about the order of the information I was not yet ready to make. Yet I was still required to hand one in, so I invented the "reverse outline." Using this technique, you write the story first. Then you index the information in the story and create an outline. I invented reverse outlining as a subterfuge but find that it provides a check on the structure of a piece. If I cannot create an orderly outline from my first draft, some revision may be in order.

4. *Show, don't tell:* This is old and good advice. A student writes a story about a teacher, whom she describes as a "good teacher and a caring, enthusiastic person." In a conference, I ask the student, "What does the teacher do that makes you think she is caring?" This question may lead the writer to describe some scenes in which the teacher spends extra time after school working with students, or applauds when students do special work, or is always wearing a smile button. When the writer shows us the teacher's enthusiasm, she opens a window through which we vicariously experience this caring, enthusiastic person.

5. *Think of past, present, and future:* This strategy helps the reporting and the writing. If a student writes a story about the new principal, he can ask questions about the principal's education and experience, her immediate impressions of her new job, her hopes for the school, and her career ambitions. At times, this pattern becomes a useful structure for the story itself.

6. *Change your technique or location:* Writers who are having trouble composing a story on a computer terminal may turn to pencils and legal pads to try to solve a problem or build momentum. A writer unable to work in his study may move to the kitchen table. Students also get frustrated or distracted and find it hard to write. Teachers can move students from a desk to a table or from a small group to a corner. A student who is having trouble composing may be able to dictate a story into a tape recorder and then transcribe it. Writers do develop comfortable habits and sympathetic spaces, but they also need a change on occasion to get things going.

7. *Borrow from fiction, film, television:* By the time students are ten years old, even if they cannot read, they have been exposed to hundreds, perhaps thousands, of narratives through nursery rhymes, fairy tales, biblical passages, movies, cartoons, sitcoms, and commercials. From these narratives children learn the structure of storytelling and immediately understand concepts such as flashback, foreshadowing, scenic construction, and point of view. They can use these structures to tell their own stories.

Chapter Ten

Editing

I once attended a meeting at which top newspaper editors attacked deans of journalism schools for graduating students who seemed to have no control over Standard English usage. "Don't blame us," said the deans, "we only have the students for four years. We can't undo a lifetime of bad teaching. You should look at what's happening in the high schools."

The high school teachers blame the middle school teachers who blame the elementary schools. To their credit, the elementary school teachers rarely pass the buck, but occasionally you hear: "Do you know what the home life of these kids is like? We can't do much if parents aren't there to back us up."

To complete the circle, parents blame the media for turning children's minds to mush, for taking them away from reading, and for lowering their appetite for learning. Or perhaps pregnant women throughout America are being frightened by newspapers, inflicting their children with permanent and irreparable illiteracy.

SAT scores decline for years, states set up batteries of tests to make sure students learn elemental skills, the president of the United States speaks from the highest podium in the land on the need for more discipline in the schools, parents line up for hours so their children can attend "fundamental" schools, a national commission claims our schools are in crisis, and, in a movie called *Teachers*, a high school student sues his school because he cannot read.

Students cannot spell, we are told. They cannot read with comprehension. They do not understand basic grammar. They have no control of Standard English. They cannot communicate basic ideas on the page.

Teachers, parents, and students all suffer from this perception of failure. A cloud of lowered expectations hangs over our schools and helps predetermine the limited achievement of our children. We have "back to basics" when we should be talking about "forward to excellence."

133

In English classes, this sensibility often results in a new emphasis on the teaching of spelling, syntax, and Standard English usage. My daughter Alison studied these hard one year. She studied the parts of speech, she learned how to diagram sentences, and she memorized long lists of spelling words. This year of study reinforced her earlier study of grammar and contributed, no doubt, to her growing language skills.

Yet I noticed something peculiar about her work. Alison would pass a grammar test on, say, subject-verb agreement, but would make mistakes in her writing. It was as if her study of grammar and mechanics was one thing and her writing another, and if the twain met, it was only by chance. For although she was taught grammar intensively in that year, she was rarely asked to write. When we teach grammar outside the context of writing, we teach students how to hate English, not how to make meaning.

When Alison was in the fifth grade, she would often hand in stories that had several spelling mistakes. But in that same year, she ran for class secretary. It was an enthusiastic campaign. She wrote up dozens of posters and hung them all over the school. Her spelling was perfect. When it really counts, the writer becomes concerned about mechanics.

Alison's experience supported my notion that what is often interpreted as ignorance is sometimes carelessness or sloth or lack of concentration in disguise. What you get is not always what it seems.

In one of the first fifth-grade classes I taught, a tiny girl came to the front of the class to share her story with the other students. I looked over her shoulder and was appalled by what I saw. I could immediately detect many serious mechanical mistakes, sentence fragments, and words left out. I was heartsick. "This girl is about to humiliate herself in front of the class," I thought.

I could not have been more mistaken. When she read the piece to the class, she efficiently corrected the grammar, completed the sentences, and filled in the missing words. The speed with which she recognized a problem and corrected it dazzled me. Essentially, she wrote a second draft in her head as she was reading.

Another day I received a paper from a student consisting of a single long paragraph that read like a stream-of-consciousness passage in an experimental novel. There was no punctuation at all. My first thought was that this student had no concept of what a sentence was. I tried to ease into the problem in my conference. "You've written a lot here. You managed to get a lot accomplished. But I think we should talk about complete sentences."

"You mean you want me to put the periods and the capital letters in?"

I nodded, dumbfounded.

"I haven't gotten to that part yet."

She snatched the paper, returned to her desk, and in five minutes brought it back to me. Every sentence was complete and the punctuation was perfect. With that dark cloud of pessimism hanging over me, I was almost ready to brand her "functionally illiterate," when the reality was that, like so many of us writers, she had not "gotten to that part yet."

When should we get to that part? Some teachers get to it during the grading of papers. They correct all the students' mistakes in red ink. Students are not asked to try to undertake the corrections themselves or to rewrite the paper with the teacher's corrections as a guide. So students get complacent. They ignore the red markings or may not have the proficiency to understand what "pron.-ante. dis." means. The most important thing the student learns is that someone else will correct the mistakes. This reminds me of the high school student whose mother typed his term papers. Mother corrected most of his mistakes. Only in college, when mom was not around, did he learn that he had a serious spelling problem.

I think we often teach writing upside down, and it may be because our model is a mechanical rather than an organic one. To build a machine, such as an automobile, you have to piece together the parts, the chassis, the wheels, the transmission, the carburetor. Unless each part is constructed well from the beginning, the whole machine cannot function as designed. In the human body, the organs grow and develop at different times, but always working together.

We tell students that before they can write they must master certain skills. They must have good, clear penmanship. They must be able to spell words. They must master the sentence, the complete thought, and learn punctuation. They must build those sentences into coherent paragraphs with topic sentences. Then they must connect those paragraphs with forceful transitions into a logical, unified, and well-developed whole.

In teaching this way, we create for students the most constricting process imaginable. The young writer's brain is clotted with mixed messages about what is important and how to achieve it. He may be so concerned about his spelling that he will never take a chance on an interesting word. He may be so anxious about paragraph structure that his final work may consist of three short paragraphs instead of ten long ones.

I will write page after page without thinking about neatness, spelling, punctuation, or the finer points of grammar. I intentionally lower my standards at the beginning of the process. This gives me the copy I need to revise, manipulate, purify, and correct. I lower my standards at the beginning so I can elevate them later on. I may ignore some of my students' mechanical problems in early conferences. I may prefer to deal with questions of information, order, and focus. But when we finally turn to grammar, spelling, and mechanics, we do so with enthusiasm. Students revise and take responsibility willingly, not because they think grammar is fun, but because they are committed to the improvement of the paper at every level and to its eventual public display.

Because I do not mark up students' papers in red, because I conduct conferences without turning every time to grammar, I am sometimes accused of "having no standards," of "being soft," of "ignoring basic problems," of being "the Doctor Spock" of writing instruction.

I believe in all the strategies the teachers of traditional grammar use. I believe in sentence diagraming, in spelling lists, vocabulary training, grammar books, and special attention to common errors. I have taught grammar using pre-tests, lesson plans, and post-tests. My argument with the traditionalists is that these strategies *do not go far enough*. In some schools students are exposed to them year after year, but the lessons never sink in. That is why students from Yale and Harvard cannot explain the difference between the active and passive voice. That is why a student is able to distinguish among "too," "to," and "two" on a state literacy test, but continues to write that her sister is "to noisy."

Almost a century of research indicates that teaching grammar outside the context of writing may actually do more harm than good. Within the context of writing, the rules of syntax and Standard English usage have direct relevance to the creation of meaning. George Orwell makes the surprising statement that correct grammar is not important "so long as one makes one's meaning clear." Clarity supersedes convention. But grammar is the lighthouse that protects us from the uncertain waters of obfuscation.

Teachers who do not teach grammar, spelling, and mechanics

should. Teachers who do may find that the following strategies reinforce and enhance what they are trying to accomplish.

Take your cues from the students' writing. The work of your students will teach you what they need to learn and what you need to teach. Grammar taught straight out of a book may be boring to students who have already mastered a skill and impenetrable to students not ready to learn it. Teachers should read the writing of their students to make decisions about how and when to teach. Students may be using quotation marks correctly but may be having trouble with "who" and "whom." Instead of using canned material, teachers can use examples from student work for lessons. These sentences can be corrected in worksheets, or revised for clarity, or diagramed.

Teach lessons in conference when the child is ready to learn. Most students learn how to use quotation marks by the third or fourth grade. Yet Donald Graves has taught their use to first graders. When a teacher sees a first grader using conversation or dialogue in a story, she can teach the child how the quotation marks help him make meaning and keep who's speaking clear. I have taught active verbs, how to correct misplaced modifiers, the difference between "who" and "whom," and many other questions of usage to young children who were ready to apply them in their writing.

Teach grammar, usage, and mechanics as tools, not rules. I learned to punctuate when I stopped asking "What's the rule here?" and began asking "How can I use this comma to help make my meaning clear?" The difference is profound. Emphasis on the rule inhibits the writer; emphasis on the tool has the writer reaching to his workbench for something that will help him. I learned the difference between the active voice and passive voice in the fourth grade at St. Aidan School. But only in graduate school did I learn that using the active voice made my writing clear, concise, and precise. It took Don Fry about twenty seconds to change a sentence like "The writing was improved by the teacher" to "The teacher improved the writing." I was ready to learn the lesson years earlier, but no one was there to teach it to me.

Highlight common problems. Every teacher knows that a class of fifth graders will exhibit certain kinds of usage problems. They will misuse the comma, write in fragments, and mix up homonyms. But not every class will exhibit the same problems in the same order. Teachers can teach lessons on the problems that are revealed in their students' writing. Some lessons are taught in conference, but some special and recurring problems need attention before the whole class, and the class should be made specially accountable for them.

Teach these skills in the larger context of revision and publication. Aaron wrote a story about his pet blue jay, which died. The final line of his first draft was "I wish I still had Floppy." Without prodding, he changed that line to "I wish I still could hear Floppy sing." That's a poet's revision, similar to Shelley's changing "To the Skylark" to "To a Skylark." Students who write six or nine or thirteen drafts of a story make dozens of revisions as they get closer to publication. Because of their commitment and time, they easily turn their attention to grammar, spelling, and punctuation. Michelle writes that Mr. Thompson is "a wonderful, and loveable and spankful Prinsapal." I tell her she has written a good sentence, and that I'm especially thankful for "spankful." I also tell her to turn her attention to her punctuation and spelling so that readers can appreciate her sentence fully, without distraction or interruption.

The Yucky List

Teaching grammar and usage effectively takes a good deal of patience and humor. The teacher must be willing to tell a student time and again that she has made a mistake. Sometimes the same one. The student needs to realize that readers will be put off or distracted by mechanical errors in a story. "Let's get rid of them," I say, "so we can get this piece published."

No mistake is more pervasive and persistent than the misspelling of the words *a lot*. I have read the first stories of first graders and the first novels of adults and have gritted my teeth over the mistake in both. I have taught the correct spelling one year and seen a good student misspell the words again the next. My guess is that students have always spelled it *alot* although I am willing to consider evidence that there was once a golden age in which students, from fear of the rack, always left a space between the *a* and the *l*.

My frustration increased exponentially until the day I heard Eliot Wigginton, the famous *Foxfire* teacher from Rabun Gap,

Georgia, explain how he handles the problem. I have adopted his strategy and it works.

When I see a number of students using "alot," I tell the class, "I want you to notice that I'm putting *alot* on the yucky list. Many of you are spelling it as if it were one word. But it's really two words, *a lot*. I don't want you to hand in your first novel misspelling the words *a lot*. So I'm telling you now, if you misspell these words, or misuse any other word on the yucky list, well . . . I'll scream." They laugh in disbelief until they hand in a paper with *a lot* misspelled. Then I shriek as if frightened by a mouse. They snatch the paper from me, scurry back to their desks, and try to find the foul blemish.

The yucky list is a long sheet of white paper displayed in front of the classroom for the entire school year. Every time the teacher pays special attention to a mechanical mistake during a lesson, that offending problem goes on the yucky list. Keeping the list in view at all times is important. It provides a daily reminder of students' most common errors, the ones to be carefully avoided. If the student comes to a problem but forgets how to solve it, he can look up at the yucky list for the answer.

The value of the list is that it derives from the daily mistakes of the students. Teachers can tailor their instruction to the immediate problems and needs of the students. Depending on the performance of the class, the list will differ from year to year. It may take a whole year for this material to seep into students' daily writing, which the teacher can use as a regular litmus test of the skills they are learning and the mistakes they are avoiding.

Teachers cannot teach a single lesson on a grammatical problem and think, "Well, I covered that." The lesson must be continually reinforced in the students' writing so that they feel responsible for finding and correcting their own mistakes. A bit of humor makes this medicine go down more easily.

"This is almost ready to be published, John. You've made some excellent revisions. But you have one sentence that's unclear because you've misused a word on the yucky list. I want you to find it yourself. And you wouldn't want me to scream, would you?"

John laughs and returns to his desk, recognizing that he has written "its" when he means "it's." He knows I will not scream at him, but the game we play defuses the usual anxiety about grammar and usage. He knows he has a job to do, and it is unfinished until we correct and clarify his work at the end of the process. When an Eliot Wigginton student makes a mistake from the yucky list (he calls it the "offal list") on a final draft, Eliot takes a point off the grammar grade. The student regains the point by rewriting the paper and correcting the mistake.

In 1975 at Auburn University at Montgomery, I helped develop English 100, a course for students who could not master basic language skills. In three years we learned that students—some of them in their thirties and forties—committed many of the same errors in class after class.

- They wrote sentence fragments.
- They wrote run-on sentences.
- They failed to make subjects agree with verbs.
- They failed to make pronouns agree with antecedents.
- They misplaced modifiers.
- They confused "who" and "whom" and made other case errors.
- They could not form the possessive correctly.
- They misspelled many words.
- They had little control of punctuation.

These college adults faced many of the same problems of making meaning, in the same order, that my elementary school children face. These stages of development have been defined by Donald Graves. First, children must represent their words through spelling. Then they must find some order for those words on the page. Then they try to make meaning. Then they revise. No wonder that a fifth-grade yucky list should contain many of the same problems that, when ignored or taught improperly, appear years later in the writing of adults.

The Yucky List

~~alot~~—a lot
there, their, they're
its, it's
two, to, too
fragment (failure to write a complete sentence)
our, are, hour
know, no
improper capitalization
Me and my brother (used as subject)
~~could of~~/could have
~~freind~~, friend
~~Baypoint Elementary~~, Bay Point Elementary
~~he be quiet~~; he is quiet (dialect)

the ~~childrens'~~ house (misuse of plural possessive)
~~he runned~~, he ran (misuse of irregular verbs)
everyone ... they (pronoun disagrees in number with
antecedent)
who, whom

The teacher teaches a lesson on the problem before it is added
to the list, which grows and grows throughout the school year.
Students have the special responsibility of finding and correcting
these mistakes in their own work. Over the course of the year,
teachers can keep a record of which skills the student has
mastered. All this is done in the context of the student's writing.

Editing Copy

When I teach grammar in context, I usually begin with a pep
talk. I tell students they have an important responsibility to
improve their own work. I even administer the "self-editing"
oath, a comic/serious promise to attend to the problems in their
own stories. They laugh and giggle while taking it, but they
know we mean business.

They learn that I want them to read their own stories more
carefully than ever before. I want them to read with critical
attention to detail so they can begin to see the problems in their
stories that need fixing. I also want them to recognize what is
good in their work so that their revisions can produce the best
effect.

I write a sentence from one of their papers on the board:

My room is yellow and pink
yellow bedspread with boys
handing little girls flowers
white dressers green carpet
flower on my wall.

Even in a sentence with so many problems, it is important to
emphasize the positive. "What works here?" I ask. "What is this
writer doing well?" The response is "She uses lots of colors,"
or "She helps me see it," or "She uses good details," or "She
spells her words correctly."

We agree that the writer has given us much to build on,
but that changes are essential to make this picture of her room
clearer and more meaningful to the reader. I quickly teach the

students four editing marks and ask them to improve and correct the sentence.

The marks are:

/ delete a letter   Roy Peter Clark~~e~~

— delete a word   ~~the amazing~~ Roy Peter Clark~~e~~

∧ insert   ~~the amazing~~ Ro∧Peter Clark~~e~~

⌐ insert from margin   ~~the amazing~~ Ro∧Peter Clark~~e~~ ——— *the conceited*

The best revisions of the student's passage looked like this:

The walls of ∧ My room ~~is~~ *are* yellow and pink. ∧ *On my bed is a*
      decorated
yellow bedspread∧with boys

handing little girls flowers.

I have ∧ white dressers, *a* green carpet, ∧ *and a*

flower on my wall.

Students can develop their editing and critical reading skills by revising sentences from their own stories. Without mentioning the name of the writer, the teacher can highlight common problems and invite students to correct mistakes. Here are a dozen sentences from the work of a dozen fifth graders:

1. they will eat their babies if they don't have food.
2. Its raining.
3. He plays alot.
4. It's name is Harold.
5. But then I get a stomickakce because Im hungry for lunch and worst of all we get homework.
6. When I was 4 years old my mother left me of at a babysitter.
7. My brother and I were aferid of him.
8. Soon we couldn't find them we looked for them for about an hour.
9. At my party we are gonna go swimming.
10. I had bring my camera and my purse.
11. I was born and raised hear in Florida.
12. We left at 11:30 and got their at 12:30.

Teachers will learn much about the students' language skills from the way children revise these sentences. Some students will be able to identify and correct the common mistakes. "Its raining" becomes "It's raining." Other students will want to undertake additional revisions for style, rhythm, and clarity. A student might revise sentence 12 to "We left at 11:30 A.M. and got there at 12:30 P.M.," or better yet, "We left at 11:30 in the morning and got there an hour later." Finding mistakes is the point of the exercise, but that process can be learned in the context of other important revisions that improve the flow and meaning of the sentence.

The exercise will also teach the teacher what the student needs to learn. One student, who speaks in dialect, revised sentence 3 to "He play alot" and sentence 4 to "Hes name is Harold." In the latter example, the student identified the problem and corrected it to match how he would say it. The teacher can take cues from such cases and teach the student how to change his dialect into Standard English.

Editing Teams

Teachers cannot grade and correct all the written work of a productive class, especially one that is writing every day. When I need help, I turn to other students. These student editors confer with their classmates and prepare work for publication. This process of "peer review" has many advantages. It creates a real audience for the work of student writers. Children begin to write for each other rather than for a single adult. This often inspires them to work more carefully and to take responsibility for the information and mechanics in their writing.

Students team up to read each other's work and to correct mistakes. They serve as "test readers" for each other before the work is published. This activity inspires careful, critical reading. Although students may overlook some mistakes in the story, they often identify the most important and distracting ones from the reader's point of view. They are also likely to find mistakes from the yucky list because these have been emphasized in class.

I often put together a team of about twenty student editors to do the final polishing of stories. Becoming an editor is a reward for students who have done special work. It is also a part of the collaborative effort of publication. Editors work in pairs and check on each other. I supply them with dictionaries. I watch them carefully, and here is what usually happens:

- They find solutions to many problems. They correct spelling and punctuation, complete sentence fragments, fill in missing words, and clear up confusion and ambiguity.
- They learn the importance of clear handwriting. Some stories are rendered illegible because of sloppy penmanship. Bad handwriting obscures the message. The editor may have to return to the writer to discover what a word says. The writer himself may not be able to decipher it. Both editor and writer learn the value of clear handwriting, that without it, a clear message is impossible.
- The editors learn the value of returning to the writer for consultation. Professional editors consult with writers to add important information or to discuss a change in the story. Students recognize the value of this strategy. The writer can answer questions and be involved in solving problems.
- Although students found many mistakes, they missed many others, especially when the mistakes came in bunches. I urged them to recheck a sentence after they found a mistake and to search for other problems in the same sentence. I asked them to read with more intense concentration than ever before.
- Students find more mistakes near the end of stories. Writers may become fatigued or bored as they near the end of a story, or they may simply lower their standards in order to get the writing finished.
- It is often desirable to have students edit each other's papers in small teams, so that each student can see the final problems in his story and have them explained. The most frustrating thing for a writer is to wake up, open the newspaper, and discover that an editor has eliminated something good or added something bad to a story. More often than not, editors help stories, but not always. That is why stories should be edited only after the writer has had several chances to make changes and revisions and corrections.

We discovered, for example, that student editors wrote mistakes into stories, changing "Indiana" to "India," for example. "Our priorities stink" became "Our priorities aren't very good," an example of the goody-two-shoes school of editing. It is important that editors not change the voice of the writer. Jimmy would say "stink" without a blink. His editor would not.

Teachers, the primary editors of student work, should remember that improvements in student work may reflect the teacher's voice, not the child's. Some teachers may reward a flowery or understated style, forcing children to develop an unnatural writing voice in order to succeed. What we are striving for as writers is an "authentic voice" expressed with clarity in Standard English. It should "sound like the writer," no matter how many corrections or improvements we demand.

Handwriting and Spelling

When my wife's aunt asked me, "What do you teach, Roy?" I replied, "I teach writing."

"Oh," she said, "Do you teach the Palmer Method?"

For how many decades have we confused penmanship and composition? And how many young writers have we turned off by focusing on the weaknesses in their handwriting rather than on the quality of their expression? The lowest grade I ever received in school was a C for penmanship in the second grade. Thank God, adult writers are not judged by their handwriting or I would have become a priest or a centerfielder.

In the future, all schools will have word processors. Children at an early age will work on a keyboard. They will write stories before they learn to form letters. Until then, we must teach penmanship within the context of writing: clarity and efficiency are the goals; readers must be able to pick up the work and grasp its meaning without stumbling over scratches on the page that have little more meaning than hieroglyphics.

Teachers have to remember that writers need to be a bit sloppy at times to build momentum. After revision and rewriting sloppy copy becomes a neat sheet. It is difficult for teachers on one occasion to preach, "Be careful and form your letters neatly," and on another to say, "Don't worry about your handwriting in your first draft," but such flexibility is necessary.

The student whose teachers insisted she compose in the neatest italic print was frustrated because she spent her energies on penmanship rather than on composition. When a teacher asked her just to write a story and not concern herself with handwriting, she felt like a person released from prison. Because she cared about sharing her thoughts and words with others in a new way, she did not abandon clear handwriting. When she found something to say she was willing, even eager, to be neat. But that came at the end, not the beginning, of the process.

Spelling must also be taught in the context of writing and communication. Students can write stories at a very early age, even preschool, if they are permitted to invent spellings. First graders can use interesting and meaningful words if they are not required to spell correctly on early drafts.

My daughter Emily once wrote the sentence, "I'm never in nervis candishin." The teacher placed a red X over the last two words and wrote on the top: "Please write words you can spell or use your school dictionary to find the correct spelling." The teacher's advice, when enforced tyrannically, can turn off writers at an early age. Some teachers give young students lists of words, and only these words can be used in stories.

Freed from the burden of correct spelling during the drafting of stories, students will attempt words like "Interreu Decurater," "Ejipt," and "pelkan." IBM has introduced a program, *Writing to Read*, which teaches phonetic spelling to first graders with such efficiency that in a short time they can represent in writing any word they can say. Other systems of invented spelling have been created and used effectively in writing curricula.

I have not found the need to teach invented spellings because most students can spontaneously create their own systems, which teachers can read and help refine. Here my daughter Emily, in her first story of the first grade, writes a long narrative about "The Sun." She was told to spell the words "as well as you can."

The Sun was good. I like the Sun. He was my
frend. I asd my mom if he cod slep over. My.
Mon sed yes and we had to Eta. now we sad o.k.
We rad books teha. We had to go to bed. Wenh
We wre in bad. We paled. I Spi gred orige yelloy
green blue prpul brawn and blak and in the moning
we ate Brefis tenh we plade hidigosek and tenh
the Sun went home.

The final story was about three times this long, all written in about twenty minutes. It contained words such as "nesxd" (next), "kasel" (castle), "lafdhde" (laughed), "rening rasis" (running races), "togatr" (together), and "mins" (minutes). To my surprise, the story contained this passage:

We hrd a sawd nok nok "how Is it"
"It's me" we sad "hos me"

Somewhere, Emily had picked up the importance of using quotation marks in a dialogue. Her classmates also wrote with ease. Inventing spellings became an easy, fun skill. Her teacher Miss Patterson and I could read more than 95 percent of the words. Most teachers become instant experts in "translating" invented spellings. "It's like learning to read a foreign language," said Miss Patterson.

The strategy works just as well in a sixth-grade basic skills class. Many of these children will not write because they are bad spellers and have been told so for years. They do not commit themselves to the page because they know they will be chided for their spelling. To further shield their work from scrutiny, they may grossly distort their handwriting so that the teacher cannot tell if it is "right" or "wrong." But if these older students are permitted to invent spellings, they will write and through the process of writing become better spellers.

The alternative is for a teacher of writing to answer the question "How do you spell this word?" ten thousand times a year. My answer is almost always, "Spell it the best way you can." That saves me work and turns the challenge back to the student.

Through normal development, reading, and traditional spelling texts and exercises, students will improve their work. But our goal is not to have students excel in spelling bees. The goal is to have students hand in finished stories with correct spellings and without distracting errors so that readers receive clear messages.

Two or three drafts into a story, students will have identified and corrected many mistakes in spelling and punctuation. After that, they may need the reward of publication to keep them going. They resist the imperative "Write it again," not because of any sense of failure, but because of tedium, especially if they are being asked to deal with mechanics. If content is the center of attention, if teachers are asking young writers what they know, students will show more pluck and stick-to-itiveness. But a student may have worked so hard on a story that the teacher is ready to say, "You've done fine work on this, improving it with every revision, so let's put it in our book," even though she knows the piece has a long way to go.

Here are some methods for helping students improve their work in the final stages of composition:

1. Have a student circle any word she thinks may be misspelled and underline any problem she suspects in grammar or punctuation. Over time, the teacher can watch a student grow in her ability to recognize errors. Students cannot correct mistakes until they unearth them in their stories.
2. If a student is close to a correct spelling, have him look it up in a dictionary.
3. If a student is way off on a hard word, for example, "numonya," give her the spelling, especially if she has checked out and corrected other words. Have her list the correct spelling of the interesting new word she has used in the back of her journal.
4. If a student fails to recognize a word as misspelled, put a tiny dot in the margin next to the line in which the word appears. This helps to focus the student's attention.
5. If there are many misspellings, say thirty or forty, ask the student to confer with another student for help. If this does not work, assign a partner who is a good speller to work with the student. Sometimes older children can team up with younger children in different grades.
6. Make the final corrections on the paper yourself. You may ask the student to rewrite the paper with the corrections added.
7. Publish the work with the mistakes corrected. This final step sends an important message to the writer: that publication is so important the editor will not tolerate errors in spelling, punctuation, or grammar. It is very important for the student to read his or her own work in Standard English. Some students have never seen their own words in that form. To them, publication says, "Here is why these things are important to learn. Now everyone can read what you have to say."

The Paragraph

Students do not need to know how to write paragraphs before they can write stories. If we teach students topic sentences and paragraph structure before we let them tell interesting stories, we may set up a serious and perhaps permanent impediment to their learning. Instead of smoothing the way for writers, we clutter it up.

I have a confession. I have rarely constructed a paragraph the way I was taught to, with a topic sentence and supporting examples, each paragraph a model of unity, coherence, and development. Instead, I write in what one teacher describes as "chunks" of information. That description appeals to me, because it is what I do.

I also create paragraphs as a function of revision, and this has been a useful strategy for teaching the paragraph to students. In the early stages of a story, I may not ask students to worry about paragraphs at all. We have other priorities at that point: getting a good idea, collecting information, finding a focus, searching for a structure for the narrative. Having solved some of these problems, the student may even develop a draft in one single unindented block of prose. This is what Willie Caseber did in his story entitled "Ouch!"

It was a crisp Thanksgiving morning, and I was ready to race! Over the intercom I heard "... All Gobbler 1 mile fun runners, go to the starting gate." So I told my mom I'd meet her in the stands, and left to get a good position in the race. "On your mark, get set, go, BOOM," said the starter. And we were off. Quickly I found my pace and started moving to the front, where I found my friend Jeff, and we ran together. We were pulling ahead of the crowd and started to go around the corner of the block. Then "Wham!!" I tripped over something and fell on the gravel road. I was bleeding and crying. My knees were cut and had some gravel in them. My hands were the same way. "Do you want me to help," asked Jeff. "No," I said, "I saw a monitor back there. You go. Win the race. I can make it back." So Jeff took off and I walked back to the monitor. Then I waited, because the monitor just had to wait for the last jogger. Finally we left for the first aid center. When we arrived there, the medic took the rocks out of my cuts and bandaged my hands and knees. Then I said thanks and left for the bandstands. When I found my mom, she made me tell her the whole story. In the end, she said, "Well, you're okay now." "Okay!" I shouted, "Tell me how I'm going to eat my turkey drumstick, potatoes, gravy, and pumpkin pie??!!"

I explained to Willie and the other students in the class the meaning of paragraphs in terms of "shifting gears." The story begins, moves along, picks up speed, shifts gears, takes a turn, shifts again, and heads for its final destination. When you shift gears, I tell the students, mark a new paragraph.

I held up their papers for them to see. I showed them that they wrote in long, impenetrable blocks of prose. I explained how paragraphs create white space, which helps readers' eyes move through the story. This is well known to journalists, who must shorten their paragraphs because their prose appears in long, thin columns of type. When you write in paragraphs, you organize the story for the reader and invite him to move through it with ease.

With that lesson in mind, Willie made the following paragraph mark (⌊) at these points in his story:

⌊It was a crisp Thanksgiving morning ...

⌊Quickly I found my pace ...

⌊"No," I said ...

⌊There I waited ...

⌊"Okay!" I shouted ...

When a student develops an interesting narrative, the logical breaks in the story become apparent even to the casual reader. The writer can mark the places where new paragraphs should begin. Then we can discuss and test each paragraph against the usual standards. So even though I agreed with most of Willie's paragraph decisions, we could confer and make additional revisions in the name of good paragraphing.

Writers' Tricks

Writers find it difficult to stop tinkering with a story. After five revisions they still make a few more subtle changes, dropping a word here and changing one there. Even after they see the story in print, they wonder why they failed to make that one last revision.

The writer's style may be as individual as a fingerprint. But writers depend upon the same devices—call them tricks of the trade—to accomplish their best work. Children use these same devices unconsciously and can be taught to use them with a purpose. These tools have been offered to writers over the years by important authors such as E. B. White and George Orwell. Student writers can use these tools during the drafting process, but also during revision, when they are correcting and fine-tuning their prose. These changes rarely involve correct or incorrect usage. Instead, they help the writer to help the reader, and make the writing clearer, cleaner, and more interesting.

Use active verbs. Verbs work hard in a sentence. Subjects and verbs together create meaning for the reader. Most writers depend on the active voice, a relationship in which the subject performs the action of the verb. The alternative is to write in the passive voice or with the verb "to be," which often weakens and inflates a sentence. William Strunk shows the improvement that results from changing "There were a great number of dead leaves lying on the ground" to "Dead leaves covered the ground."

"It was announced by the principal that the appearance of the school would be improved by the custodian" can become "The principal announced that the custodian would improve the appearance of the school," saving about a third of the words.

Children use active verbs in their first stories. Teachers can encourage and reinforce this tendency through the early grades so that students can become verb masters by middle school.

Laura Sullivan writes:

A couple of days later, I went to the beach and met him there again. This time he was over with a group of other kids a little way down the beach from me. I walked over to see what was going on. When I got there, I saw Charley throwing rocks at a group of rays. All of the rays swam away except one little one that was farther away than the others. When he came, Charley threw a rock at it, and hit it close to the backbone, killing it.

He picked it up by the tail after poking it with a stick to make sure it was dead, and waved it around by the girls trying to scare them. After a while, his mother told him to put it back in the water.

Later it washed up on the shore. I picked it up and brought it down to the pier where the water was low, and I buried it. Still later that day, Charley ran up to me and asked me if I would play with him. I said "I'm not going to be friends with anyone that kills helpless animals. I always knew that you were stupid, but this proves it." I walked away and ignored him. I haven't seen him since. I'm glad.

The underlined verbs are in the active voice. They help Laura develop her narrative in an interesting way.

Use specific, concrete language. Good writers will revise "supermarket" to "Kash 'n' Karry"; "cereal" to "Froot Loops"; "a good place in the stadium" to "two seats on the fifty-yard line"; and a "fancy car" to a "cherry-red Corvette." Concrete words and images help readers enter a story and vicariously experience an event.

Frank Witsil explains how he suffered a bad cut:

> ... I had been playing in the house, jumping around, like many 8-year-old boys do. I fell into a carton of 8 Coca Cola bottles. One of the bottles broke under my weight and sent shattered glass everywhere. My arm went into a sharp and jagged end of the bottle, and my skin curled up....

Frank could have written "I hurt my arm on a broken bottle." But words like "carton of 8 Coca Cola bottles," specific and concrete, help us relive Frank's experience.

We get more of this after Frank is driven to the hospital and treated by a doctor:

> ... When the doctor came in, he cleaned the wound again, just to make sure. Then, he used a needle of Novocain to decrease the pain. I thought it was pencil sized! ... The doctor used black surgical thread and a small curved needle to sew up my arm. Even though I had been given Novocain, I could still feel the tugging of the thread pulling my skin. Eventually I had 12 stitches in my right forearm.
>
> When the doctor finished I sat up. I bent my elbow and in-spected the stitches with my Dad. They looked something like an unraveled black sock. Later the doctor wrapped my arm in bandages, gauze, as he called it. He also gave me instructions to keep my arm clean, not to get it wet, and not to move it around too much.
>
> As we were about to leave, the doctor got a new surgical glove, blew it up like a balloon, and gave it to me. When Dad and I came out of the room I was happy because I had a real doctor's glove. Dad was relieved it was over. We walked out in the waiting room, Mom had calmed down, and I was all right.

Frank combines active verbs with words we can see, words like "unraveled black sock," "surgical glove," "gauze," and "bal-loon." He makes us experience the anxiety over the pencil-sized needle of Novocain. And I feel a bit squirmy when the thread tugs at his skin. In fact, I cannot imagine a more vivid description of this event.

Teachers can work in conference with students to discover better verbs and more concrete language. The student who writes "I have a poster on my bedroom wall" can learn to write "A life-sized poster of a dancing Michael Jackson hangs on the wall at the head of my bed."

Vary sentence length. Fifth graders can learn that using sentences of various lengths sets the pace for the reader and makes the experience of reading more pleasurable. Long sentences carry the reader down a river of meaning, passing rocks, meadows, trees, animals, and other details, the result of which can be a smooth flow of images and ideas. But the river cannot flow forever. So the short sentence stops the reader. It makes him pause. It makes him think.

Fifth grader Stephanie Carrington writes about being a contestant in a beauty contest:

Before I got off the stage, I had to answer questions about what my favoirite color is, and what I would want to be when I grow up. So I told that lady that my favoirte color is red, and I also said that I would like to be Wonder Woman when I grow up. Everyone laughed and giggled.

Stephanie sets the pace for the reader, opening the paragraph with two long sentences and resolving it nicely with a short one.

Here my daughter Alison, now a seventh grader, writes about her passion for dancing:

I love to dance and I do it well. Just ask my Dad! It's great to dance. When I hear good music I can picture myself dancing to it in my head. If I am in my living room listening to the radio, I will jump up, push back the furniture, and start making up steps. I'm always being asked to dance by my family members and I do it willingly. My father said to me, "You should take some sort of dance lesson!" So I do.

Alison gives rhythm to this paragraph by using sentences of different lengths to accomplish different purposes. When she expresses a positive statement, she uses short sentences that carry a lot of weight:

- "I love to dance and I do it well."
- "Just ask my dad!"
- "So I do."

Almost by instinct or the natural flow of the language, she writes longer sentences to convey action or process:

If I am in my living room, listening to the radio, I will jump up, push back the furniture, and start making up steps.

In the hands of a less skillful or experienced writer, this paragraph could have been written in choppy sentences of the same length. Clear perhaps, but without imagination or reader appeal:

I love to dance and I do it well. Every day my dad says so. It's really great to dance. I like to listen to good music. When I do I picture myself dancing. I do this in my head. I usually listen to the radio. . . .

And so forth. Teachers can sometimes get students to combine sentences or to divide them in half in order to create a better flow with greater emphasis.

Place important words at the end of a sentence or paragraph. Here are three sentences from a story by Kristyn Whetstone on a medical emergency following a chlorine leak at a public swimming pool:

Kay, in charge of the kids, took DeAnne and me to the far end of the park to keep us away from the smell. DeAnne kept spitting up and I kept coughing. Michelle hopped over a low fence and went next door to call 911.

All three sentences are written in the active voice and conclude with an important or emphatic word. "Smell," "coughing" and "911" are specific, vivid words enhanced in emphasis by their location at the end of the sentence. Perhaps the middle sentence could be given further emphasis by inverting the clauses: "I kept coughing and DeAnne kept spitting up." This puts more emphasis on the predicament of DeAnne, which is more serious.

When young writers end a sentence or paragraph with a special word or image, they can be rewarded for it. The teacher can point out how this trick works, and it can become a new tool in the student's repertoire of writing devices.

Cut. Because we traditionally teach the fill-up-the-space school of writing, students find it difficult to cut useless or lazy words from their stories. If we teach students to be word counters ("I want you to write five hundred words on . . .") we will find it difficult to teach them to be tough-minded, to make every word count. They believe that cutting out a word is like performing an appendectomy on themselves—without anesthesia. In fact, the work of many young students is admirably compact and precise, a state of innocence spoiled, I would speculate, by the combined experiences of puberty and high school.

I have cut thousands of words from this text, and should cut a thousand more. I learned to do this from reading William Zinsser's *On Writing Well*, in which he demonstrates how he cuts clutter from his own work, even after four or five drafts.

Over time, I teach students to do the same, to make great demands of each word they use. Sometimes we focus on adverbs because they often repeat the meaning of the verb. When Melissa writes, "I asked him what was wrong and he totally ignored me," we can inspect *totally* and consider whether we need it. When she writes, "Quickly I unlocked the door and opened it immediately," we repeat the sentence aloud and find that we prefer its rhythm without the final word.

When Holland writes, "The dwarfs quickly went into the theater," I ask questions about the meaning of "quickly went." Can she find a single, more descriptive verb—"hustled," "ran," "scurried"—to replace two weaker words? She writes, "They were dancing and singing and got to use the ten dressing rooms," but we discover that a simple "danced and sang" allows us to cut "were." So the search continues, a relentless, painstaking process to prune dead limbs from our sentences. In so doing, we permit our best words and phrases to grow and give meaning.

Three is the magic number. Three wishes, Goldilocks and the Three Bears, Three Blind Mice, Snow White and the Three Dwarfs ... uh, you get the picture. Four examples seem too many, two not enough. Three is perfection. Dante took it to extremes in the terza rima and three-part structure of *The Divine Comedy*. Lincoln wrote "of the people, by the people," and we would not have remembered his address with such fondness if he had not added "for the people."

Children tap into the rhythm of this structure at an early age, and teachers can take advantage of it. When I tell them that a story has a beginning, a middle, and an end, they see the story in threes. If they write about the Salvador Dali Museum and describe two paintings, I may ask them to go back and find a third. In an opinion piece we look for three reasons. The threeness invades the texture of their sentences.

"People like Johnny Mathis, Dionne Warwick and John Davidson have performed at Ruth Eckerd Hall," writes Tracey.

Janet writes of her adopted sister, "We got her a bathing suit, a dress, and a couple of shorts outfits just so she would have more than one thing to wear."

Writing about the misadventures of yard work, Clark writes that after being stung as a young child, "I'd always stayed away from all bees, hornets, and wasps." Later he adds, "After interruptions, danger, and buckets of sweat, I was done."

Writers collect dozens of other tricks from many sources. They can be learned in the same context as grammar, spelling, punctuation, paragraphing, and other similar skills, as tools for making meaning and making it clearly. We apply them throughout the process but often near the end as we polish, clarify, and revise.

We should look forward to the day when most students write on computer terminals, for then handwriting will not be the same obstacle to meaning it is now, and the process of revision, so cumbersome with pencil and paper, will be accomplished with the speed of light.

Chapter Eleven

Publishing Stories

I wrote hundreds of stories and papers before I got to college, but the only ones I remember are ones that in some way got published. In fourth grade I wrote and performed a skit about the Lewis and Clark expedition. In sixth grade I wrote a Christmas poem for the school newspaper: "On a cold winter's night in a land so far away / A babe was born in Bethlehem, born on Christmas Day. / They laid him in a manger, no place for a King, / But it seemed just like a palace when they heard the angels sing." The next year I wrote a love poem to a frog ("Oh, your skin of greenish hue") and a news story about a Boy Scout outing to Town Hall. In the eighth grade I wrote my first short story, about a failed criminal lawyer, which I read before the class.

I wrote much more in high school, but I remember only a few pieces written for a homeroom newspaper called *The Mustang*; two speeches written and read in front of the student body; a parody of *Moby-Dick* read to the class by my English teacher; an essay on *The Catcher in the Rye* that Father Horst flashed on a screen for the class to admire and discuss; and a couple of skits written and performed at pep rallies and talent shows.

I can reach back in my memory to the days of first grade. I remember when some paper I wrote was stapled to the board for special praise or carried home for my parents to fawn over. What I craved was an audience for my work, which usually brought attention and approval. Without this, writing seemed pointless to me. With it, I could write as often as possible, looking for funny or compelling ideas and listening for an appealing voice.

In his autobiography *Growing Up*, Russell Baker of *The New York Times* recalls a high school moment of epiphany when he found his true vocation. The occasion was an eleventh-grade English class taught by a certain Mr. Fleagle, famous "for dullness and inability to inspire." Until that time Baker had been bored by English classes. "I found English grammar dull and baffling. I hated the assignments to turn out 'compositions,' and went at them like heavy labor, turning out leaden, lackluster paragraphs that were agonies for teachers to read and for me to write."

One day Mr. Fleagle handed out a list of essay topics, and one, "The Art of Eating Spaghetti," caught Baker's eye. It reminded him of large family gatherings in which his relatives argued about the etiquette of spaghetti bending:

Suddenly I wanted to write about that, about the warmth and good feeling of it, but I wanted to put it down simply for my own joy, not for Mr. Fleagle. It was a moment I wanted to capture and hold for myself. I wanted to relive the pleasure of an evening at New Street. To write it as I wanted, however, would violate all the rules of formal composition I'd learned in school, and Mr. Fleagle would surely give it a failing grade. Never mind, I would write something else for Mr. Fleagle after I had written this thing for myself.

When I finished it the night was half gone and there was no time left to compose a proper, respectable essay for Mr. Fleagle. There was no choice next morning but to turn in my private reminiscence of Belleville. Two days passed before Mr. Fleagle returned the graded papers, and he returned everyone's but mine. I was bracing myself for a command to report to Mr. Fleagle immediately after school for discipline when I saw him lift my paper from his desk and rap for the class's attention.

"Now, boys," he said, "I want to read you an essay. This is titled 'The Art of Eating Spaghetti.'"

And he started to read. My words! He was reading *my words* out loud to the entire class. What's more, the entire class was listening. Listening attentively. Then somebody laughed, then the entire class was laughing, and not in contempt and ridicule, but with openhearted enjoyment. Even Mr. Fleagle stopped two or three times to repress a small prim smile.

I did my best to avoid showing pleasure, but what I was feeling was pure ecstasy at this startling demonstration that my words had the power to make people laugh. In the eleventh grade, at the eleventh hour as it were, I had discovered a calling. It was the happiest moment of my entire school career. When Mr. Fleagle finished he put the final seal on my happiness by saying, "Now that, boys, is an essay, don't you see. It's—don't you see—it's of the very essence of the essay, don't you see. Congratulations, Mr. Baker."

I have quoted this anecdote at length because it represents
a high point of educational enterprise. It involves a teacher helping
a student find himself and his voice. It shows a teacher using
praise to reinforce a student's best work. And it reveals a teacher
using the best student work as a model for others. By simply
reading a student's work before a class, a teacher can change
a student's life forever. If the work is good, the effect can be a
good feeling that lasts a lifetime. If the work is bad, the effect
can be demoralizing, even devastating. I ask dozens of professionals how they came to be writers, and in almost every case
I hear a story like Baker's, of a young writer whose work was
appreciated by a concerned and thoughtful teacher.

No effective writing instruction can take place without the
publication of student work. Publication accomplishes great good
and puts writing in proper perspective for the student.

- Publication allows the student to communicate a message with an audience beyond that of the teacher.
- The student can learn from the variety of responses to
  the work.
- Publication permits the writer to discover the sound of
  his own voice on the page and to develop it.
- The writer learns from reading and hearing the work of
  other students.
- Publication creates a goal for multiple revisions of the
  student's work. The writer endures with publication as a
  reward.
- The writer is much more concerned with grammar, spelling, handwriting, punctuation, and form because the
  work will be shared with others.
- Publication allows the teacher to display the best work
  of every student in a collaborative effort inspiring both
  competition and cooperation.
- It gives students "something to show" for their work, the
  equivalent of a painting for art students or a play for
  theater students. It gives teachers a chance to show off
  the work of the class to parents, administrators, and
  other teachers.
- Continual publication of the best work allows teachers to
  chart the progress of the student throughout the year.
- It creates goals and deadlines for student writers.
- Teachers and students together create a permanent, last-
  ing record of the young writer's accomplishments.

Whenever I teach a new group of students, I promise them that "before long you are going to write and publish the best story of your life." I go on, "I'm not just talking about a few of the very best students in this class, I'm talking about every single one of you. I know you are going to work hard on your writing every day and that you have some things to say. So we'll read our stories aloud to each other, and we'll swap some, and we'll display some on the bulletin board, and we'll put our stories together in a class book, and we'll show them to the principal and to your parents, and who knows, maybe some of you will get published in the *St. Petersburg Times.*" That pep talk offers a range of publishing options. During the course of a school year, teachers can use all these forms of publication to motivate students to achieve the fruits of the writing process.

Reading Aloud

I have been told that one of the things I do best as a teacher of children is to read their stories well. This is the first form of publication, and it often happens on the first day of class. "Who would like me to read his or her story for the class?" I ask. A few hands, usually those of the more confident students, go up. I read the story slowly, in a hearty voice, with feeling, emotion, humor, and emphasis. In other words, I try to distill in my reading the best parts of the student's work. If the student is trying to be funny, I may add emphasis with a comic little voice. If the story is dramatic, I will contribute to the suspense. If it is touching, I will read with great sympathy.

Many students are fine writers but weak oral interpreters of their own work. They have tiny voices, or are shy, or scratch their behinds. If the other students react badly, the student associates the embarrassment with the writing, a setback that may be permanent.

When I read a passage, I do it justice. I edit out little mistakes and fill in a missing word. More important, I can let the writer hear her own voice coming off the page through my reading. Other students can hear it as well, and respond to it.

Here is the ending of Chrissy Metz's story, "The Embarrassing Adventure of the Mayo Squirter," in which she describes what happened when she tried to open a packet of mayonnaise at a restaurant:

All of a sudden, the mayonnaise squished out everywhere! It went all over my dad and brother, on the ceiling, and all over the mirrored wall. A big blob even landed on the lady and her daughter behind my dad!

I was so embarrassed that I started laughing. Everyone thought I was nuts!

By the time everything got cleaned up, everyone was in hysterics; even my parents and the people behind my mom and me.

The lady behind my father was really nice about it. She didn't get mad, but she didn't laugh either. When my dad tried to get it out of the lady's hair, her husband sort of got mad. I could tell because his face got really red and his eyes started bulging out! He watched my father like a hawk!

The people that worked at the restaurant were real nice about the accident. In fact, they thought it was pretty funny, too!

From now on, I am going to try spreading my mayo, instead of squirting it!

All those exclamation points cry out for a vigorous and humorous reading of this passage. I want you to imagine Chrissy's enjoyment of her own story as her teacher reads it aloud in front of the class, his own eyes bulging out at the appropriate moment, a hint of laughter in his own voice. Now imagine a bad reading of this passage by a student who stumbles over the words or holds the page close in front of his face.

Good teachers read poems, short stories, essays, or newspaper stories to their students all the time. When teachers read a student's story out loud, they pay that student a high compliment.

Students Reading Aloud

When teachers read stories aloud, they also provide a model of excellence for the student. It is important that all students become accomplished readers of their own work. To read your work before a school assembly or a group of parents or the principal, to read it well and be rewarded by applause, is an experience that gives confidence and satisfaction. This rarely happens without training and practice.

When I told a sixth-grade basic skills class that in two weeks they would be reading a story in front of the principal, the students did not believe me. But we spent a third of our time reading stories aloud to each other in small groups, and then in front of the whole class. I told them to stand up straight

Young writers find their voices through public reading of their own stories. This often demands hours of rehearsal. Here Kristin Klinkenberg practices oral presentation of her story on being a volunteer at a nursing home.

and stand still, to hold their papers down from their faces, to speak slowly and distinctly, and to project their voices to the back of the room. The teacher can use a tape recorder so students can hear themselves performing.

The teacher has to be an active coach during this process, mixing encouragement with useful criticism:

- "Your voice is fine, John, but look down, your legs are crossed."
- "You have a handsome face, Michael, so don't hide it behind your paper."
- "Donna, you've written a terrific story, but you're not at a race. Slow down so we can enjoy it."

But before we get to the grander performances of student work, we start in small circles of three and four students. This is sharing time, when each student gets to read a story to other students. It is the writer's job to read it well, and the other students' job to listen and receive it.

After reading a story, the writer gets to call on students for their reaction. They respond to the story with positive reactions, "I like the part when the dog wrestles with you," or with questions for more information, "How did you get the dog?" The student then has some basis for possible revisions or additions to the work.

During this process, the teacher has to be on guard for inappropriate responses from negative students. Some students have received harsh criticism of their work for so long that their critical vocabulary is limited to things such as, "Why don't you ever put description in your story?" or "You said 'dog' too much. Why don't you say 'puppy' instead?" The teacher can cut off demoralizing blitzkriegs of criticism by reminding students, "That is not how we respond to the work of other writers."

When stories are published by oral reading, the students in the class get to know other students' work. Students in a writing class often quote the work of others and share in a colleague's developing expertise. John may learn something new about astronomy, and he shares it with Wesley, who is writing a paper about a visit to a planetarium.

When children read their work aloud to others, they find mistakes invisible in silent reading. A word is left out or repeated, the handwriting is illegible, a sentence trails off into incoherence. The student can make corrections and revisions on the spot, while she is reading the paper, and follow this with editing changes.

There was a time in our culture when all reading was done aloud, even when the reader was in a room alone. Even now, we may read a student's story to ourselves and say, "It sounds good." Since we can never escape the orality of the experience of reading, we should take advantage of it by training students to write and to read in their best voices.

Posting

Teachers make creative use of the limited classroom space available to them and their students. They create special learning spaces, corners filled with books and magazines. They decorate their rooms to connect the classroom with the seasons or the subject matter. They often use bulletin boards to display special writing, some of which is the work of students. I look at my second-grade class picture and know it was taken in November because the walls are decorated with turkeys and pilgrims and what are obviously student papers on Thanksgiving.

Hanging things on the wall was the primary form of publication in my elementary school, and I can remember feelings of personal triumph and intense disappointment depending upon whether Sister Leone decided to display my work or not. If she did not, I redoubled my efforts to produce work worthy of being pasted to a piece of colored paper and stapled on the cork board above the alphabet strip.

Teachers can use this strategy to accomplish a number of goals. They can display the best work of the day or of the week, creating some healthy competition among students. They can also display the best work of a single student, even if that work is not among the very best in the class. They can create instant models for other students to emulate. And they can illustrate both process and product by displaying, for example, a number of drafts of the same story.

Mrs. Collins liked to display in large letters the steps of the writing process—FIND IDEA, COLLECT, FOCUS, DEVELOP, CLARIFY—so students could hold the model in mind. She would also display interesting stories or photos from the *St. Petersburg Times* so that when student work was published, students could see their work as part of a higher calling.

By posting work in this manner, teachers can literally surround a class with good writing: poetry, essays, famous words from famous authors, and of course, the work of students. The reaction of students is usually one of pride and interest in reading their own work and that of other students, and in seeing who has gained the honor for the day or week. The greatest pride and satisfaction comes to the weak or average student who, through hard work, rises above himself to produce a work that shows progress or promise, a work that finds itself on the bulletin board next to a story by a professional reporter.

The Writing Folder

During the month of January 1980, I kept a daily journal in which, for twenty minutes a day, I would record my reactions to the morning's news. I would never write for longer than twenty minutes, and sometimes for only five. I wrote quickly, sometimes as fast as I could, not even stopping to check my spelling. At the end of the month, I typed out my journal entries and was surprised to count sixty-five double-spaced pages. Little drops of writing form puddles, then streams, then rivers.

Over a school year, my students produce an impressive folder of writing. Kept in chronological order, the folder becomes a form of publication itself. Students can share it with other students, with teachers, and with parents. If you want to see how Melissa is doing, all you have to do is pick up her "finished folder" and browse. If you want to see what she is working on now, she can open her "work folder" and show you early drafts being prepared for publication. As we shall see, these folders become vehicles for the evaluation of student work as well.

Class Books

The best work of every student is published in a class book. These stories are written and edited by students, who themselves decide which of their stories will appear in the book. When possible, these stories are typed by parents and bound with cardboard or wallpaper samples. The books are displayed prominently in the classroom and sometimes in the school library. They can be read and reread, aloud or in private. They can be checked out by students, many of whom prefer reading them over their basal readers because they contain real stories written by writers they know. They can be produced once a month, or

Students take pride in publication. Here Sonja Felton shares her story, published in a class booklet, with her father. Earlier she had a chance to read her story before a large assembly of parents, students, and teachers.

more often if parents and principals are supportive, as they usually are. Even if published only twice a year, they prove to students that writing has a purpose and an effect.

The class books are a collaborative learning venture. Students take pride not only in the display of their own work but also in the book containing many writers. I once watched Wendy Witham pick up a class book and flip through the pages to find her own story and show it off to her mom. Then she flipped through some more and showed off the work of her classmates, stories she especially liked.

Each student has his or her own page in the book. Even if the story is only three paragraphs long, or even a single paragraph, it appears as the work of a single writer. The students seemed unconcerned that "her story is longer or better than mine." That sentiment is replaced by "it's great to see my story in a book" or "I never thought our stories would be good enough to appear in a book."

Some students are so productive that they want to publish more often than once a month. In these cases, I encourage students to put together a collection of the best stories from their folders to be published in their own books. I have had students publish as many as twenty stories on the same topic during a period of two weeks.

Mark Jackson and Mark Beery collaborated on a book called "The Writing of Our Vacation Stories," a tiny bound volume illustrated with a colored picture of the two of them waving from an automobile. The two Marks were so proud of the work done on these stories that they published the "early drafts" as well. Any reader can pick up this collection and read nine drafts of these stories.

Teachers do not have to wait until students can write on their own before they begin publication of student work in this way. Many first-grade and kindergarten teachers get students to dictate interesting stories. The teachers copy the stories for the students and publish the work in books. Because the students know what the stories say, they often learn to read more effectively from their own stories than from basal readers.

Writer Joelle Sander tells the story of how she used this process years ago with her son Jason. "Making books had been Jason's idea. Early on, he had loved to be read to, was fascinated by the sound and rhythm of words, and was thoroughly enticed by the adventures of characters he was beginning to know. So it was no surprise when he wanted to write his own stories. The only problem was—he couldn't write. He was three years old."

At the age of thirteen, Jason was still very much interested in writing. Sander attributes his language skills and his creativity to those early collaborative experiences between mother and son when Jason told her interesting stories and Joelle transcribed them into little books.

Publication is one of the writer's greatest rewards, right up there with money. Howell Raines, a political reporter for *The New York Times*, once told me that he experiences profound discomfort when he opens up a newspaper and his byline is not in it. A talented young writer can gain great satisfaction from publication of work in a class book, which usually results in the writer wanting to have that experience again and again.

It may be that such experience is more important for the weaker writer, the child who has been told over and over again, year after year, that his work is inadequate. For such a person to write a story, even of two or three sentences, and see it typed with his name above it, is an experience that can change a student's perception of himself. He can use the experience as an anchor in his memory, a reminder that he can accomplish something.

The Class Newspaper

The motto of our fifth-grade newspaper was "If a fifth grader needs to know it, we print it." By class vote, the newspaper was entitled *The Cougar Chronicle.* Published twice a year, it contained the very best work of the children of Bay Point Elementary School. More than twenty-five mimeographed pages presented the work of as many as sixty fifth graders: news and feature stories, teacher profiles, school activities, poetry and the arts, book reviews, humor, and puzzles. The *Chronicle* published stories on presidential elections, space shuttle flights, professional and student sporting events, Halloween celebrations and safety, field trips, and special visitors to the school. Reading them over four years later, I get the sense of a group of children connected to their school, their community, and their country. The publication is full of life, adventure, and controversy, and seems peculiarly American in the best sense.

In one edition Shelley Cook writes about a fire at Lakewood High School; Leslie Gillespie describes a trip to the Art Museum; Adam Roessler writes about the good work of the March of Dimes; Tommy Coy tells how a tornado hit his family's trailer; Cesar Alvarez writes about a trip to the Nature Trail; fourteen students write about a blast-off of the space shuttle Columbia, which was visible in the sky from outside one of their classrooms; Jennifer Merrick explains a science experiment; nine students cover the school's Halloween Carnival as if it were the World's Fair; John DeMouy pleads in an editorial to "get rid of boring books"; Alison Clark profiles poet Peter Meinke; Laura Bonanno covers poet Guy Hoagland's visit to class; and Buddy Snider reviews *Elvis and His Secret.*

Students love the collaborative effort of producing a newspaper. They carry out the roles of reporters, editors, and artists.

All their efforts at writing interesting stories about their world reach a crescendo when the stories are prepared for publication, typed, mimeographed, stapled, and distributed. Even children who may not produce stories for publication in the newspaper contribute with their work as artists or production workers. The class takes collective pride in the *Chronicle*, a pride that can be shared with other students, teachers, and parents.

The Newspaper

When students produce their own books and newspapers, they come to see themselves as part of a larger community of writers. This is why they sometimes seek publication beyond the classroom.

Eighth grader Zaneta Seay wrote this letter to the editor, which was published by the *St. Petersburg Times* on August 22, 1983:

Editor:

Women today are being exploited just for their looks. They are not being hired for their ability to be able to report the news.

When I grow up I hope to be a news anchorwoman. I would get to interview people and to travel all over the world. I also want to be an anchorwoman because of the interest I have in the news media.

Right now there is a controversy over news stations hiring women just because of their looks instead of their qualifications. That is not fair, because a woman may be beautiful but incompetent to report the news in a professional manner.

One such case of sex discrimination was taken to court by a news anchorwoman, Christine Craft. She accused the producers of firing her because they said she no longer looked good on camera. She sued them and won $500,000. I'm very happy that she won.

By the time I grow up I hope the issue of sex discrimination will have cleared up. When the producers hire women only for their looks, they are really robbing the public of listening to someone who really knows how to report the news.

Zaneta Seay
Age 13
Southside Fundamental School
St. Petersburg

It is not unusual for the *Times* to publish letters from children on the editorial pages. They provide an interesting perspective on issues ranging from the quality of education to animal abuse to nuclear war.

On Christmas morning, 1982, Nicholas Heinzen awoke to find his Christmas story on the front page of the *St. Petersburg Times*. It was introduced by an editor's note:

In 1897 a letter from an 8-year-old girl inspired Francis P. Church, editor of *The Sun*, to pen his immortal editorial: "Yes, Virginia, there is a Santa Claus." Fifth graders at Bay Point Elementary School were asked to write on the same topic and all agreed that Nicholas Heinzen, 10, best captured the spirit of the original. But then, his name is Nicholas. And he played Santa Claus at the Christmas assembly.

Yes, Virginia, I can truly say there is a Santa Claus. How do I know? Well, I could tell you how the legend started.

About St. Nicholas, the patron saint of boys, young men and sailors of Greece and Sicily. About how his reputation grew and grew. It reached many countries. When it reached the English, they attached the custom of gift-giving on Dec. 25. But that's not the real reason I know there's a Santa Claus.

I know there's a Santa because of all the love that fills the air as Christmas gets closer and closer. Something changes people from complaining discontents to singing, caring. Suddenly, the poor are fed, the old are visited and cared for, families come together, sometimes far apart. Even countries at war take time out from fighting.

This kind of miracle takes a special spirit. That spirit is Santa Claus. The best part is he lives in all of us!

So, Ho! Ho! Ho! Merry Christmas.

One young writer, Katrina Clark, understands the excitement of publication. On September 11, 1983, she wrote this for a special section of the *St. Petersburg Times* called Alligator Express:

As I sat and listened to my teacher, Ron Hoddinott, in my 6th grade PFG (Program for the Gifted) class explain how to write short stories, I never even had the slightest thought of being a published author one day. But sure enough, that summer vacation I saw my story, my illustrations and my name in the children's magazine *Stone Soup*!

Stone Soup is a magazine with only children's work in it. You must be 12 or younger to get your work published in the magazine. My story, called "Jeff's Encounter in the Woods," is about a young boy who is bitten by a snake while hiking and because of the bite decides to take out his anger on all animals. It also has a lesson to it—that animals have feelings just like people.

I enjoy writing very much, in addition to my hobby of

stamp collecting and foreign doll collecting. Although I'm only 13, going into 8th grade at Azalea Middle School in northwest St. Petersburg, I think I have a pretty good idea of what I would like to be when I grow up. I would like to write and illustrate children's books.

Alligator Express is a full-color page in the Family section of the Sunday *St. Petersburg Times*. Its creator is Nancy Green, who produced a similar page for a newspaper in Montreal. Alligator Express first appeared on July 31, 1983. Its goal, according to Nancy, was "to get kids into the newspaper."

By 1985 Alligator Express had published the writing of hundreds of students, most of whom were nine to thirteen years old, but some of whom were as young as three and as old as seventeen. Nancy receives more than one hundred stories a week from the children of Pinellas County.

Green understands the consequences of publication for these children. "I know it spurs them on to write more," she said. "Some parents say their children are thrilled to death to have their work in the newspaper." It is not unusual for the parents of these young writers to buy dozens of copies of the newspaper so they can send copies to relatives across the country. One grandmother was sent a poem and a drawing by her grandson in Madison, Wisconsin, and she arranged as a special surprise to have it published in Alligator Express.

This section has generated much enthusiasm in the schools, where teachers help students prepare stories to be submitted, where teachers and students read and discuss the page each Monday morning to generate new story ideas, and where major celebrations are set off when a student makes the page.

In March 1984, Mrs. Osborne's class at Sandy Lane Elementary School published their book, *How I Write a Paper*, and here's what some of the students said about being published:

Amy Makosky wrote, "I keep on writing drafts until I make my final draft then I have someone edit it. Then if I have any mistakes I go back and correct the mistakes. Then it's usually ready to be put in a book or my final draft folder."

Ricky Van Emburgh: "Then I read it outloud. My classmates ask questions and give comments. If they say it can be changed, sometimes I will."

Todd Rice: "I cross out words and erase things that are unneeded. And then I write a final draft and turn it into my teacher so she can make a book for our class to read."

Marciann Skidmore: "Then I ask the teacher if I can read

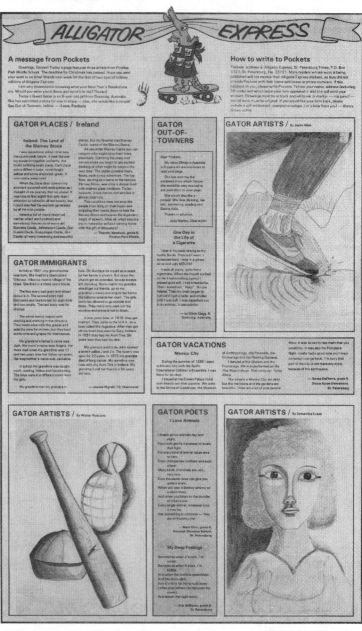

Alligator Express displays the writing and artwork of children each Sunday in the *St. Petersburg Times*. Children, teachers, and parents celebrate when a young writer they know makes the page. Teachers use examples from the page to inspire students to publish their own work. The page is printed in full color.

it to the class. She reads over and says yes. After I read it, the class snaps their fingers because clapping is too loud. Then I go sit back down feeling proud of my pencil, brain and hand."

Jenny Cavins: "After my teacher reads my paper over and makes corrections, I may start my final draft. I make a few final drafts before I get one that's perfect! When I get one that's perfect I sometimes publish it in the *Saint Petersburg Times*. So when my mom and dad see it they'll be proud and say pointing to the newspaper article, 'That's my girl!' "

Performance

Jenny Cavins has revealed the secret to success in education: Parents want to see their children succeed. What parents crave most is specific evidence that their children are learning and growing. Teachers who produce that evidence gain parents' support and cooperation, which makes all learning possible.

The best example of this is the Christmas assembly. On the Thursday before Christmas, more than 500 people cram into the Bay Point cafeteria to watch their children perform. Parents, grandparents, brothers, and sisters crowd into a long room, the latecomers so far back they can barely see the stage or hear the public address system.

All the children in the school perform at the assembly, singing Christmas and Hanukkah songs, playing in the band, all dressed in their best clothes. The crowd madly applauds every song, with special adulation for the cute child who forgets the words but sings anyway, off key, or the young trumpet player who trudges, note by note, through "Deck the Halls." The children can do no wrong, and parents rush to the front to flash cameras at the stage and take credit for their kids' sour singing.

Performance is important. It reflects preparation and accomplishment. It allows parents and principals to share in the achievement of students. It makes the children feel good about themselves. And it can work with writing as well as music.

That is why we have conducted award assemblies in which young writers read their best work aloud to friends and parents. That is why Bob Drafahl, a fourth-grade teacher, invites parents on special evenings to hear their children read their writing aloud.

Good performances do not just happen. Obviously, the writing must be good. But it must be interpreted well by the student writer and projected to a large audience. Some students need lots of rehearsal, both in class and at home. I remember one student, Michelle, who was so shy and withdrawn that she found a way to answer all questions with a nod or a shrug. It was necessary to take her aside and have her read her story to me, over and over, her voice growing louder and louder. But we still had to cross our fingers and toes on assembly day, hoping she would not wilt in front of a large audience that included her parents. Her voice was soft and steady. When she finished, the audience broke into applause, both out of relief and genuine admiration.

The goodwill in the air that day was palpable: children looking great in suits and dresses and shiny shoes, parents applauding and embracing their children, their faces glowing with pride. It took hours and hours of writing and revision and conferring and more rewriting before we could experience that moment. But when parents left on the last day of class, they congratulated the teachers and said how much the children had gained from the experience of writing and how much they hoped their children would have a chance to write in the future.

"My son says he wants to be a journalist," said the mother of one fifth grader.

"My daughter wrote every night at home," said another.

"This is what education is all about," said a teacher.

Chapter Twelve

Evaluation and Grading

During my first year as a full-time newspaper reporter in 1978, I wrote more than two hundred stories for the *St. Petersburg Times*, including news and feature stories, columns, and reviews. I keep those stories in what reporters call a "byline file," and I review them occasionally for my own enlightenment and amusement.

If I had to grade myself for that year of writing, I would give myself a B+. I see a person growing in confidence in a new craft. The stories show enthusiasm and innovation. Routine stories—high school graduations, daylight savings time, the new phone book—are written with flair and an eye for interesting human detail. I am proud of these and would give myself an A+. Other stories I am not so proud of. One, on the threat of a postal strike, is not well organized and has a bad lead. Others seem overripe and overwritten, as if I were trying to write with words instead of information. Some lack a hard news edge.

It was a year of peaks and valleys, the peaks getting higher but the valleys not so low. I might chart my progress like this:

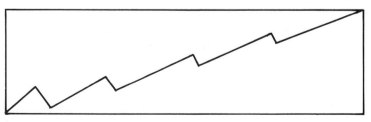

In retrospect, I am inclined to grade myself by the body of my work. I also recognize that, as a writer, I will hit high notes on some days that I will not be able to reach on others. I accept the irregularity of my progress as a given. What I want, over a period of time, is to make significant movement, to raise my game a notch, as the tennis players say.

If I do not expect daily or even weekly progress from myself, a professional writer, I do not expect it from my students. Tiffany refused to write for two weeks, a dry well, and then wrote eighteen stories in a single week. Joshua writes personal narratives with skill but stumbles when he has to take notes and report a story. Despite their highs and lows, by the end of the school year both students have produced a thick folder of stories that is, in itself, the best evidence of their progress.

Parents or other teachers or principals can examine these files, kept in chronological order, and see dramatic growth in many areas. Some teachers record skills that have been learned and story ideas that have been developed on folders; the folders help teachers and parents keep track of what the child has accomplished and what he has to work on next.

Teachers who do not grade or mark up every student paper are not abdicating their responsibility to evaluate the work of student writers. In fact, they are much more scrupulous than those who grade in the traditional way. When my daughter comes home with a B in language arts on a report card, I have only the most general sense of how she is doing. Is she a strong reader or a weak writer, good in spelling or weak in grammar? Who knows?

In contrast, when I examine a student's writing folder, I may be able to tell that he has good story ideas but needs work in punctuation. The writing folder reveals this information because when we evaluate the total work of student writers, we do so according to specific criteria that reflect the process we are trying to teach:

- Does the student write with enthusiasm every day?
- Does the student demonstrate good work in a variety of writing forms?
- Does the student discover interesting story ideas?
- Does the student collect information for stories effectively through notes, interviews, reading, and brainstorming?
- Does the student write good leads that focus the stories?

- Does the student write stories that reveal planning and organization?
- Does the student undertake various strategies for revision, including working through several drafts?
- Does the student show strength in grammar, punctuation, and spelling?
- Does the student show a love of words and a concern for the proper use of the English language?
- Does the student respond well to deadlines and make significant progress toward publication?
- Does the student respond well to conferences and show an ability to articulate problems in his own work?
- Does the student show a willingness to collaborate with other students in the sharing of student writing?

These are exacting standards that take into account the mastery of skills, effort, and attitude. These standards can be shared with parents at the beginning of the school year, so that they can understand the criteria by which their children will be evaluated and participate in the effort to move them in the right direction.

Even as we evaluate the progress of the writer, we must not fail to evaluate the work. A student who writes every day may produce dozens of finished stories during the school year. Sometimes it helps both student and teacher to select together (during a marking period) three stories for detailed scrutiny and grading. When teachers evaluate the best work of students, they concentrate on how far the student has come and how far he needs to go.

Traditional grading of student writing is often done whimsically rather than according to a set of objective standards. I well remember in high school trying to adjust my writing style to the grading personality of my teacher. One teacher liked metaphors and similes, another liked spare prose, another liked theological jargon. Those of us who played the "guess what teacher likes" game well received high grades.

When teachers ask me how to grade student papers, I ask them this question: Can you describe for me in specific terms the difference between an A paper and a B paper? I also ask whether members of an English department have ever gotten together to formulate criteria for the grading of papers and whether these criteria are ever made known to parents and the students themselves.

Groups of teachers who analyze the work of their own students can devise categories of excellence that can become standards of achievement. The weakest stories go in a pile marked 1 and the best in a pile marked 5. Stories in between are classified 2, 3, or 4. The more difficult task is to describe the strengths or weaknesses of a work in a way that makes sense to children, parents, and other teachers. Once these descriptive categories have been created, teachers can collectively or individually mark the whole paper. Such categories might look like these, which are adapted from a system developed in Grosse Pointe, Michigan:

1. This paper is incompetent. The writer may be incapable of committing any words to the page. More often the paper is a jumble of confusing language and thoughts. The writer shows a basic inability to make meaning. She has no control over the basic tools of language. Thus she cannot communicate clearly or reach an audience. Bad spelling, grammar, punctuation may block the reader's understanding.

2. This is a weak paper from a writer who cannot find something to say or who lacks the means to say it. The language may be immature, the sentence structure repetitious, and the meaning unclear. Such a paper is usually weak in mechanics, but not always. The story lacks information or details that would attract a reader. Or, if the information is there, it is so poorly organized as to be incoherent. No human voice comes off the page. With revisions, it may become a competent paper.

3. This is a competent paper with obvious flaws but potential for improvement. The writer has something to say or a story to tell. It contains information worth reading. But it may be badly organized. The writer uses inappropriate language; weaknesses in mechanics get in the way of meaning. Sentences may be unclear and the thinking hazy.

4. This is a good paper. It conveys meaning in a generally organized way. The writer has control over information and uses clear language. She has something to say and gets the job done. But any number of deficiencies stand in the way of excellence. The story may stray from its topic, have a weak beginning or ending, reveal confused thinking, or contain some mechanical mistakes that distract the reader.

5. An excellent paper need not be perfect. But it should show strength and accomplishment in every category. The writer writes for a real audience. She creates a human voice on the page and uses language appropriate to the topic. The writer focuses on a single idea, theme, or issue. She writes with specific information and concrete details. She pays attention to an effective beginning, middle, and ending, and achieves an organized structure. The writer uses mechanics powerfully to reinforce meaning.

Such categories help teachers in numerous ways. First, they serve as a diagnostic tool. Through timed writing assignments or in the course of daily writing, teachers can analyze and evaluate student work. Both teacher and student then understand where the student needs to go and, eventually, how far the student has come. The categories can be adjusted depending on grade level. They are not meant as pigeonholes that stereotype and eventually frustrate students. Teachers of writing hope for dramatic improvements in student work. A student who in a year moves from a 1 to a 3 or from a 2 to a 5 inspires serious rejoicing.

I have already described the assignment in which fifth-grade students were asked to respond to the famous letter of young Virginia on the existence of Santa Claus. For this assignment, students worked on their own, without conferences or teacher oversight. They could write to any length and revise as often as they liked.

Jimmy handed in a paper entitled "Virginia's answer" that read:

Santa Claus' spirit is alive in the
way pepole care about eachother
   and give present's at christmas
and be to eachother

The reader is invited to analyze and evaluate this and other stories in this chapter with care, and to imagine what grade would be assigned and in which direction the teacher should move with the student. It is not important that you agree with every detail of my evaluation of student work, but that you use it as a springboard for creating a useful system for analyzing and judging student writing.

I would give this paper a $1\frac{1}{2}$. It is not incompetent. Jimmy can make meaning and communicate it to a reader. Most of the words in this sentence are spelled correctly. But the other mechanical problems indicate serious weaknesses and distract the reader. The writer cannot process and convey information effectively. The piece is too short and undeveloped. My guess is that, recognizing some of his own weaknesses, he has intentionally kept this paper as short as possible. My conference strategy with Jimmy would be to ask him a lot of questions about the Christmas spirit: When do you feel the spirit? What was the nicest thing that happened to you on Christmas? What are you planning for this Christmas? I would pay primary attention to information and content, giving him enough momentum to inspire more attention to mechanics. I would also give him a mini-lesson on the use of the possessive.

To Virginia

> Snata Claus is in your hart. Some people say there is know Snata Claws. And other people say there is.
>
> > Your friend,
> > Sue

Most obvious in this paper are the spelling mistakes. They should clue the teacher that the student needs work in that area. But to place immediate emphasis on the mechanics may make the student's next paper even shorter and simpler, which is to say safer. The main problems are lack of information, no focus, and no organization. Like the previous paper, this one receives a $1\frac{1}{2}$.

An obviously stronger paper comes from John, who tells Virginia:

> Although parents and older children will tell you otherwise, I happen to believe in Santa Claus. Not as a common mortal, but as love and joy personified. He is a symbol of the love and joy of the Nativity. Yes, there is a Santa Claus, not in a common sense, but in the hearts and minds of us true believers.

Unlike the previous papers, John's work reveals a clear message, an interesting vocabulary, an authentic voice, an organization, and a control of mechanics. I would grade it a 4. The paper does not contain enough concrete and specific information to be superior student work.

Analyzing stories in this way helps the teacher recognize

the strengths and weaknesses of student work in some sort of balance. Here is another example:

Dear Virginia.

if you belifve in Santa Clas I belifve
in him to, if you come down here to
Florida, you will se a Santa Clas
in The Shopping Mall I went to see
him and he gave me a Strawberry sucker
but, I all ready ate it.
Have you been good? I have once I saw
Santa Clas up in the sky in his sleigh.
he brings toys to all the girls and boys,
who are good if you are bad he brings
you coal and tomatos.
I have been a good girl, I am
11 years old, I was born in October 18, 1971.
I am pretty, and I have brownhair,
I have no brothers or sisters, my name is
Julie and my Parents are not
devoris.
Do you put up your Christmas Tree?
We do, but ours is fac is your's fac?
Do you have Grandparents? I only have 1
The rest live in Boston Mass.
     Well I better go now.

From: Julie

This letter is clearly inferior to John's in economy and clarity of expression and in the use of language and mechanics. In fact, John will wind up in an advanced English class in the sixth grade, while Julie will be assigned to a basic skills class for remediation.

Ironically, I see ways in which Julie's letter is superior to John's. Knowing both students, I see much more effort in Julie's. John wrote a good paragraph, but it probably took him little time. He kept it short and clear. Julie's letter is longer and more detailed. It has wonderful details: the strawberry sucker, the coal, and the tomatoes. It has a sympathetic and interesting voice. You can hear a friendly child in the letter. Unlike the first two letters, this one takes chances with both language and meaning. Julie is willing to attempt words she cannot easily spell, such as "devoris" (divorced).

The problems in the letter are manifest. They go beyond the spelling and punctuation errors to questions of focus and organization. Julie rambles from Santa to herself to Christmas trees to grandparents. I would turn my attention in conference to finding out what one thing Julie wants to tell Virginia. Then we would turn to writing complete sentences and then concentrate on spelling and mechanics. This story rates a 2.

This evaluation system is flexible enough for special cases. Consider the story of ten-year-old Maria entitled "When I first came here":

> When I first came here I was a little asited because these is my second airplaen that I tride so my Mom said come [calm] down Maria When I saw those womans coming to me to hive me a little game, then I whent to the bathroom. so when I was doing py [pee] the airplaen start to muve I was a little sacare [scared] but then I start to laught.

The story is easier to read when you know that it was written by a girl recently moved to Florida from Venezuela who had been speaking English for no more than two years. Even though this represents one of her first attempts at writing a story in English, she manages to tell a neat little narrative with a sharp focus and a little earthy humor. I would give Maria a 3 with an asterisk. It turns out that writing can become an excellent vehicle for a student studying English as a second language.

When we evaluate writing in this way, we try to take into account all that the student has learned, as reflected in his story. The bottom-line question is: "How effectively does the child communicate meaning through the writing?" When Thomas writes "All about my Plays," he offers a paper that is basically clear and technically correct:

> OK now. The first play was "Gypsy" and I worked back stage. I met a lot of people. It was fun but when it was over I was sad.
> The next play was Brigadoon. I worked back stage. I saw a lot of friends from Gypsy. I liked it. It was fun but it was sad when it was over. But she was a good actress.
> The best play was Anything Goes. I worked back stage. My mom was good. She was in the chorus. I liked going a lot. It was fun. I liked it but it was sad when it was over. I cried.

Thomas has organized his story into three paragraphs, each of which concerns a single play. Almost every word is spelled correctly, including tough words like *chorus* and *Brigadoon*. He also knows that titles should be set off in quotation marks, although he uses that tool only once. But Thomas lacks a story. He depends, instead, upon repetitious sentences that express generalized emotion. Thomas was sad, or he had fun. As readers, we lack telling detail, a meaningful narrative, or a human voice. This young writer is playing it safe.

Beth tells a more effective story with "The funnest bick trip":

My Girl Scout Troop went on a bick trip to Bay Vista Park. Frist Sue tire got flat. We rod to go get another bick. And then Anns seat came off but we fixes it. Then Kims bick won't ride right. But still more I furgot my lock and had to lock my bick up with Jennifer. Then Ms Davies made a sharp turn and fell over. But we made it back all right.

Despite her obvious problems with mechanics, Beth gives readers a basic chronology they can follow. Unlike Thomas's story, things happen here in some kind of meaningful order. Beth needs more information to fill out her narrative, and she must correct the numerous spelling, punctuation, and grammar errors that distract the reader. Though her story is weaker in mechanics than Thomas's effort, it warrants an equal grade (a 2) because of its superiority in narrative and detail.

Traditional grading would make the grade the end point, but with this system it can become a new beginning. Thomas needs to loosen up while Beth needs to tighten up. Both can be encouraged to do so in conferences that lead to rewriting. This approach to grading shifts attention from the grade to the skills learned, the process completed, and the work published.

Deemphasizing grades will make some children uneasy, if not downright queasy. Their grading gyroscope will wobble; they may fear the prospect of writing without grades and be intimidated by a new system of evaluation that is both detailed and specific.

Children who complain about ungraded papers are mostly bright students for whom the grade has become an end in itself. Teachers admire students who exercise ambition in the quest for high grades, but those sacred grades must be placed in a broader educational context. We expect more of students than that they adjust their behavior to match a teacher's grading idiosyncrasies. Students who write well are eagles, not chameleons. They want to see their words in print, informing and amusing audiences of real readers. A good grade is one more symbol of their effort and enthusiasm.

To summarize, although they cannot mark up and grade every story, every day, teachers of writing do not abdicate their responsibility to analyze and evaluate student writing in different contexts. Dedicated teachers have at their disposal creative strategies that inform students and parents of the writer's progress, and build the foundation and the incentive for personal and intellectual growth. These strategies include:

- Grading the body of work produced by the student over the school year.
- Evaluating students according to the skills of the writing process they have learned.
- Grading whole stories selected from a student's best work.
- Grading timed assignments periodically to see how well the student writes without teacher guidance or endless rewriting.
- Using the graded paper or assignment as a springboard for revision and instruction.
- Establishing descriptive guidelines so that teachers, parents, and children understand and become involved in the process of evaluation.

These methods provide tough but flexible standards that inspire effort, creativity, and experimentation rather than timidity and rigidity.

Chapter Thirteen

Writing Anxiety

One day Sam Ficarrotta strolled into the library of Sandy Lane Elementary School in Clearwater, Florida, where he was principal, and found two sweet-faced children doing research for a term paper. One was reading up on chipmunks, the other on hummingbirds. Ficarrotta ruled his school with the tender passion of an Italian nobleman, exchanging lines of poetry with members of his staff and talking effusively about the need to introduce children to a world of truth and beauty. He pulled a volume from the library shelf and displayed it for the children, two fifth-grade girls named Carri Lantto and Becky Miller. The book contained the plays of Shakespeare, written in language children could understand. He convinced them that *A Midsummer Night's Dream* and *King Lear* would be more engaging than chipmunks and hummingbirds.

In the days that followed, Becky and Carri devoured the plays, wrote reports on the life and works of Shakespeare, and introduced the Bard to their classmates. In March of 1984, Ficarrotta introduced the girls to me. We talked about the universality of Shakespeare's plays, his marvelous plots and intriguing characters, and even got down to the nitty gritty, chatting about the humiliation of Bottom and the blinding of Gloucester.

We then walked into Becky and Carri's classroom, where about seventy-five students waited to show me their work. They had been writing every day since the beginning of the school year for their teacher, Mary Osborne.

She had them explore ideas for stories, plan their work, write rough drafts, rework the story after consultation, make changes and corrections, and publish their work in a class booklet. Mark Beery handed me his story on "Teenagers and Drugs." He wrote: "It is easier to prevent drug abuse than to stop the practice after it has started. If you know what drugs do to you, then you will have a better chance of not taking them. I wrote this opinion paper because teen-agers need to know what drugs can do to them." The final version of his story was stapled to eleven other drafts! Each draft brought the paper closer to publication, and Mark was as proud of his revisions as he was of his final story.

Mrs. Osborne had so thoroughly converted her class to the values of good writing that her students became ambassadors of writing to other classes. Groups of fifth graders took second graders to the library, where they wrote stories together. The older kids consulted with the younger children, evaluating the stories and suggesting revisions. The fifth graders compiled a "yucky list" to help the little ones avoid common second-grade errors, and even created a handy model of the writing process in language that second graders could understand.

These little miracles of collaboration are being worked throughout Pinellas County by teachers turned on to the teaching of writing. In school after school, I have seen students and teachers writing their way toward excellence in education.

The teachers, arm in arm with dedicated language arts supervisors, believe writing is a way of seeing, learning, and communicating. They shout one message from the schoolhouse rooftops so other teachers, principals, and parents can hear: Please do not use writing as a form of punishment.

In Aldous Huxley's *Brave New World*, doctors took infants into rooms filled with pretty books and flowers. The infants crawled over to feel the silky petals and stroke the bright pages. Then something happened. A nurse threw a switch, and "there was a violent explosion. Shriller and even shriller, a siren shrieked. Alarm bells maddeningly sounded. The children started, screamed; their faces were distorted with terror."

The mad scientist behind this experiment explains: "They'll grow up with what the psychologists used to call an 'instinctive' hatred of books and flowers. . . . They'll be safe from books and botany all their lives."

With Huxley's parable in mind, imagine a scene in which a fifth grader misbehaves. He throws spitballs, or drops books on the floor, or laughs in the library, or gives the finger to a teacher. Imagine the teacher saying, "Johnny, because you've been bad, you have to draw a picture." Or, "You have to do a scientific experiment." Or, "You have to play something on the piano."

These forms of discipline seem absurd. Yet for years teachers have told Johnny, "You were a bad boy, so you have to write." Perhaps a student will have to write an essay under the title, "Why I Must Not Laugh in the Library." Perhaps the teacher will work over the paper with a red pen, marking every flaw in crimson hieroglyphics. The exercise leaves an indelible mark on the psyche of the student: WRITING IS PUNISHMENT.

In crude Skinnerian terms, it works this way. Teachers try to modify the behavior of students by creating negative consequences for misbehavior. In one school, students who misbehave badly are given a choice between suspension or writing an essay (the death penalty or life imprisonment). The unintended side effect of this process is to create in the mind of the student a perpetual association between punishment and the act of writing, in the same way that the protagonist of A Clockwork Orange was conditioned to hate Beethoven.

A teacher described for me how her colleague in a Miami high school gets students to show up for exams. If they show up, they get to take an objective test, multiple choice and the like. If they miss the test, the makeup is a ninety-minute essay exam. In other words, writing is the punishment for missing a test. Attendance for his exams is almost perfect. "Do anything, sir, but don't make me write."

My daughter once had a teacher who assigned writing as punishment. Alison stalked into the house, slammed her books on the table, and marched to her room to write fifty times: "I must not talk in the library." I noticed that the next time she sat at her desk to undertake a real writing assignment, she did so with less enthusiasm. She came to associate the act of writing with punishment.

Watching her made me recall my early days. My cronies and I developed clever defenses against different types of punishment assignments. If the teacher told us to write one hundred times, "I will not talk in the library," we would write one word at a time.

I
I
I
I
I
I
[etc.]

I must not leave the classroom without permission.

I must not leave the classroom without permission.

I must not leave the classroom without permission.

I mustnot leve the classroom withoutpermission.

I must not leie the classroom without permission.

I must not leave the classroom without permission.

I must not leave the classroom without permission.

I must not leave the classroom without permission.

I must not leave the classroom without permission.

I must not leave the classroom without permission.

I must not leave the classroom without permission.

I must not leave the class room without permission,

I must not leave the classroom without permission.

Old traditions die hard. I attended a Halloween Carnival in 1985 at an elementary school. I was eating a hot dog and went to throw away the wrapper when I found this punishment assignment in the school dumpster, where it belongs.

If the teacher ordered us to write a hundred-word essay, we would inflate each sentence with clutter and redundancy, and count the words after every sentence: "The library should always be a quiet place, a very quiet place, a place where no talking goes on, a place where people come to study because there is always quiet there, at least in my opinion." Two more sentences like that, and the snow job is complete.

Sometimes a teacher would tell us to write an essay that would be "two sides of a piece of paper" in length. It was always fun to outsmart her by writing in our most immature cursive, puffing out the length and width of each letter so that a big title and a few worthless sentences filled up the space.

The tendency to equate writing with punishment is so deeply ingrained in our educational system that it has been reflected in popular culture. During an episode of the television comedy "Diff'rent Strokes," an otherwise enlightened teacher gives Arnold and his classmates a one-hundred-word essay to write as punishment for misbehaving in the hallway.

In a nostalgic reminiscence of his Indiana childhood, Jean Shepherd remembers a teacher this way:

Miss Bodkin, after recess, addressed us: "I want all of you to write a theme. ...." A theme! A rotten theme before Christmas! There *must* be kids somewhere who love writing themes, but to a normal air-breathing human kid, writing themes is a torture that ranks only with the dreaded medieval chin-breaker of Inquisitional fame. A theme!

In a recent film version of Shepherd's story, Miss Bodkin is portrayed in a dream sequence as a cackling witch who marks student papers with an F.

In the popular teenage movie *The Breakfast Club*, several high school students are sequestered during a Saturday detention session and told that they cannot leave until they write an essay on the topic "Who You Think You Are."

The criminal justice system has caught on. In March 1985, a judge in Fort Lauderdale made a nineteen-year-old shoplifter write "I will not steal" 250 times. The judge may have been inspired by a colleague who earlier that week sentenced a child molester to write "I will keep my hands off other people" twenty-five times a week for eleven years. One reporter described it as "a 14,300-sentence sentence." The judge said, "It reminds [offenders] every week that they must behave. If they seem to forget, they go to the big house." Writing or the big house!

Fred Hechinger of *The New York Times* reported the story of a father, a professional writer, who complained to a teacher after his child was made to write a punitive essay. "Only once have I written an angry letter to one of my children's teachers, and that was when our son was made to write an essay as a penalty for some transgressions in class." The teacher admitted that she never considered the consequences of using writing as punishment.

The issue was addressed by Linda Lewis, principal of LeMay Elementary School in Bellevue, Nebraska, in an article in *Principal* magazine. During job interviews she asked three candidates how discipline could be maintained in the classroom. "I make them write something for me," said one. "I have offenders copy pages from the dictionary," said the second. A "fresh-faced 1981 college graduate" said, "Oh, I make them memorize poetry." "Is it any wonder," says Lewis, "that English teachers find it difficult to whip up kids' enthusiasm for writing?" In the *Times*, Hechinger argued that "the joy of writing is not dead in today's children unless it is killed in the bud by adults."

What then is the appeal for some teachers and administrators in using writing as punishment?

- It is easy to control, requiring little supervision. Students can be stuck in a room and required to write till their hands fall off.
- It creates the illusion of an educational and counseling purpose. Students who write essays about why they should not smoke are thought to benefit from the exercise.
- It seems a humane alternative to suspension or paddling.

None of these reasons justifies the practice. Students are not encouraged to plan these essays carefully. They may not be required to consult with teachers, to discuss the issues and strategies of the essay, to write several drafts, to polish and correct their own work, and to share it with others. When writing becomes punishment, all the positive elements of learning—organization, discovery, and communication—disappear.

A 1984 survey revealed widespread use of writing as punishment in the Pinellas County schools, a system with almost 90,000 children. Despite protests from many English teachers, principals refused to abandon the use of punitive writing. The language arts supervisors carried the fight to a state organization of English teachers, which supported a ban on writing as punishment. This and similar efforts inspired the National Conference of Teachers of English meeting in Detroit late in 1984 to condemn the use of punitive writing. They found such writing inconsistent with their aims: "The writing act should include the process of imagining an audience, setting goals, generating ideas and notes, producing drafts and revised text, and editing the product to meet the audience's expectations."

One of the best ways to create a positive, disciplined atmosphere for learning is to teach writing the way Mary Osborne does at Sandy Lane. Her students seem too busy to be bad. This goes for her weaker students as well as her champions because Mary has discovered, like so many other teachers, that writing is for all students.

The weakest students, many of whom receive writing as punishment and fear the act of writing, need desperately to discover the value of their own words. Fear of writing, argues John Daly of the University of Texas, "is related to low self-concept and low self-confidence" as well as various kinds of academic failure.

In too many schools, writing is a recurring nightmare for students. They learn, like Huxley's infants, the negative consequences that flow inevitably from the act of writing. Their writing anxiety, their "instinctive" hatred of writing, is not instinctive at all, but learned. We take the first step toward healing the writing wounds of students by banning writing as punishment.

The next step is for teachers to burn their red pencils. Students associate the red marks in the margins of their papers with anger, failure, and loss. The students learn nothing from these except that writing wreaks evil consequences. And when teachers mark up papers in the traditional way, they learn that the teaching of writing is punishment—for the teachers.

I once worked on a college student's paper for an hour. I marked each mistake in red. This was a C paper, so the margins were decorated in red. My marks said things like AWK (for awkward), CHECK SP, and PROBLEM IN AGREEMENT. I returned it to the student with the hope that he would learn from my efforts, avoid such errors in the future, and appreciate my concern for his education. It was no fun to watch him take the paper, read the final grade, ignore my comments, crumple the page, and slam dunk it in the trash can. Two points. I should have slapped him with a technical foul.

I overheard students describing what teachers did to their

papers. I was surprised how often their language had images of violence: "He cut up my paper." "She tore it to shreds." "He bled all over it in red ink."

So I turned positive. I copied the best papers and distributed them to the class. Occasionally, I let students read and grade them. Students passed over anything good in the papers. They marked the margins in red and assigned low grades. Moral: the abused child becomes the abusive parent.

I graded the papers the way my teachers graded mine, the only way I knew. But I converted to black ink while teaching at Auburn University at Montgomery, Alabama, where I taught a course in Advanced Composition. One of my students, a truck driver, cared about his writing. I tried to be balanced, to show him his strengths and his weaknesses. Truck reappeared a year later and rushed up to me in the school parking lot. "Good to see you, Doc," he said. "I'll never forget what you did for me last year." I prepared myself for one of those comments a teacher waits a career to hear, the one about "changing my life." Instead, Truck said, "You were the first teacher who didn't mark up my papers in red ink."

I learned a more dramatic version of the same lesson at Bay Point Elementary. One day I talked to the class about why teachers write on student papers.

"To show us our mistakes," the students said, almost in one voice.

"When Mrs. Collins writes on your papers," I said, "what color pencil does she use?"

"Red," they agreed by acclamation.

"Are you sure?" I held their papers behind my back.

Gillian Gaynair timidly raised her hand and suggested that Mrs. Collins had switched to a different color. She was jeered down by about forty students. "It's red. I know it's red," said one boy with fiery conviction. I held up the papers for them to see. The marks were black.

We have trained our students to see red. We can retrain them to enjoy writing, to accept criticism, and to revise their own work. Here are some strategies that have worked for me:

- Mark papers in black or blue or green, never in red.
- When you mark a paper, build on its strengths.
- Avoid useless comments like AWK.
- Help students recognize the good in each other's work.
- Use short conferences in class to review a student's work. Help the writer take the next step.

IDEAS OR BUST!

"NOW I KNOW HOW GOD FELT"

Fifth grader Marty Solomon gives us two illustrated versions of writer's block.

- Think of writing as a process. Don't spend all your time on the final product. Confer more and grade less.
- Get students into the spirit of rewriting. Teach them to mark up and revise their own papers in a useful way.
- Make them care enough about what they have to say, so that they will be moved to perfect and correct their own work.
- Help them to understand that writing is hard work, not punishment.

I often share my feelings toward the act of writing with students. I tell them that when the writing goes well, it's more fun than Ping-Pong or *Star Wars*. When it goes badly, or when I cannot think of anything to write, I get nervous or frustrated. When faced with writer's block, I get lazy, unwilling to do the hard work necessary to overcome it.

They agree that writing can be difficult, even painful. They love the expression "writer's block." They have all experienced it, and they envision it as some sort of oppressive ogre who stifles creativity or imagination.

"What do you do when you get writer's block?" I asked.

"I break pencils," said Mitch Bayliss.

One student drew a picture of writer's block, a dark, snarling, fanged blockhead who, I thought, vaguely resembled one of his teachers.

Another student, Robbie Allison, decided to write about writer's block and about the way he tries to overcome it, by brainstorming.

Writer's Block is funny and mostly weird. It's when you just sit there with your head on your desk not knowing what to write about. And if you try to write you still won't know what to write about. But when you do write it doesn't make much sense.

A Brain Storm is like a rain storm in your head. You keep thinking about different things and you aren't sure what to write about and it's hard to decide. And it really makes you mad. And your face turns red, blue, yellow, purple and orange and your stomach starts to boil.

Robbie is coming to realize that the boiling stomach is one form of initiation into the world of writers. It is a product of the natural tension between the writer and the blank page. The teacher who uses writing as punishment turns the tension into loathing. The enlightened teacher, like Mary Osborne, helps the student transform his anxiety into the creative energy he needs to write.

Chapter Fourteen

The Writer at Home

At the age of nine, Lisea Lyons and her friends took a tiny piece of paper, a pencil, and a strong sense of injustice and plopped themselves down in the middle of a St. Petersburg sidewalk. The result of that impromptu brainstorming session changed the direction of my career as a journalist and a teacher.

That was in 1980. Lisea was a fourth grader at Shorecrest Elementary and felt a bit frustrated that the world's great flow of information was rushing past her life and her interests.

"I would hate it," she remembered, "because I never got any mail. I would read the newspaper and there was never anything in it about me or my friends or my neighborhood."

The notion nagged at her until that golden day when she and some pals found themselves a few blocks from home with paper and a pencil and nothing to do. A thought came to her that could have been inspired by an old movie: "Hey kids, why don't we write our own newspaper?"

"We sat down right in the middle of the sidewalk and started writing down stories," she said. She returned home, rewrote them by hand, and distributed free copies to neighbors. The *Neighborhood Times* was born, and the world of communication is still trying to catch its breath.

"Everyone was so excited," she said. "I promised to do it every Saturday. A lot of people would look forward to it. I would have fun writing it. I would make my own deadlines. And it was fun handing it out."

A neighbor and journalist, Peter Gallagher, handed me a

copy of the inaugural issue of *Neighborhood Times*. I had been working as a newspaper writing coach and developing a series of professional seminars.

"I don't know why you waste your time working with grown-ups," said Pete. "If you want to find the real writers in this town, you'd better read this."

"This," of course, was the *Neighborhood Times*, and I found in the stories of Lisea Lyons a charm and economy of style that comes when children are free to write without interference from adults wielding red pencils.

The Pigeon That Can't Fly

Marc Mosley has a pigeon. It is recovering from a hurt wing. Before when the bird couldn't fly at all, Marc would throw him up and he would fly and come down. The bird is fed corn. Marc has a dog. But the bird and the dog behave well around each other.

(I love the surprise transition at the end connecting the bird and the dog.)

The Butterfly Lady

The Butterfly Lady lives on 13th St. It is the house with the long path in front. She raises butterflys on her back porch. She'd be glad if you would visit every once and awhile. But lots of times she isn't always home. But if you go over there she will show you her butterflys.

(Peter Gallagher expressed a special fondness for the graceful flow of that last line.)

The Babysitters

Most everyone knows Kim and Patty and Lynn. They are the most famous babysitters in the neighborhood. They live across 12 St. on 15th Ave., 2nd white house. Kim is turning 15 in two months and Patty is turning 17 in 1 month and Lynn is an adult.

(We learn something here about kids' definition of adulthood, but we learn about simplicity and economy of style as well.)

Things Stolen

There are 2 people that had things stolen. Marc Mosley had his new bike stolen. Mrs. Knippen had a lot of plants stolen. We never got those things back.

(Why don't adult newspapers ever tell us whether people get stolen things back?)

The rest of the newspaper contained interesting graphics, puzzles, riddles, and jokes: "A guy went to the priest and said I want to be holy, so the priest took out his shot gun and made him holy."

I've cherished that little newspaper like some precious heirloom and compared it with subsequent editions. A year later, when Lisea was ten, her stories were getting longer and her style more mature.

Can an Egg Survive?

Well, it sure can!
Have you ever wondered what an egg and an astronaut have in common? Well they are both fragile, whether they are traveling to the moon in a space capsul or in a grocery bag to your house. Chances are they will get banged, squeezed and slammed. I made an egg survive, can you? What you will need is a fresh egg, a plastic sandwich bag, tape and packing materials such as cardboard boxes, old newspapers, cotton, styrofoam etc. Pack egg however you desire. If you try experiment, let me know the results.
Good luck.

At the age of twelve, Lisea Lyons is still writing and publishing occasional editions of her newspaper. She still searches adult newspapers for items of relevance to her, her friends, and her neighborhood. She makes a quick list: "I read Alligator Express [a page of stories written by children in the Sunday *St. Petersburg Times*], the comics, and Ann Landers."

Some students enjoy writing so much, they practice it at home or as a recreational activity. They find it fun, interesting, and rewarding. Sometimes they keep it to themselves and sometimes they share it with friends, siblings, or parents.

Then something happens in school. Children learn to be "careful" in their work. They realize that the teacher reacts differently from a parent. Perhaps no praise will result from writing, only punishment.

Anecdotal evidence suggests that many talented writers learned their craft without teachers or in spite of them. James Carey is dean of the College of Communications at the University of Illinois. A prolific writer and scholar, Carey writes with clarity, style, and passion whether the topic is journalism ethics or the Chicago Cubs.

Jim was so ill as a child he was unable to attend school until the age of fifteen. "They didn't know what to do with me then," he remembered, "so they put me in the tenth grade." There he learned that he could not parse or diagram a sentence. But he could write, more effectively than his peers who had attended school for years. Unlike them, Jim had no fear of committing his thoughts to the page. He learned his craft at home, as a diversion. He wrote without teachers and without direction. He wrote for himself and for fun.

In childhood writing, we begin to discover our voice, our areas of expertise, and the value of our own experience. Jeff Klinkenberg is the talented outdoors and feature writer for the *St. Petersburg Times*. He writes colorful narratives about the fishermen and hunters who inhabit the west coast of Florida.

He grew up in Miami and fished with his father in places like Key West. Thanks to a scrapbook kept by his mother, Bea, we have some record of Jeff's early development as a writer. At the age of six, he wrote and illustrated a tiny booklet on that great American outdoorsman, Davy Crockett. Jeff wrote about how Davy had fought a bear and how he met his fate at the Alamo.

"Too bad he was killed," wrote Jeff the first grader. "He wooda been 185. That is very old. Well that's the way the ball bounces."

At the age of six, Jeff Klinkenberg was writing about outdoorsmen, and, more than thirty years later, he still is.

When she was in the third grade, my daughter Alison decided to write a story for me. She selected one of her favorite topics: the unicorn. She proudly showed me the story knowing that a daddy who teaches writing must approve such activity. It was a sweet little story showing lots of excitement over the beauty of unicorns:

The Land of the Unicorns
What woud it be like,
to live in the land of
Unicorns? But of
coruse their is nothing
like a unicorn!
Unicorns are the
most Beatiful things
in the world. But like
most every person
on eath knows that
unicorns are Beatiful!

I read the story with enthusiasm, praised her for it, and asked her a question: "Can you tell me a story that shows how beautiful a unicorn really is?"

She looked a bit flustered, perhaps slightly suspicious, as if she thought I were playing some teacher's trick on her. But she disappeared for about ten minutes and returned with a story three times longer than the first. It had a new title:

The girl and the Unicorn.
once a girl saw some twickeling stars that
shine like a fairie's wand. But wasn't
strange that she thougt that she was
dreaming but she was not. The stars turned
into a Unicorn! But a fuw minets
later the littel girl was riding the Unicorn.
She saw horses that color of pink, yellow,
puple too! The mancen the she saw was
20 stories high. But all of sudden everything
in the land frose and the unicor disipered
with littel stars behind him.
The End

I was impressed, not only by Alison's story, but by the effectiveness of my first writing conference with an eight-year-old. When I asked her that one question, I did not expect to receive a third-grade version of the Legend of the Holy Grail complete with mythic implications and psychedelic transformations.

I have reread that story many times, and I wonder how I would have handled it ten years earlier when I was teaching writing the old way, which is to say "not at all." Certainly there are enough mistakes to correct. I count twelve misspellings, for example, and a few other words missing. But now I see writing the new way, and as both a teacher and a proud parent, I am inclined to catalogue the good and interesting things Alison does in her story:

- Most of the words are spelled correctly.
- She invents spellings for difficult words, and comes pretty close on *twinkling* (twickeling), *thought* (thougt), *minutes* (minets), *froze* (frose), *little* (littel) and *disappeared* (disipered). I had a hard time decoding *mancen* as mansion.
- She can use the period, the exclamation point, capital letters, and complete sentences.

- She has a good idea of how the story should look on the page.
- She weaves an interesting chronological narrative.
- Unlike the first version, which told us how beautiful unicorns were, this version showed us. She accomplishes this by using descriptive details, interesting verbs, and even a simile ("like a fairie's wand").

As I study the scales, these strengths outweigh those dozen spelling mistakes.

I learned a few things about teaching writing from this experience.

- That students enjoy writing on their own.
- That they want to share their work with people who will respond with praise.
- That they are willing to rewrite under certain circumstances.
- That a conference can be a sentence and last fifteen seconds.
- That even young students can use sophisticated rhetorical techniques.
- That students will use interesting words in their stories (*twinkling* and *mansion*) if they can invent spellings.
- That young writers enjoy publication, even if it only means posting stories on the refrigerator.

The story does not end there, for Alison's sister Emily does not like her sibling getting all the praise and attention. Emily was only four at the time, but she wanted to write too.

She handed me a pencil and some paper and dictated to me a story about a prince and a princess. As her amanuensis, I was to write down every word. This I did, although her tale was a lurid one filled with suggestions that the prince and princess did more than just live happily ever after.

One day there was a princess. There was
a beautiful horse with a prince on it.
And the princess married the prince.
They had a picnic. They ate a cake.
And she wore a beautiful dress. They
fell asleep kissing each other. She
brought him back to her castle.
They ate supper. They kissed and hugged
and went to bed. It was snowing outside.

They took a shower. They got dressed.
They built a snowman. Then they rollerskated.

Emily had me read it to her several times. Then she took the page, illustrated it with a colorful drawing, and posted it on the refrigerator. Take that, older sister.

Four-year-olds want to write, I thought, scratched my head, and laughed. Where will this end? I learned the answer two years later. It was Christmas 1981 and Emily was an older sister herself. Her baby sister Lauren was a year old. The girls received a toy called Printer's Kit, which permits children to set a few words of type and stamp them on a page. The result of this was a tiny booklet written and illustrated by Emily, using words she could spell without any trouble.

Meticulously, Emily printed out two sentences: THE CAT ATE THE RAT. THE RAT ATE THE CAT. This epic of violence and revenge was illustrated with two color drawings. Emily left the last two pages of the book blank. She received lots of praise for her effort, but the next day something mysterious happened. I found Emily's book on the floor, inspected it, and discovered that the final blank pages contained a few suspicious squiggles in pencil.

The scribbles looked familiar, and the whole family was shocked by the recognition of what had transpired. Baby Lauren had taken a pencil and marked up those blank pages. She did not want to be left out. She wanted to make her mark on the world—and on the page.

I wondered at that moment when writing instruction should begin? Why not start as early as possible? As educators or parents, we should not be distracted by the fact that our children may be too young to speak, or to read, or to spell. Writing instruction can enhance development in these other areas.

Hand a two-year-old a crayon and a large slice of white paper and see what happens. Take dictation from a three-year-old, let her illustrate it, read it back to her, and see what happens. Scribble, draw, illustrate, dictate. Read a child's words aloud. All contribute to a young writer's intellectual and personal growth. No six-year-olds I have worked with were afraid to write. They learn that later.

The first step to effective language arts instruction is the simple act of freeing students to write. I learned that lesson in a special way during a writing workshop at the University of Tampa in January 1983. I worked with twelve elementary school teachers in a place called the Dome Room, a round chamber with terrible acoustics. It was like trying to conduct a seminar in Carlsbad Caverns.

The teachers brought fifteen fourth graders with them, and I brought three fifth graders I had worked with. My kids set up shop in the back of the Dome Room. The idea was to get the children writing on their own, while the teachers talked in front. Later the teachers would join the students for observation and conferences. If you believe in your methods, I said to myself, test them out and show them off.

The fifth graders handed out paper and pencils, suggested some writing topics, and got the group started. I went back and told them they could write on any topic in any form, fiction or nonfiction. For the next half hour, they made a racket. The sound wrapped around the circular walls and disrupted my discussion with the teachers. I lost heart. Finally a teacher, looking disgusted, said "I'm sorry. This is not an environment in which I can learn."

I apologized, blamed the whole thing on the acoustics, and begged her to endure for a few more minutes. I talked louder against the growing din of what I assumed was student mis-behavior. When we joined the students, I was amazed that they, including one first grader who had tagged along, had filled their pages with writing.

Some students read their work aloud. Others applauded. They responded well to questions. When I asked, "What sentence do you like the best?" they pointed quickly to their favorite lines. When I asked, "What would you like to do next?" they responded, "Finish the story" or "Add more details."

One of the best stories, by a Tampa fourth grader named Frances, was called "Dream." It was the story of a character called the Bad Christmas Spirit, and she read it with enthusiasm:

One night I was sleeping when I head a "BANG!"
I pulled back my curtain and looked. I saw a
rust colourd car. It must have been the door
I heard because I saw a white figure coming
towards our front door. It had an empty sack.
It was Christmas Eve, and I wouldn't be surprised
if it was the "Bad Christmas Spirt" coming to
take our presnts.
So I rushed to the living room with two (2)
cans of tennis balls and a tennis raucket.
When he floated in the living room window,
I pointed to him and said "This Christmas

you retire!" Then he and the car dissaperd.
In the morning a news report came on and
said, "There were no sins of bad spirit
attacks last night, but at the station
I found a note saying . . .

Christmas Eve

Dear Everyone,

I have retired to taking presants,
I now have decided to give presnts!

Love
The Good Christmas Spirit

On hearing the story, teachers and students applauded.

I told the teachers at lunch that I thought their fourth graders were strong writers. I said, "Maybe next workshop I should put in a request for some weak writers."

"That's what you got today," said one teacher to my surprise. "That girl who wrote about the Christmas Spirit. She hardly writes at all in class. She just sits there so tight, afraid that she's going to make mistakes. You worked wonders with her."

I had to laugh. Frances had done the writing before I even met her. What I did, of course, was to sit her in the back of the room with a pencil and paper. I left her alone. I let her write without a bunch of adults looking over her shoulder. And those annoying sounds that disturbed us so, I now realize, were the sounds of happy writers at work.

Writing at an early age helps a child find her own voice. *Voice* is the word English teachers use to describe the illusion of a writer speaking directly to a reader. "When I read your story," a friend said to me, "I could almost hear your voice speaking the words." I took it as a compliment.

Teachers are not sure whether voice changes as a writer matures or whether it is like the marks on a zebra, unique, identifiable, ingrained. Poet David McCord tells of the time he was reading an old copy of *St. Nicholas* magazine, which contained a section of children's writing. "I had come on a few paragraphs signed respectively Edna St. Vincent Millay, Cornelia Otis Skinner, Robert Hillyer, and was suddenly struck by a prose passage much more earthy and natural in voice than what I had been glancing through. This sounds like E. B. White, I said to myself. Then I looked at the signature: Elwyn Brooks White, age 11."

Hearing this anecdote for the first time led me to wonder

whether my own writing voice had changed much in the past twenty-five years. The best evidence comes from a piece called "The Unsuccessful Failure," which my mother exhumed from some grave of memorabilia. It was an important act of archaeology.

I wrote the story in the eighth grade. It concerned a defense attorney who dies at the instant he wins his first case. The story exhibits a good writing vocabulary and a smooth style:

As Devon walked back to his seat, he was exhausted. He had given his best just now; had it been good enough? After the customary charge by the judge to the jury, they retired to reach a verdict. Devon's head throbbed with pain to the point where his vision blurred.

Parts of the story contain too many clichés, and the language is never concrete or specific enough: "Here they waited for what seemed like eternity."

Yet I find myself pleased with the reading of this courtroom melodrama. At the age of thirteen I was a better writer than I thought I was. I am struck by several observations:

- Just as Jeff Klinkenberg was influenced by Davy Crockett, I was influenced by Perry Mason and other televised dramas. For my generation, television can be a stimulus for writing.
- I used words such as *adroit, multiplicity* and *circumstantial*. I learned these from a thesaurus, which improved my vocabulary but led me to use words which now seem unnatural to me.
- I considered the law (along with sports) to be my special area of knowledge. I knew something that other children did not know, and I wanted to convey this in my writing.
- I had control, but not total control, over mechanics and punctuation, even the semicolon. I checked my spelling carefully because I knew the piece would be published for the class.
- I used a variety of sentence lengths, emphatic word order, and active verbs even though I did not know at the time that these led to effective prose.
- The name of my hero was Joe Devon. My girlfriend lived on Devon Road. All writing is autobiography.

Can it be demonstrated that most of the important work in writing development is accomplished by the eighth grade, by the fifth grade, by the second grade? Is the rest only fine-tuning?

What I sense in my childhood writing is the sound of my own voice. It is an illusion, I know, but I recognize it as I would my face in an old photograph.

I have vivid memories of my childhood writing, but only of pieces that were in some way published. I remember poems published in a mimeographed sixth-grade newspaper. I wrote news stories and funny essays and serious satire, which teachers read aloud in class. Most stories, like my parody of *Moby-Dick*, were not assignments. They were done for fun or because I had something to say. These always aroused the most interest, laughter, and outrage.

I never thought in those days that I wanted to be a writer, but I did derive great pleasure from the notion that I could play with language and that my work could move an audience to laughter or anger. The teachers who helped me the most were those who let me write, read my stories aloud, inspired me to rewrite, and gave me some new insight into the process that would make my writing better.

By teaching writing early, in the elementary school years, we will inevitably inspire some young people to writing greatness. The seeds of good writing, planted early, will blossom into famous writing careers. This is what happened to Donald Murray, who, in *A Writer Teaches Writing,* describes how a childhood love of language grew into a vocation:

I never lost the excitement I must have felt, as every child does, at making a mark on paper. That squiggle is me, I made it. It is my meaning. But as I got older I found writing harder and harder. I started searching for the writing process under the illusion I could find a way to make writing easy—the sword would come right out of the stone. I didn't realize then that the importance of writing lies in the fact that it is not easy, and should not be. The writer should be exploring new territory with writing, seeking important meanings that are beyond the glib, easy sentence the writer has already mastered.

By the time I was in fourth grade I was publishing a newspaper, using a sickly yellow gelatin spread out on a cookie sheet with purple ink. In junior high I was reading about writers, fascinated at how they made up stories. Ever since then I have been reading about writers, collecting what they have to say about writing, observing them when I can, listening to them, trying to understand how language creates worlds that are more real than the one in which we live, how language creates and communicates ideas, how language keeps surprising me at my desk.

• • •

An alliance between teachers and parents helps ensure that children will be nurtured in their growth as writers. The alliance can be struck by parents who crave enlightened writing instruction in their children's schools; and it can be struck by dedicated teachers who know the importance of parental support of their work.

To get parents on her side, fifth-grade teacher Mary Osborne informs them of her goals and teaching philosophy. Usually a September letter to parents does the trick:

September 12, 1985

Dear Parents,

This year your children will be spending a lot of time writing. They will be learning the process of writing and working toward the publication of their stories in class books. The first emphasis will be on the content and structure in each piece of writing. We will tackle specific problems in spelling, punctuation, and grammar during revision and final editing.

I'll need your help and support in order for this program to be successful. If your children bring home early drafts of their writing, try to resist the urge to correct any spelling, punctuation, or grammar mistakes at first. We want to give students the primary responsibility for finding and correcting their own mistakes. I'd appreciate your concentrating on the content and details of their stories, making sure they've included enough information for their readers to understand.

I'll also need your help when we publish our class books. There will be a lot of typing involved, so if you're interested in helping let me know.

I'm confident that your children will grow as writers this year by experiencing the same process professional writers use. Through this program, I hope your children will enjoy writing and improve their English skills at the same time.

If you have any questions or concerns about this or any other part of your child's Language Arts program, please don't hesitate to let me know.

Sincerely,

Mrs. Osborne

Mrs. Osborne

Parents love to see their children writing well. Some parents want to know how they can help teachers help students. A group of writing teachers in Pinellas County, Florida, developed this list of suggestions. Teachers using this book are invited to copy the list and share it with parents:

Interview. Have children interview family members. Have them take notes and write stories about each member. These need not be life stories but might instead tell about one special event in each member's life. Interview the oldest members of the family on important historical anniversaries (such as the ending of World War II) to evoke memories of those events. Interview an older relative about a craft or activity that is no longer common (using an icebox, or playing marbles).

Read. Read to and with your child a few minutes each day. Read stories at bedtime, even with older children. Share the newspaper in the morning and highlight for each other the day's important news.

Diary. Encourage your child to keep a private diary or journal. Many bookstores carry beginner diaries containing blank pages along with starter ideas for children to write about. Make little booklets with blank pages for your children to write in and illustrate.

Television. Watch television with your child. Occasionally, have your child write about a show you've watched together. The child can retell the story, or better yet, focus on one part he or she liked. The child might also relate a television event to something similar he or she has done or felt. Don't be afraid to discuss television shows critically, leading to conversations about values, which might inspire some writing. Why do little girls like Barbie dolls? What are the best and worst videos on MTV?

Special things. Have your child write down directions for doing something he or she enjoys: playing soccer, making ice-cream sodas, or break dancing. Perhaps there is a special object in the house, an old watch, a sports trophy, or a wedding picture that could become the subject of an interesting story.

Trips, special events. After a special family trip or event, have your child design a travel brochure or poster advertising or explaining where you've been.

Share. Don't be afraid to try some of these ideas along with your child. Let your child see you writing. Write about your own experiences for your children.

Letters. Encourage your child to write letters to relatives or friends to tell of a day's adventure or an important event. Encourage relatives to write back.

Albums and yearbooks. Review your old high-school yearbook or a family album with your child. The child can turn your reminiscences into stories.

Brainstorm. Explore story ideas with your children. Talk about interesting characters or events in your neighborhood. Inform the teachers about these as well.

Publish. Have a place in your home (a bulletin board, the refrigerator) where you display the good work of your children. Keep an album of their writing.

Praise and question. Be generous with praise and be open to your child's ideas and approaches to stories. Don't just criticize mistakes. Ask questions to inspire additions and revisions.

Dictation. Take dictation from your children. Type out their stories and turn them into little books that they can illustrate.

Spend time. If you have tried all these ideas, you might as well become a teacher of writing. Just try one or two, as the spirit moves you. Any time you are able to spend with your child will contribute to his or her education.

Ask. Ask the teacher if there is some way you can help.

Chapter Fifteen

Learning from Children

The second-grade class picture shows me standing against a row of lockers in the back of a classroom jammed with children. That's me, third from the right, among a row of boys clad in neat St. Aidan School uniforms. The girls are seated, prim and smiling, in long rows. They wear large yellow bows in their hair, a bit of color to offset bland green and tan jumpers.

My daughters think the picture looks "weird." They marvel at the number of children in that one class, sixty-three in all. I tell them eighty was the school record. One teacher.

The time was 1955. I look at that photo and see the baby boom in full bloom, postwar white America mushrooming in the Long Island suburbs. We weren't born with silver spoons in our mouths, only stainless steel flatware. But we were happy and prosperous and learned in spite of ourselves.

In that era, the raciest thing on television was the sight of Annette Funicello outgrowing her Mouseka-T-shirt. We had mothers and fathers and lived with both of them at the same time. We did not know any children whose parents were divorced. We lived within an hour's drive of a small tribe of relatives. Nobody had sex, not even our parents. I thought "dope" was my brother Vinnie. When I got home from school, my mother was waiting for me with a hundred questions including, "What did you learn today?" and "Do you have any homework?"

The education of children has changed because the world has changed, and it is remarkable that we have achieved certain kinds of educational progress in a social atmosphere poisonous to children. Second graders today must worry about not only their multiplication tables but also the division of their parents. Too often, they return from school to empty houses where cable TV serves as babysitter. Neighbors may be strangers. The closest relative may live 1,000 miles away. Grandma is a voice on the phone.

Indiana humorist Jean Shepherd wrote this description of the differences between childhood and adulthood for those who grew up during an earlier generation:

> Life, when you're a Male kid, is what the Grownups are doing. The Adult world seems to be some kind of secret society that has its own passwords, handclasps, and countersigns. The thing is to get In. But there's this invisible, impenetrable wall between you and all the great, unimaginably swinging things that they seem to be involved in. Occasionally mutterings of exotic secrets and incredible pleasures filter through. And so you bang against it, throw rocks at it, try to climb over it, burrow under it; but there it is. Impenetrable. Enigmatic.

The wall of adulthood is a thin veil for today's children. I once asked a group of fourth graders what their favorite movies were. Some students said *Star Wars* or *E.T.* But others said *Animal House*, *Halloween*, *Lipstick* (in which a teenage girl is raped), and *Last Tango in Paris.* Children can see these movies in their own homes on cable television.

The music video is an exciting new genre, but too many videos designed for young people are filled with sex and violence. Inevitably, the video narratives show women being slutty or submissive or masochistic.

Even those parents who carefully monitor their children's television viewing have probably lost control of what their children know. The existence of the technology means that, one way or another, children gain access to the secrets of adult life, a phenomenon aptly described by Neil Postman as *The Disappearance of Childhood*.

I thought about that phrase as I drove across Tampa Bay one morning with three ten-year-old girls in the back seat. During a thirty-minute drive, they talked nonstop. They discussed R- and X-rated movies, miscarriages, abortions, and dark family secrets. One girl asked me to tell her the worst thing that my daughter had ever done. "Well, I can think of something pretty bad," I said, "but those things are secret and personal."

"Well," she said, undeterred, "I'll tell you the worst thing I ever did."

She went on to describe a night when her parents were out of the house. Her brother was scaring her by telling her that a burglar had broken in. In a scene that suggested the movie *Halloween*, she went to the kitchen and got the biggest, sharpest butcher knife in the house. With arm cocked, she went searching through rooms for a burglar. When she got to her mother's bedroom, she saw a long lump under the blanket. She stabbed it and poked a hole through her mother's pillow. I shuddered to think what would have happened if a child had been hiding there.

The morning's conversation troubled me. Why were these lovely girls talking about the grisly realities of adult life rather than about childish things? Graphic violence, sex films, and adult secrets were all part of their world.

Neil Postman cites evidence from television, advertising, films, and news programs to argue that the traditional definitions of childhood are disappearing in the age of television. It was once necessary to learn to read before one was privy to the world of adult secrets. Book learning and childhood education set children apart, nurtured them, and protected them from the realities of the adult world. Now the images of television wash over young and old alike. We must accept the loss of innocence as a given. We can do nothing to prevent it.

This has profound implications for all teachers, especially teachers of reading and writing. As Postman concludes, "In one form or another, no matter how diluted the effort, the school will stand as the last defense against the disappearance of childhood."

Writing is a form of communication but also a path to learning and self-knowledge. In an age when children are vulnerable, the student writer can communicate problems to nurturing teachers. Teachers can then begin to help students better deal with a world that no longer provides children with a safety net of love and security.

Some young people have always used writing as a way of making sense of a harsh or hostile world. Tennessee Williams said this about his profoundly unhappy childhood: "I discovered writing as an escape from a world of reality in which I felt acutely uncomfortable. It became my retreat, my cave, my refuge."A different kind of writer, George Orwell, relates a similar sentiment about how writing made him feel comfortable in an uncomfortable world:

I was the middle child of three, but there was a gap of five years on either side, and I barely saw my father before I was eight. For this and other reasons I was somewhat lonely, and I soon developed disagreeable mannerisms which made me un-popular throughout my schooldays. I had the lonely child's habit of making up stories and holding conversations with imaginary persons, and I think from the very start my literary ambitions were mixed up with the feeling of being isolated and under-valued. I knew that I had a facility with words and a power of facing unpleasant facts, and I felt that this created a sort of private world in which I could get my own back for my failure in everyday life.

Part of becoming a writer does not involve technique or process at all. It concerns developing the personal strength, resources, and habits that make undertaking the process possible. When an athlete is in a slump, coaches sometimes say, "It's in his head." Understanding the process can give a writer confidence to overcome whatever personal obstacle stands in the way of the writing. Writing makes self-discovery and maturity possible.

The teacher plays different roles here, and I am amazed by the skill and versatility of the teachers I work with. They are not only teachers, they are substitute parents, psychologists, po-licemen, wardens, entertainers, sex counselors. . . . Each student presents a different and special challenge.

During her career as a fifth-grade teacher, Mrs. Collins has worked with students who suffered from severe dyslexia, who drank alcohol before coming to school, who were beaten at home, who were the victims of bitter divorces, who were hy-peractive or lethargic or who pinched themselves or hit themselves in the face. How a teacher finds the special way to communicate knowledge to each student is the miracle of modern education.

Sometimes the response of the teacher must be to get counseling for the child or to take emergency action. Fifth-grade teacher Janie Guilbault remembers how one writing conference with a child took a surprising turn: "Joan's story was about her dog, but it soon turned into a nonstop sentence about live rats in her house, running through her bedroom and keeping her awake at night. If it hadn't been for that conference, much more time may have elapsed between getting a social worker in, and Joan out of that situation."

Effective writing instruction creates a beautiful symmetry out of the skills of the teacher and the complex needs of the student. The act of writing permits the student to deal with his own fears, accomplishments, feelings, and experiences. The teacher learns more about the student through the writing. The student grows in self-knowledge and develops a sense of self-worth.

The writing conference permits the teacher to help the student move and grow as a writer. The conference takes advantage of the teacher's skill and ingenuity in meeting the needs of each student. The result is the marriage of academic skill and personal growth.

• • •

Miranda sits at her desk with her arms crossed while everyone else is writing. She obviously resents the exercise. Her teacher knows the girl is a perfectionist, upset by her inability to master something new and different. How much praise should the teacher use, and how much discipline? What strategy will move her?

• • •

Joan, two years older than her classmates, is tall, beautiful, and suffers from a reading disability. Her brother is twenty-five years old and can barely read. Joan writes through a veil of fiction about another girl named Joan who is tall, beautiful, older than her peers, and has trouble reading. For the first time, the teacher comes to understand the full force of the girl's insecurity and embarrassment and uses a conference to bolster her confidence.

• • •

Drake comes into class one day and tells his teacher that he is "upset and depressed." It turns out to be the anniversary of the death of an older brother, a difficult tragedy for Drake and his family. Drake seems to be carrying a special burden. His writing is filled with superheroes and fantasy characters, narratives of power and escape. When you ask him to write about something real, he writes "I was at the book store yesterday. It has a great comic book section . . ." and he is off describing superheroes again. The teacher wonders whether the fantasy writing offers therapeutic escape or whether the boy should be encouraged to write directly about his feelings and experiences.

• • •

Malcolm was having trouble with his writing. He could not construct any sentences on his own, even with lots of help and

The teacher as student

The teacher reads the student's writing and listens to learn about the student's world and experiences.

Student as teacher

Student as person

Student as writer

The teacher as parent

The teacher works with the student to make the writing possible.

The teacher as editor

The teacher confers with the student in order to improve the writing.

encouragement. He could copy a sentence if I wrote it on the board, but that was it. At times, when other students were writing, Malcolm would be drawing. His drawings would illustrate the lesson. One day I brought in a collection of color slides to test students' ability to observe and describe. There were photos of clowns, circus performers, children, and hot air balloons. Malcolm was very excited by this exercise. He knelt on his chair and responded to almost every question. He saw things in the pictures that few other students could see. He noticed contrasts of colors, textures, small details, and ironic juxtapositions. He could not write a story for the class newspaper, but he drew a beautiful picture for the cover. When the paper was published, ninety students cheered and applauded Malcolm for his work. At the end of the school year, Malcolm received an award for his artistic ability. He had also begun dictating poems and stories that other children wrote down and he copied.

• • •

Mary writes the story of how her father died three years ago on Christmas Eve. The teacher comes to realize how deeply the child has been affected by this event.

• • •

Keith concludes a short story about his mother with the sentence, "I hope she lives forever"—the day before his mother is hospitalized from an overdose of sleeping pills.

• • •

Michele was playing with her friend Janet when Janet ran out into the street and was struck by a truck. The girl was killed instantly and Michele had to run and tell Janet's grandmother the terrible news. A picture of a distraught Michele appeared in the newspaper the next day. The day was a nightmare for Michele, who wound up in tears when curious students demanded to know all about the accident.

I was surprised months later when, without encouragement, Michele chose to write about the incident. She included a news clipping about the accident to hammer home the details and explained in her own words what happened in simple, direct, and poignant prose:

My Best Friend Died •
By Michele West
One day on the way home we were walking on the sidewalk. We decided to cross the street. Janet crossed the street. She wasn't

supposed to cross the street. I was watching her cross. A truck was going so fast. I saw her get hit. I said "She's hit!" My sister ran home. I went to her grandmother and told her about Janet. She was really scared. I was just shaking. My sister and brother were screaming. That day we had a police officer ask us how the accident happened. I told the police officer that the truck was going over the speed limit. The next day was Friday. We woke up, got dressed and ate breakfast. We read the newspaper. Our picture was in the paper. We went to school. We had a very sad day.

In a conference, I asked Michele, "Is there anything else you can tell me about the accident? It must have been terrible for you."

"I don't think I can," she said.

So be it. I understood that her plain, understated narrative was her way of dealing with the tragedy, of expressing her sadness, and of making it part of her personal history.

Even when the world seems most sinister and threatening, children take control of it through their writing, as when Glenda writes about "A Strange Man":

A long time ago I was going over to my friend's house at 7 o'clock p.m. On the way I saw a man and he said, "Do you know where Maximo Middle School is?" I said "No, I don't know where it is." Then he said, "Do you want to look on my map?" "Well, OK, if you get it out." Well I showed him where it was, but he grabbed me! So I kicked him in the leg and he let go of me, and I ran for it, I ran all the way home. I told my mom what happened, and my mom asked me a lot of questions. I answered all of them. My mom had called the police station. The next minute mom said, "I love you and nothing is going to hurt you!"

Most of the daily writing of students does not concern matters of life and death, but describes the normal anxieties and problems of being in the fifth grade. Nichole writes:

It was the first day of school. I brought things for my friends and when I stopped bringing the stuff, they started floating away. Well, I can't depend on my friends. I am the only person I can depend on. Take my advice, do not get best friends because when you try to do something, you just will get disappointed.

Well, the next day, it seemed like I didn't even meet anyone. I said I would never be bringing things again. If we could not be friends just because I did not bring things, I don't need them.

When I bring things, I don't know they're just not being true friends. I don't need them. So everyday when I come to school I just sit down. Maybe I'll get a good friend that will like me, not for the things that I bring.

Through these stories students hear the sound of their own voices on the page and learn the value of their feelings and experiences. Writing becomes a process of self-discovery.

Mrs. Driver was pleased when Cory came into class excited about a Sea Food Festival he had attended. Cory's oral story was filled with sights, sounds, and smells, the crisp details of an effective narrative. Yet, when it came time to write, he produced a routine story about his friend. He could not yet create his own voice on the page. He did not yet believe that he could develop an interesting written narrative out of his own experience.

To overcome this reticence, teachers can work in conference, receiving information from students about their experience, offering praise and encouragement, and getting them to feel comfortable with the sound of their voices on the page. When a student finds his voice through his writing, it can come off the page loud and clear, teaching all sorts of things about the student's values.

Trent is a bright and personable student from a family that has had to work hard to make it. His parents have taught Trent the lessons of industriousness. That was brought home to me when Trent wrote a response to the famous letter of eight-year-old Virginia wondering if there was a Santa Claus. I had read Virginia's letter to the students and asked them to respond.

Trent told Virginia flat out that Santa Claus was only make-believe and then apologized for his candor. He explained, "The reason why I don't want you to believe in Santa Claus is you might think you don't have to work or earn money. But you do."

The weakest students are the ones who most desperately need to discover the value of their own voices in their writing. I spent two weeks teaching a group of sixth graders who had been grouped together at the "basic skills" level. The group referred to itself as "the dumb class."

I am uncomfortable with the grouping of students according to skill level in a writing class. I prefer a group of diverse students, a class where stronger students can be taught to help weaker ones. Collaboration benefits the weak and the strong.

Students in the "dumb" class had low expectations of themselves and distrusted me at first. They seemed beaten down and demoralized. They did not laugh at my jokes. I saw a look of collective hopelessness on their faces.

When I asked them about their writing, many answered in

one-word responses and spoke so softly they could not be heard. Some students wrote their names in the tiniest script as if they were trying to hide their identities in the farthest reaches of the paper. Their body language was defensive. They were trying to protect themselves from me. Over the years they had developed sophisticated strategies for avoiding teacher scrutiny.

I tried to break through these barriers by being unshakably positive and optimistic in my response to their work. I told them that at the end of two weeks, each student would have written the best story of his or her life, published it in a class booklet, and read it aloud in front of the principal. They looked at me as if I were a wild-eyed used car salesman.

In two days we began to learn, through the writing, that there were many different paths into the dumb class: learning disability, physical illness, social disadvantage, and unsettled home lives.

Chester wrote about his fragile health:

I was born on the 21st of November, the year of 1969 at 10:35 a.m. It was on a Friday. I didn't get to go home for 2 weeks because I had breathing trouble. Finally I got to go home when I was 4 weeks old. My mom had to flip me on the end of my foot so if I stopped I could start breathing.

I had epilepsy from the time I was 2 till I was 9 years old. I was really scared cause I didn't know what medicine I was taking. My mom told me to take it so I did. The day I stopped was Wednesday, February 23rd, 1978. How I remember so well is that it was like a special day for me. My mom came in and told me I didn't have to take the medicine any more. I jumped up and gave my mom a hug and said "Ya."

When Chester's teacher read this story, she looked up and said, "Now I understand."

Another student seemed fairly bright but often looked lethargic and scored poorly on standardized tests. I began to understand why when I read her story:

On October 17, 1971, I was born. It all began the 3rd week of October that my doctor told my mom and dad that I was going to die. The doctor told my mom and dad that I had two holes in my heart.

One day while my dad was at work, my mom took me and my sister shopping. After shopping we went home. On the way home this drunk man was driving down the road and hit my mom's car. It killed my mom, but my sister and I were OK. Now I'm adopted and so is my sister. My sister is 13 and I am 12.

Many students have personal histories that are strong impediments to learning, emotional health, and maturity. When we test them for proficiencies and basic skills, we may fail to consider the needs of the whole person. We see 1, 2, or 3 on the stanine scores and stick the kid in the dumb class.

The great moments for teachers of writing come when students turn personal tragedy into triumphant stories that enlighten the mind and lift the spirit. Such a story comes from a tiny, quiet girl, only three years in America at the time of the writing. Published in the *St. Petersburg Times*, her story revealed to thousands of readers the good that comes from the freedom to write:

A Child's Escape to Freedom •

By Phonephet Xayavong, eighth grade

I remember the night we left our country. That night, I experienced a nightmare that I won't forget for the rest of my life.

My journey from Laos to the United States was very long, dangerous, and unforgettable. It took us about a year to get here.

Laos is a small country in Southeast Asia. It is surrounded by Thailand, China, Vietnam and Cambodia. In 1975, the Communists took over Laos. Many Laotians were afraid of them, so they tried to escape.

It was August 1980. After my parents, brothers, and I had discussed for several weeks about escaping from Laos, we finally reached the decision.

The reason we risked our lives was because we were seeking freedom. We don't like communism and business was slow. My father was the boss of the sawlumber company and my mother owned a small store.

My parents also wanted my brothers and me to have more education and to have a better life. In Laos, we learned only what the communists wanted us to learn. They also could come into our house at any time and take whatever they wanted. Our lives were in their hands.

They could come up, accuse us of something, and then arrest us. However, these things had never happened to us because we lived in the city. It only happened to the people who lived outside the city.

Many people escaped and were killed by the guards. Only about 60% of them survived. Each morning, there was news about more people being killed.

There are five members in my family. My big brother was about 13 years old and my little brother was about 4. I was about 10, so we didn't really know what was going on. My little brother thought we were going on a trip.

The night we left was very dark and there wasn't a single star in the sky. We walked quietly and slowly into the dangerous forest, trying not to make a sound because it could mean death to all of us. Our hearts were tumbling because if the guard saw us, they might kill us or put us in jail for the rest of our lives.

Suddenly, we heard footsteps coming closer to us. Our hearts were pounding harder and harder and our faces turned white. We quickly hid behind big trees and thick bushes. The only thing that was on our minds at that time was fear. Fear of being caught.

We tried to be calm. In our minds, we could see thousands of guns pointing at us and ready to fire at any time. My hands and legs were shaking although at that time I was very little and didn't realize what death is like. We were so scared.

After a while, the two night guards walked past us without noticing us at all. We were so relieved that we felt like screaming. However, we still knew that danger was within a mile.

We walked nervously to the small boat near the water. We pushed the boat into the river and got in. Quickly, we sailed across the Mwkong River.

I looked back once more at my country. The country I once loved and trusted, once full of beauty, now full of evil. The homeland that I was born and grew up in. Once I left it, I knew I wouldn't be able to see it again.

I looked forward and saw my dream of starting a new life in America grow warm. Then, I fell asleep.

When I awoke the next morning, we were at the Thai Police Station. They asked us many questions and then sent us to a refugee camp. We stayed there about six months. In between that time we were interviewed many times. Each time was very hard. If we failed it, we would have to start all over again. If a family was suspected of being Thai, the members weren't allowed to go to America.

We had to tell the truth about everything the interviewers asked. We also had to remember what we told them the first time and then we had to tell them the same thing ever after. They had a record of everything we said.

When we passed all the interviews, we were sent to the concentration camp in the Phillipines. There, we learned what life is like in the United States. When five months had finally ended, we were very anxious to come to America.

We came to San Francisco by plane. We stayed there for two nights. Then, in July 1981 we came to Florida.

Through their writing, students give teachers a chance to learn about them as persons. When we confer, we say to each student: "I care about you and what you have to say. Tell me more about what you know. I trust you to improve your work." It may be the first time in their lives students have ever heard that.

Chapter Sixteen

Celebrate Student Writing

She was a teacher of English in a south Florida high school, in her early thirties, friendly and articulate. We met at a dinner party on a Friday evening. That morning I had taught writing to a class of thirty students, and the high of that experience carried me into the evening's conversation.

I found myself bragging about the stories my students had written, marveling at how productive they had been that day and confident that I was finally doing things right. I was probably overdoing it, at least that was the impression she gave me.

"If you got them to write for fifteen minutes, you were lucky," she said.

"Oh, I don't know, I think there are ways you can get students to write every day."

"It's impossible."

She taught at a supposedly good high school in an affluent community, where we might expect students to be high achievers. Yet she discussed her students in the most negative and bitter terms. They were discipline problems. It was impossible to teach them anything.

I felt anger and then sorrow.

My anger was over the persistent negativism of this teacher. What must it be like to be one of her students? Would she assume that I, too, could not learn? Would she never give me a chance to write because it was "impossible" for me to succeed?

My sorrow was over her unwillingness to see her own predicament. If her current method of teaching led only to frustration and bitterness, why not open herself to something new? What was there to lose?

As she ranted on about her students, I thought of teachers of writing who were enthusiastic about their work, who shared their sense of excitement with others, and who were always bragging about the work of their students. What I loved about these teachers is that they were always willing to be surprised by a weak student who suddenly, through writing, caught fire.

I sensed at that moment that there are two schools of contemporary teaching: the School of Hope and the School of Despair. Most teachers of writing wind up in the School of Hope because they come to see possibility where others see failure. They come to know students more personally through their writing and share in the little triumphs that keep them optimistic. It is rare to see a teacher from the School of Hope become a burn-out case. There are too many challenges, chances to change children's lives for the better, opportunities to show good example to other teachers.

The good news is that teachers can be saved from the School of Despair. The door of salvation is the teaching of writing, but to enter through it the frustrated teacher must experience the equivalent of a religious conversion, one borne out of years of dissatisfaction and wandering.

I am not using the religious imagery of the last paragraph frivolously. I am talking realistically about the chance for teachers to be renewed in their profession, to be happy in the accomplishments of their students, and most of all, to see themselves as part of a profession dedicated to the love and nurturing of children.

That is why I am devoting this chapter to a celebration of student writing. Each story represents the best work of the student in a particular year, the kind of work students and teachers should be proud to display in class booklets or school newspapers.

Readers are invited to analyze each story, to list the story's strengths and weaknesses, and to consider conference strategies that might help the student make the story better.

● ● ●

New York, New York •
By Alison Clark (fourth grade)

The morning I went to New York I was excited. When I
got on the airplane I had a nervous stomach. I got a little
sick. The breakfast they served wasn't my favorite thing,
but I survived. But there was something good about it, I
met Vitas Gerulaitis.

My grandma and grandpa were looking good. The
first night I was in New York I saw a play called Godspell.
It was sad, funny, good in a mixture all together. I got
three autographs from Jesus, John the Baptist and from
the director.

The second day I was there I went to a place called
Hick's Nursery. It was full of bright and beautiful Christmas trees. There was a Christmas mouse and lots of
other things.

That night I went out for ice cream and bought
something for my sister Emily.

On Saturday it was my big day. I went to New York
City! Saturday was pretty cold. First I went to the Museum
of Natural History. It was interesting and pretty and a
little scary because of the dinosaurs. Then I went on the
World Trade Center. It was taller than the Empire State
Building! It was very expensive and pretty. It took 56 seconds to get to the 107 floor. Do you believe the men
"had" to wear dinner coats!

After that I went to my Uncle Pete's house. I saw my
cousin Teresa and cousin Peter. When we got home I was
tired. I slept like a baby! Sunday morning I got ready to
go. But before I went, I went to see Mary and Pat Cregan.
Pat gave me some perfume called Timeless.

Then it was time to come back to Florida. When we
got on the airplane the generator broke down. I was a
little scared. I got over it. They had very good food and
we had a safe trip back. The first thing I did when I got
home was hugged my mom. It was good to be home.

(The journey is one of the most reliable story forms for children.
The trip offers the weight of its own chronology to the student
and the details fall in an order that seems natural to both writer
and reader. I was especially proud of the details in this story:
the anecdote about *Godspell*, the time it took to reach the top
of the World Trade Center, and the name of the perfume. When

children write about their travels, the journey itself is sealed in their memory in a new, more profound way.)

• • •

What It's Like to Be a Shoe •
By Leilani Anderson (fourth grade)

My name is Nike. I'm a sneaker. Do you know what a hard life a shoe has? Well, if you don't and even if you do, let me tell you from a shoe's point of view.

When I first left the store, I was bright, young, and happy. I didn't even know what it was like having a foot in me. The first time I got put on it felt weird. But then I got used to it, but that was only the beginning of being uncomfortable.

Then the foot went outside. He was running and jumping. I felt like I was going to tear. Fortunately I didn't. I got so dirty that his mom threw me in the washing machine. If you only knew what it's like to be thrown, after being hit and after feeling the sunbaked sidewalk through the bottom of you, you would know why I was so mad.

If people only knew that sneakers breathe air not water, they wouldn't throw us in the wash. I had a hard enough time staying on top of the water. Especially when the clothes are pulling you under the water while they pull and swish from side to side.

Being in the wash was bad, but when they try to hang you on the clothesline it's even worse. They try to hang you. After a half an hour passes and you fall they try to hang you again. Those clothpins pinch, you know.

After a while you get holes. Then they use you so much that you get stained. Then they put bleach on you. Do you know how much that stuff stinks! Then you lose your color.

Then finally they leave you in the closet. Now they only use you for clamming so their feet don't get cut up but we do instead.

Now that you know what a hard life a shoe has, please be more careful with what you do with us.

Sneakers have hard lives.
The End

(This story grew out of an exercise in point of view and personification. Students were asked to see the world from the perspective of an inanimate object. While the resulting story is fiction, it grows out of Leilani's real-life observation and her thinking about the plight of the average shoe.)

• • •

My Funny Dream •
By Regina McGrew (fourth grade)

I was six-years-old and often thought about animals before going to sleep. Well, I guess my brain was telling me to think about pigs because that's exactly what I was doing. "It's fun to think about pigs," I said in a soft voice. After thinking about pigs for quite a while my eyes grew heavier and heavier and I soon fell asleep.

My dream had started sometime later. I was in a dark room lying in a soft bed. All of a sudden pigs started to jump and play around me. I was very scared and tried to scream but only a squeak came out. Then there was this big hog licking at my legs like I was its Thanksgiving dinner. I tried to scream again and nothing came out. It moved to my head. It was licking all over my face. It must have weighed 800 pounds because when I tried to push it, it wouldn't budge. Then I saw my mother and father. I knew it was them but when I yelled for help they laughed. The wet, sticky, smelly tongue was now licking at my arms. I couldn't stand being licked any longer so I pulled at its ears until it jumped off of the bed. I jumped up and ran for the door. It wouldn't open. So I looked around and spotted a window. It was locked. I unlocked it and jumped out of the two story house. Luckily, I fell into a pool. Ouch! When I landed in the pool it felt like I had fallen on rocks. I was hurting all over.

Then I was awakened by the barking of my dog Sheba. My back was still hurting. I noticed I had fallen out of bed. I got up to get into bed and saw that I had fallen on a couple of toys. "That explains the rocks," I said to my dog.

(When children write about their dreams, they write about real things in imaginative ways. The comic narrative of Regina's dream grows out of an introduction that prepares us for the dream itself and a conclusion that brings us back to reality. Vivid language helps us vicariously experience the dream with Regina.)

• • •

My Experience at the Dali Museum •
By Michael Serbanos (fourth grade)

One day, for the first time ever, the Dali Museum chose thirty kids from the gifted program, not adults, to be docents. (A docent is someone who tells about an object in a museum to a group.) I was one of them.

The Dali Museum is a museum of art created by a man named Salvador Dali who lives in Spain. His art came mostly from his mind. He had a wife named Gala who died three years ago. Dali is around 75 and is very sick, weighing only 90 pounds. He's been heartbroken since Gala died.

On December 17, 1982, I was allowed to tell about the painting entitled "Slave Market With the Disappearing Bust of Voltaire." Before this, I had learned about the painting from adult docents of the Dali Museum once a week for three weeks. We learned at the Museum. Then I received a speech that I could switch around. My choice was to switch it around.

This painting is interesting because it is a double image. There seems to be a hidden face of Voltaire. Also because there is a plum and a pear and the plum becomes the bottom of a man. The pear becomes part of a distant hill in the painting.

Channel 8, the St. Pete Times, and the T.V. show Black Forum were there on December 17. I was interviewed by all of them. That night I was on Channel 8 and on Monday there was a paragraph on me in the Times newspaper. This was an interesting, exciting, and a learning experience for me.

(Michael is an efficient collector of information and a clear writer. He takes advantage of his interesting experience and converts it into a story with lots of information about the museum and his adventure there.)

• • •

My Hearing Aids •
By Lydia Abrams (fourth grade)

I have something in each ear that is called a hearing aid. Hearing aids are electronic mechanisms. Most of a hearing aid is brown, the plastic parts are called ear molds and tubes. I have to wear them every day because I was born with a hearing loss.

Every time something gets close to my hearing aid, and it is switched on, it will sound like a beep. I take off my hearing aids when I go to bed. If I don't, they will beep when I lean on my pillow.

My hearing aids will break easily if you drop or get them wet. So, I take them off when I go to the pool, go to the beach, when I take a bath, and when I take a shower.

I like and don't like hearing aids. The reason I don't like hearing aids is because I am different and other children tease me, and they ask me what hearing aids are over and over again. I like them because I am special when I'm different, and when it gets noisy I get to switch them off.

My father is an Audiologist. An Audiologist is an ear doctor. My dad knows everything about hearing aids! He can fix them if they are screwed up.

I think hearing aids are wonderful. Hearing aids seem special and different to me. I think they are wonderful because they help me hear. If I didn't have them, life would be silence and dark inside me. You might feel the same if you had them.

The End

(Lydia came into class wanting to write about rainbows and unicorns but became quickly convinced that she could tap into her own rich experience. This story reveals much of her character—intelligent, sensitive, confident, with a good sense of humor. The story has voice; it creates the illusion that the writer is speaking directly to the reader from the page.)

• • •

My Day of Shark Fishing •
By Kristin Klinkenberg (fifth grade)

This summer my family spent our vacation at the Keys. We stayed in a crowded hotel room at the Marina Resort. There were only two beds and two cots but we had six people so I ended up sleeping with my 3 yr. old sister. It was very hard to sleep because the air-conditioner kept breaking down. When I finally started falling asleep, my sister would start slurping on her thumb.

The next day we were all up early because we were going shark fishing. First we went to a bait store and bought live shrimp to catch barracuda which we used for shark bait. We caught five barracuda.

Once we got to the bridge, we cut up the barracuda and put a piece of it on the hook. Dad casted it out. We waited and finally a shark came. I got a huge tug. The shark that was on started swimming out. "Hold your pole up!" someone yelled.

The shark was brown and three feet long. It was a nurse shark. I think it's called a nurse shark because its head is wide and shaped like a nurse's cap.

Dad walked under the bridge with a camera in one hand. He unhooked the hook with pliers and took a picture of me holding it. Afterwards we fished for snapper which we'd have for dinner.

About half of our vacation, we went to Miami to spend the rest of vacation with Grandma. She is always glad to see us. Grandma lives on a canal called Granada Canal. There used to be a 14 foot alligator in the canal, but in May the Florida Game Commission killed it because it was out of hand. We went fishing, and when we got hot we jumped in the pool.

The next day Dad took us to the Miami Seaquarium. We saw a tank full of manatees. We also saw a whale and sea lion show. We saw Flipper, the dolphin who used to be on the T.V. show.

I would have to say my vacation was the best vacation ever!

(One of the great clichéd assignments of writing class is "What I Did On My Summer Vacation." Kristin shows that such a topic need not be dull. The daughter of outdoors writer Jeff Klinkenberg,

Kristin organizes her story around Florida wildlife: the barracuda, the shark, the alligator, and the dolphin.)

• • •

Living Construction •
By Dalia Baseman (fifth grade)

My first floor is multi-colored, reminding me of the song that was sung to me while I was fed baby-food. I loved the soft mass of colors on my spoon. When I got candy I said "yucky" Dalia, instead of "lucky."

The second story is pure white with black spots, the color of the cupcakes Mom made for my birthday. I took them to nursery-school. I remember the very familiar song, "Happy Birthday," sung out of tune in young, childish voices.

Third floor is a gaudy, light yellow. That's the color of my old plastic baseball bat. I can still hear the crack of the bat connecting with the ball, for a single second, before the ball whizzed past two houses. Before my Dad would shout, "Beautiful shot, babe." Before Mom called us in for dinner.

Down the next stairway the walls and floor are gray. The color of the faded, old pictures of Mom, with her bouffant hairdo, Dad's funny-looking old glasses, my sister's baby pictures, and my baby pictures. I loved looking at them.

Now, on the next story, the rooms are painted blood red. Bloody, from the fall I had while I was roller-skating. We were playing follow-the-leader down a driveway. I turned the wrong way and before I could hold on to something, I fell. I had bit thorough my lower lip and my two front teeth had moved forward. I needed braces on them for a month.

My last floor is silver and brown. These colors represent my braces and glasses that I wish I didn't have or need. My braces hurt sometimes and make you feel like you're carrying a hardware store. My glasses are different but are just as much of a problem. I wish I didn't have them.

(This story/poem was inspired by poet Jason Bell. He asked the children to picture their lives as a building, with each story of the building telling a different story. The first floor would be a memory from early childhood and the top floor a recent memory or feeling. This turns out to be an excellent strategy for brain-storming story ideas. Each mini-story can be elaborated on in a different context.)

• • •

Two Hours 35 Minutes to Florida •
By Hallie Shapiro (fifth grade)

I got on the plane and looked for a seat in the front. No such luck. I looked around. It sure was crowded. Finally I saw an empty seat. I asked, "Anyone sitting here?" "No," came the answer. I sat down. I couldn't wait to see Heidi and her family. Then I saw the baby.

"Oh no," I groaned to myself. "A plane ride of $2\frac{1}{2}$ hours next to a baby! As if getting up at 4:30 AM isn't enough! Oh, well," I got out my flight pass and money.

"Hello," said the man next to me.

"Hi," I said with as big a smile as my face would allow.

"Sarah, what's the matter, do you need to be changed?" I figured the guy wasn't talking to his wife, so the baby's name must be Sarah.

Sarah's mom removed the diaper and said "You're right."

Boy was he right!! (Phew)

"What's your name?" the man asked.

"Hallie," I answered. "How old is Sarah?"

"Around 6 months old," he said.

"Welcome to Flight 275 to Florida. We expect to have a smooth flight. We should arrive around 8:35 AM. I'd like to introduce you to the flight attendants, Blah Blah in the middle. . . . . . ."

When the pilot was through talking, I settled back in my seat.

"Sarah, say hi to Hallie," said her dad. "Daruh," said Sarah. I just smiled. Sarah stared at me and smiled back for a while. She was cute and chubby. She had no teeth.

She stopped staring when her father took a blanket out of a bag and placed both baby and blanket on his knee. He started to sing the Barichu, an old Jewish prayer. He sang softly, and she was soon fast asleep on his lap.

When the stewardess with the pay cart came Sarah woke up. I paid for my ticket first. The stewardess said "Have a good flight." Then Sarah's parents paid. When the food cart stopped by us I bought Orange juice. Sarah's parents bought Apple juice. Yuck. Everywhere I see a baby I see Apple juice!

I took out my squashed, crumbly, gross looking corn muffin. Sarah reached her hand towards me and said "Du."

Her father saw the muffin and asked, "Wanta straw?"

"Hah, Hah," was my brilliant reply.

We ate in silence. Actually, I drank.

The rest of the trip was boring so I'll skip to the end.

At 8:28 AM the pilot said, "We are going to arrive in 17 or 18 minutes, at about 8:45 AM."

Amazing! We landed at exactly 8:45 AM! To myself I said, "Hello, Florida!" To Sarah and her parents I said, "Goodbye! Have a nice time." They said the same.

I grabbed my bag. As I stepped off the plane the pilot said goodbye to me and a lady. I waved as I looked for the Kluesses.

(Once again the trip provides the structure for an interesting student narrative. The time on the plane provides Hallie with the chronology she needs. But most of the story derives from a sophisticated use of dialogue. The conversations, flavored by Hallie's sarcastic asides, create the humor which makes this piece a delight.)

● ● ●

A Day in the Life of an Overworked Boy •
By Clark Blomquist (fifth grade)

It was that dreaded kind of day. A hot, boring, T.V. day. "Gilligan's Island," "The Flintstones," and "The Price is Right" comforted me, but I knew what would be asked of me sooner or later—most likely, sooner. I was right.

My mom casually walked over to the sofa I so comfortably sat upon and said those immortal words, "Mow the lawn."

"Me, mow the lawn?" I knew the answer.

I slowly left my beloved couch and headed for the garage. There it was, the lawn mower. I pushed the primer a few times and switched the knob from Off to

High. Then, I reached for the cord. Many a time I had not been able to start the mower—at a younger age, of course. What an embarrassment it would be if I had to ask my mom for assistance now.

I yanked the cord with all my might and started the mechanical monster.

A feeling of fear crept up on me. Could I beat this lawn? Was it too tough for me? I pondered the idea for a minute or two. I could do it! I could do it! I knew I could do it!

I charged the yard and mowed down eight consecutive rows. Hurray! But on number nine, I froze. A wasp!

Memories of wasps buzzed through my mind. When I was very young, I was stung by a wasp on the bottom lip. After that, I'd always stayed away from all bees, hornets, and wasps.

I pushed the mower forward with tremendous speed, not stopping to look back. When I returned, the wasp was gone.

After the incident with the wasp, I thought everything would go smoothly. Nothing could go wrong now. I sure was mistaken! With eleven rows to go, the mower stopped. After a quick check, I discovered that the mower was merely out of fuel. No problem. I filled it up and returned to the lawn.

After interruptions, danger, and buckets of sweat, I was done. I quickly ran into the house and listened to the fizz bubble up out of the Coke bottle. Music to my ears!

(Clark weaves a wonderful little story out of the threads of ordinary experience. What happens, after all? He watches TV, is asked to mow the lawn, has trouble starting it, goes by a wasp, runs out of gas, and gets himself a Coke. Nothing very dramatic. But the tale has a Tom Sawyer quality to it, a wise innocence communicated in a likable voice.)

● ● ●

Backstroke •
By Lisa Denner (fifth grade)

"Swimmers! In the water!" I jumped into the pool and gripped the bar with my hands and held on tight. My toes hugged the gutter. Four other swimmers did the same.

"Take your mark!" I pulled myself up to the bar. "Go!" Five swimmers sprang off the blocks. I could hear my name being shouted. The water felt good but I kept going.

I looked across the pool and found that so far I was first. I could see the second set of backstroke flags coming up and I pulled harder. I did my back fly-turn, hit my head on the wall and lost time. I kept going. I had never gone as fast as I did that day. I could still hear my team cheering for me. I thought I could make a first. I could see the backstroke flags nearing again. I kept going. I counted the strokes. Five, six, seven, eight. My hand touched the wall. I came in third place.

"You did great, Lisa! What place did you get? Second?" my mom asked. "Third," I said reaching for a towel. People were beginning to leave Northwest Pool even though the meet was only half over. "It was fun," I said wrapping the towel around me.

(Athletic events provide young writers with opportunities for description, suspense, and dramatic narrative. Lisa does not waste the reader's time. The action starts with the first sentence and builds through the tightly organized story.)

● ● ●

Down in the Dirt •
By Shad Mullins (fifth grade)

One morning when I was in second grade, I was running late for school. I jumped out of bed, put on some clothes and asked my mom if I could ride my bike. She said, "Yes, be careful." I got on my bike and raced for school.

Today was the same as every other day, very boring. When I got to my bike after school let out, the bike racks were crowded. Then I saw Jody Nicholas walking to her mom's car. Jody has blue eyes and blond hair and is very smart. She also makes the A-B Honor Roll.

I unlocked my bike and started riding towards the patrol. On the way I said "Hi" and she said "Hi" back to me. Then I pulled a wheelie. I was riding it very far when all of a sudden my back tire hit a big rock. "Oh, no!" I said to myself and before I knew it I was down in the dirt. I picked up my bike, brushed the sand off of me, and started riding off as fast as I could.

When I got home, I put up my bike and went in my room. I lay down in my bed and thought about what happened. Boy, I felt embarrassed.

The next morning when I woke up, my mom asked, "Are you riding your bike today?" I answered, "No way."

(Shad's embarrassing moment results in a short, tight narrative in which few words are wasted. The lead introduces the bike, a key object in Shad's downfall. The paragraph introducing the little blond girl nicely sets up Shad's trick ride to impress her. The ending echoes the lead, adding a bit of humor as a reward for the reader.)

• • •

Grandpa's Death •
By Rebecca Barrett (fifth grade)

November, 1984. I came home from Nature Trail to a sad, gloomy house. "What's wrong?" I asked. Daddy motioned for me to sit on his lap. "Honey, Grampa's dead." Silence. Then a yell, my yell. A scream of pain from inside me. I asked how and I'm told that he was driving somewhere last night and bumped his head. He became unconscious. He was on a bridge and went right off it. He was killed instantly because of the way he bumped his head.

November, two days later. We are pulling into the funeral hall. We go inside. We have second row seats, but we don't immediately sit down. I go and stand up by Grandpa's body with my family. I go back to the car and get the flower I got him. I loved him very much. I go back inside, and put the flower on him. I do it very carefully. It is a rose. I am very, very sad.

November, same day, after the funeral. Everyone meets at our house. We have punch and hors d'oeuvres. Everyone seems happy, including me. But I know we aren't. But then I think back to the happy memories, about the things he got me, the places we went, especially the time we went to Texas. Then I realize someone is talking to me. It is my Aunt Patty. She had come over to ask me if I wanted to spend the night. I ask Ma if I can, and she says yes. So I go. But through the night I am restless. I always wondered what it was like to have a loved one die ... and now I know.

(Writing permits children to share with teachers and other students their feelings and experiences. In this story, Rebecca reveals the depth of her affection for her grandfather and her sadness at his death. Her use of the present tense invites readers to share in the immediacy of her suffering. And yet the piece is never maudlin. Her story balances the sad experience of the funeral with her happy memories of life with her grandfather.)

• • •

The Blue Heron Who Struck Oil •
By Amanda Tantum (fifth grade)

Ralph Heath from the Suncoast Seabird Sanctuary came to visit our class. He told us many of his seabird and land-bird rescues. My favorite rescue was about a blue heron who struck oil.

One day a vet in Dallas, Texas, phoned Ralph. He said a lady brought in a blue heron covered from the tip of his head to the tip of his claws in oil. The vet said the blue heron was walking along an alley and while investigating a vat of oil, fell in. The vet told Ralph that he had seen him on 20/20, a television show, and thought he could tell him how to clean the bird.

Ralph explained how he should clean the bird. He told the vet to wash the blue heron. Once more. Again. Again. Again and many more times to get all the oil from his feathers. The vet used a special soap for washing its feathers and a clean rag for his beak. Ointment was put in his eyes again and again.

After the bird was cleaned, he was set free. The vet, the lady, and Ralph Heath were happy that the bird was saved, but happiest of all was the blue heron.

(Ralph Heath, a world-famous rescuer of injured seabirds, visited our class to share his many adventures with the children. He spoke quickly in rapid-fire anecdotes. Many children found it difficult to keep up with him. Amanda solved the problem through selectivity and focus. She does not attempt to recount all the high points in Ralph Heath's illustrious career. Instead, she focuses on one good story that says much about Heath's work.)

• • •

Our Chinese Friends •
By Amit Rajadhyaksha (sixth grade)

We were told in Writers' Camp that it is a tradition for visitors to come so we could interview them during their visits.

But in the last three years of Writers' Camp, no one has come farther than this group of Chinese delegates from Peking, China.

As they came in one by one, we were all in awe! I asked myself,

"Could this be the group of the Chinese delegates?"

By golly joy! It was them.

As soon as they came in, representatives of the groups graciously led them to their groups side by side.

As soon as everyone was seated, we began asking them many interesting questions about the People's Republic of China.

One of the questions asked was,

"What is common between the United States and China?"

One of the delegates answered,

"China and the United States have a common desire for world peace, stability, and friendship."

Another question asked was,

"What is the Great Wall of China used for now?"

A delegate answered,

"The Great Wall is used to bring tourism in, instead of keeping it out!"

Still another question asked,

"Is there any specific kind of bamboo trees Panda bears eat?"

One of the delegates answered,

"Yes, there is only one specific kind of bamboo trees Panda bears can eat."

Soon enough our time was up with our Chinese friends. They had to go. I felt so sad they could not stay for some more time. But at least I received an autograph from one of my Chinese friends.

In such a short period of time, I had met a foreign friend.

Whenever I look at the autograph it reminds me of the flicker of the flame representing friendship between the United States and China.

(The students at a summer program called Writers' Camp had the rare opportunity in 1985 to interview five young politicians from the People's Republic of China who were touring the United States. Through a translator, students were able to ask questions about Chinese life, culture, and politics. Visitors to a writing class almost always inspire interesting stories. Amit shares with readers his special enthusiasm at meeting some new friends from the other side of the world.)

• • •

China •
By Shannon Tierney (fifth grade)

Have you ever wanted to live in China? In case you do, here are some facts about it.

China is probably one of the most crowded countries. One out of every four people live in China. It is also similar in some ways to the U.S.

The children start elementary school when they are six or seven and go for six years. They go three years for junior high and three years for high school. But most children do not get a chance to go to University. By 1990, they hope every politician will be a college graduate. In China all schools are free. The main subjects are math, Chinese and foreign languages which are Japanese, English, and French.

The Spring Festival is probably their most important holiday. They get new clothes, better food, and have family reunions. The second most important day is National Day. In 1949, there was a liberation where there was more freedom. The Spring Festival is like our Christmas, and their National Day is like our Fourth of July.

The government has contributed money to help the famine in Africa, and people have also contributed their own private donations.

Drugs are totally forbidden for young people and are very rare for adults.

The way that they punish young people is to limit their freedom. In a worse crime, all they do is study and work. But in a felony, first they work and then they are sentenced to prison.

The Great Wall of China is a lot like our Statue of Liberty. They are both being fixed up to look better and be safer. The Great Wall is 3,000 miles long and 2,000 years old and it's the only man-made thing able to be seen from outer space. At first it was used to keep people out, now it's used to get people in.

Chinese pets are mainly dogs, cats, and pigeons. The way they name them is by number!

They have many parks which they name "pioneer houses." On holidays they stay there where they have food and utilities. They split up in groups which are sports, management, and study. Michael Jackson is popular. The Chinese politicians that visited loved the Space Mountain at Disney World.

They do have writing skills classes for elementary and high school called training classes.

China is still trying to protect the giant panda but it is hard because the bamboo they eat is a very rare kind. The other countries are also helping. China is very grateful for the U.S.A. helping.

The reason I learned all of this is that on July 30, 1985, five Chinese politicians (one speaking English) came to visit Writers' Camp. The men and woman said,

"Chopsticks are easier to use, but it's better to use a fork with steak."

I wish if I ever get the chance that I could go to China!

(Two reporters may respond differently to the same event, and so it is with Amit, in the previous story, and Shannon. Amit emphasizes his personal reaction to the Chinese visitors, sharing with readers his excitement and anticipation. His story is about the visit. Shannon chooses to tell what she has learned about China. She has listened carefully, taken detailed notes, and written a story filled with information. Hearing two versions of the same event helps students judge the quality of their work and make plans for revision. Perhaps in subsequent drafts Amit might be inclined to add more hard information about China, and Shannon may decide to deal with the Chinese visitors as human characters. The visit provided teachers with an opportunity to discuss with students aspects of history, politics, and propaganda.)

• • •

It's Torture Going to the Dentist! •
By Heidi Kluess (sixth grade)

It was my third dentist appointment since I first got my braces. Every experience so far had been very painful. I was hoping this one wouldn't be.

My dad and I were walking up the cement walk to the braces dentist, as my brother calls him.

Then we finally got to the black-tinted door that had my dentist's name on it in small white letters. My dad opened the door and I sat on the couch while my dad checked me in.

I began to look around the familiar room full of magazine racks and many people with retainers and braces. But there was always one thing that caught my eye every visit and that was the plaster molds of other people's crooked teeth. I imagine he put them there for people who are nervous or bored to see that other people have more crooked teeth than they do.

Soon my name was called and I was shown into the bright yellow room with bright yellow dentist chairs and posters on the ceiling.

One of the ladies showed me to the second chair.

Then Dr. Kochenour, my dentist, came over to me. He asked the normal questions. How are you doing? Are you liking summer? Things like that. Then the torture started. He took out my bottom brace to recement it while my back teeth began to bleed.

I read every poster on the ceiling while I was waiting for him to finish cementing. My favorite poster was of a duck standing in water up to his ankles and the writing over in the corner of it said, "You can't be expected to skate through life if you don't get your feet wet."

Again the friendly looking brace Doctor smiled a metal grin as he leaned over me to force back in my recemented bottom brace. That part didn't hurt but when he widened my top brace, that hurt!

When I got home it hurt to do anything but breathe. The next day I could barely chew.

It's torture going to the dentist!

(Heidi tells a universal children's story: the torture of going to the dentist. She is alive to every detail of the visit, not only the physical discomfort, but also the details of the waiting room and the dentist's office. I especially like the perspective Heidi gives us from the patient's chair, the view of the dentist's metal grin and the duck poster on the ceiling.)

● ● ●

The Mosquito •
By Michael B. Nigels (sixth grade)

It was a hot and humid night. The bugs were tapping up against my bedroom window and the shadows were dancing along my wall. There I was, lying half asleep, when a buzzing sound brought me to consciousness. I quickly snapped open my eyes and waited for them to adjust to the darkness.

There it was, its huge round eyes peering at me through the darkness, its broad opaque wings flapping rapidly, its long straw-like mouth ready to bite. I panicked! Where was the bug spray when you needed it?

We sat staring eye to eye, my hand feeling along the windowsill for something to swat it with. Ah ha! There it was! My hand met up with the book I had been reading earlier. I reached up with my left hand to grasp the hardcover copy of J. R. R. Tolkien's *The Hobbit* when the buzzing became louder. I spun around just in time to see him coming right for me!

With the book in hand, I jumped up and gave a valiant swing, catching it in mid-air, stunning it. It landed on my foot. But I knew it was alive; its legs were still kicking. I lifted the book high above my head and brought it down five times as hard.

So there it lay on the ground. Its eyes no longer stared back, its wings no longer flapped, its mouth closed tight. And as I looked down in agony at my foot, I realized the mosquito wasn't all I hit!

(I love this little story because of its simplicity and humor. Michael takes advantage of a common experience, an attack by a pesky mosquito, and exaggerates in his description for comic effect. Although the writer makes this adventure seem larger than life, specific details, such as the title of the book, ground it in reality. Michael takes full advantage of the details he uses, especially the "hardcover copy" of the book that will prove fatal to the mosquito and painful to his foot.)

● ● ●

A Stitch in Time •
By Frank W. Witsil, III (seventh grade)

I didn't feel it at first, but after I saw the blood streaming down my arm I ran to the bathroom in pain. Bright red blood was dripping off my elbow in small drops and falling to the floor, hitting it with a splat.

I had been playing in the house, jumping around, like many 8 year old boys do. I fell into a carton of 8 Coca Cola bottles. One of the bottles broke under my weight and sent shattered glass everywhere. My arm went into a sharp and jagged end of the bottle, and my skin curled up. I didn't scream, yell or even cry. I have gotten hurt enough times to know that it would only make it worse. I just acted as if it were a little scratch, which led my parents to believe it was not serious.

My Mom was talking in the doorway to a neighbor, and Dad was very absorbed in a long distance telephone call in the library. When Mom heard the crash she came to see what was going on. Then she saw the blood and shattered glass, and she assisted me to the bathroom to help me clean up.

As I passed the library, Dad saw the blood on my arm. Mom figured Dad could probably bandage it up. My parents thought this was just another every day injury. I was scared. Blood was literally pouring down my arm. Mom grabbed a very cold compress and pressed it on my arm, and tried to get Dad off the phone. Although he knew I had been injured, he was talking long distance and he thought it was just a minor thing. He decided to finish the phone call first. It made me angry. I started yelling at him to get off the phone, and Mom did, too. What was seconds, seemed like hours. It was then, I guess, that he realized the urgency of my wound. Dad politely hung up the telephone and hurried over to take a look at my arm. When he saw it he looked at my Mom and said, "He will need stitches." Now I was really frightened, and Mom seemed to be even more shocked than I was. She was really upset. I had no idea what stitches were, except something to hold the skin together as a wound heals.

The neighbor's car was on the street just outside the door. It was still running because she was going to leave. She offered to take us to the hospital. We gladly accepted this offer.

In the car, on the way, Dad put direct pressure on my arm, pressing the compress hard against me. I began to relax a little as my Dad explained what would happen and what I should do. It was nothing like open heart surgery which I had imagined. Mom also calmed down slightly. Nearing the hospital my cut stopped bleeding.

In the hospital the doctor commended my parents for cleaning my wound and putting pressure on it. A nurse led me to a small room and told me to lay on the table because the doctor would be in soon. Dad went with me in the room and Mom stayed in the waiting room. I suppose she was too upset to see me get the stitches. Dad seemed to be under control the whole time. He was very calm and relaxed. When the doctor came in, he cleaned the wound again, just to make sure. Then, he used a needle of Novocain to decrease the pain. I thought it was pencil sized! Now, after he stuck the needle in my arm, he was ready. None of this hurt me badly, the needle felt like a brief poke. The doctor used black surgical thread and a small curved needle to sew up my arm. Even though I had been given Novocain, I could still feel the tugging of the thread pulling my skin. Eventually I had 12 stitches in my right forearm. When the doctor finished I sat up. I bent my elbow and inspected the stitches with my Dad. They looked something like an unraveled black sock. Later the doctor wrapped my arm in bandages, gauze, as he called it. He also gave me instructions to keep my arm clean, not to get it wet, and not move it around too much.

As we were about to leave, the doctor got a new surgical glove, blew it up like a balloon, and gave it to me. When Dad and I came out of the room I was happy because I had a real doctor's glove. Dad was relieved it was over. We walked out in the waiting room, Mom had calmed down, and I was all right.

(Frank writes straight dramatic narrative in chronological order. The action begins in the first paragraph and races breathlessly to the end. The vivid language and concrete descriptions force us to share in the pain and anxiety.)

● ● ●

The Library •
By Anita McDivitt (seventh grade)

It was one of those Saturdays when the sun was scorching hot, you feel tired and extremely bored. My house doesn't have air-conditioning so I also got unpleasantly sticky from the humidity. My mother was preparing to leave the house and go to the library. I asked if I could come along. She muttered under her breath a few words about me pestering her, but finally consented. I ran into my room, picked up my library card, and sped out to the car. I suddenly had what I call an anxiety attack. That's when I get hyper with excitement and expectations. Right then, anything was better than staying at home.

The library was not just a library to me. It was a palace of knowledge, and I was a knight ready to besiege it. Besides, it was cool and air-conditioned, and also very quiet. I had to get away from all the noise of the house.

It seemed that a million cars were driving down our small, unpopulated street. Also, our neighbor is eighteen and plays the radio incessantly, always blaring and shouting out at someone.

Mom got into the car and tried to start it. To our despair, the light on the dashboard lit up—check engine. Mom tried again, but to no avail. It was a new car, and mom cursed it, calling it a lemon on wheels and worse. We got out of the car, and mom went to call dad. All it needed was a little oil.

With that problem solved, we drove to the library. The outside walls always seemed so bland, like the white shell of an egg. Yet once inside, it was as colorful and exciting as a circus come to town.

We passed through the gates to this palace of knowledge and the cool air and quiet hit us like a brick wall.

In front of me were an endless amount of shelves, holding a thousand times more books. I went to the card catalogue, the master brain of the place.

I was always looking for a specific book, and soon found out where it was located. It was on a shelf down one of the vast corridors created by the many outrageous ideas put into print by many authors. As I walked down this corridor, I felt a million eyes watching me, beckoning me to enter their world. I stood fast, using all my willpower to avoid those eyes. Yet, as I walked on, I felt I could no longer resist. I turned to face many book titles. At first I just gazed with longing. Then a feeling of jealousy seized me. What if when I came back, someone else had them? What if they were gone, or lost? I wished I could live there and guard these books. There was always so much I wanted to read.

Abruptly the scene changed, as my mother appeared.

"Anita, are you ready to leave yet? We've been here almost two hours."

(Anita writes with flair and imagination, using a rich vocabulary for someone her age. She turns a visit to the library into an adventure. She accomplishes this with a slightly inflated style that forces us to see the library in a new way. In the process. she reminds us of the excitement of reading, that we don't have to visit an amusement park to experience an exciting day.)

• • •

Stacey •
By Janet McKay (seventh grade)

I'm sure just about everybody has had a visitor come to his or her house at one time or another. I'm sure though, they haven't been as different as the one I had. It was on the 21st of July that she came.

I got up at 6:00 in the morning. My family and I left for the airport at 6:30. I had butterflies in my stomach. I don't know why. If there was anybody to be scared or nervous, it was our visitor, Stacey Elizabeth McKay. Her real name is Kim Mee Kyung, but we felt she should have an American name considering the fact that we were sponsoring her for six months and may even adopt her. Also, because she was living with us for awhile, she had to have our last name. Mee Kyung McKay didn't seem to fit. Stacey was abandoned on the streets of Korea about nine months ago and taken to a local Korean orphanage. No one knows who her parents are, where they are, or if she has any living relatives at all.

We arrived at the airport at 7:00. The plane was scheduled to come in at 7:22. A lady who had already adopted four Korean children had come to meet and help us. My whole family was by the gate with big smiles waiting for her arrival. I had a doll ready to give to her.

A long line of people started coming out of the plane.

Finally, at the end of the line, I saw a little figure in a green dress with big white polka dots and about forty-two inches high coming out of the plane. She had short black hair and dark brown eyes, which were very big for a Korean. She was very skinny and had little bowed legs with scars on them. In addition to that, she didn't even speak English.

The first thing Stacey did when she got off the plane was throw up. We then had her sit in a chair for a little while, so she could rest. When she felt better, she started running all around the airport terminal looking through windows and checking everything out. That minute we knew she was curious.

She was having a great time on the way home except for the fact that she threw up again in the car.

When we got home, the first thing Stacey did was take off her shoes. She wouldn't move until she took off her shoes. In fact, a couple of hours later my dad wanted to take Stacey outside to play on our swing set. Stacey put on her shoes and was ready to go outside, but my dad wanted to go out the back door which meant she had to walk across the house with her shoes on. So Stacey got on her hands and knees and crawled across the kitchen to the back door with her feet off the floor so they wouldn't touch. We assumed this was a Korean custom.

When Stacey came back inside she watched T.V., looked at books, and drew pictures the rest of the morning. Boy, could she draw pictures. The adoption agency told us she was five and a half, but from the mature handwriting she had and the fact that she had a lot of permanent teeth for a five and a half year old, we knew she had to be about six and a half.

For lunch we had soup and rice. My dad and I had the soup. We gave Stacey the rice. About one minute after we started eating, Stacey put her spoon in my soup, took a taste, and decided she wanted some Manhattan Clam Chowder. Then she put a little bit of soup on her rice and boy, did she like that. She had orange Gatorade to drink and tried putting it on the rice. She didn't think too much of that. Then she got the idea to pour the soup all over the rice and mix it up like they do at Japanese restaurants.

The second day my mom and I took Stacey to Belk Lindsey to get clothes. The only clothes she came with were the clothes on her back consisting of a dress, socks, and shoes. We got her a bathing suit, a dress, and a couple of shorts outfits just so she would have more than one thing to wear. After shopping for clothes, we went to a house where a Korean couple lives. We wanted the lady to ask Stacey some questions and tell her some things. We had the lady to tell Stacey in Korean that she would be going to school, camp actually, but then she was coming back home. These Korean orphans have been to so many places, it's hard to know whom to trust. She might have been afraid that she wasn't coming back home. Stacey had some Korean books that we showed to the lady. They had some writing in them and we wanted to know what it said. Stacey didn't respond to the lady at all. The books, the language, and the questions brought back a lot of bad memories for Stacey, so she cried. Crying was good for her though.

As the days pass, Stacey and my family grow closer and closer. She's picking up the language rapidly. She can already read and write the words: Mommy, Daddy, Janet, and Stacey. Mommy is her favorite word. She's learned to say, "Thank you and you're welcome." She also learned that it's OK to wear your shoes in the house. We'll have problems, of course, but Stacey's a survivor and no matter what happens, she'll keep on living.

(This story represents the very best work I have received since my work with children began in 1980. I read it over and over and enjoy it more with each reading. The story is an uplifting one, and Janet tells it with compassion but without sentimentality. There is an honesty in her voice that reflects a caring young person who writes very well.)

• • •

A Pain in the Foot •
By Bonnie Harris (seventh grade)

It was a very hot Saturday afternoon when it happened. My friend, Molly, and I decided to go to the beach. When we got there, we rolled out a blanket and set out the cooler. It was so hot, her mom made us put on tons of sunscreen that smelled like coconuts. Then we decided to go swimming. The thing I hate about sea water is that I don't know where I'm stepping.

At first we just clowned around, being carried out by the waves and trying to swim to the sandbar. Then, just to scare Molly, I pretended that I had stepped on something. I screamed and jumped back. Molly screamed too, and swam away while I laughed hysterically. She became furious!!

Then, when we were only a few feet away from the sandbar, I really did step on something. It was hard, and had sharp spikes on it. My foot hurt so bad, I screamed and told Molly I cut my foot.

For some reason, Molly didn't believe me. She laughed right in my face and said, "You're not going to fool me *again!*"

I was in such pain, I had to drag her to the sandbar where I could stand up. I lifted up my foot. There was a big slice right on the bottom and blood was gushing everywhere. Molly's eyes were so big, I thought they'd pop out!

She helped me swim to shore, telling me to hold my foot up in the air to keep the blood from attracting sharks. That almost made me faint.

At shore, I limped over to her mom, who let out a sort of gasp when she saw my now blood-covered foot. There was a trail of blood all the way down the beach where I had been walking.

My foot hurt real bad, but I had learned my lesson. Now I knew how "The Boy Who Cried Wolf" felt!

(This story is typical of Bonnie's work, an interesting narrative, funny, detailed, and tightly focused. Her lead cleverly foreshadows her accident. The detail about the shark adds humor at just the right point. Her writing appeals to our senses: we can see the blood, hear the screams, and even smell the suntan oil.)

● ● ●

The Best Hike I've Ever Taken •
By Katrina Clark (seventh grade)

Last summer my family and I took an unforgetable trip to Tennessee. We stayed in a friend's house that was isolated on a mountain. It was surrounded by woods which gave it an eerie yet exciting feeling.

One day my father was looking at a trail guide map that showed many hikes you could take through the woods. He thought the thirteen mile hike up Mount LeConte and back down sounded like a good one. My mother, brother, and I all agreed so we decided to take it.

We had to drive for about 45 minutes to the place where it began. When we got there, there was a sign at the beginning of the trail that said "Mount LeConte—13 mile hike." "We're in the right place," my dad said, "Let's go!" We got our walking sticks out of the trunk of the car and started out.

The first part of the hike was pretty flat and followed a cool mountain stream. There were many log bridges across it as part of the trail. The woods were so peaceful—all we heard was the wind rustling the leaves on the trees and the soft roar of the rushing stream. As the trail got steeper it got more narrow and rocky. We began to get into some fog. The air felt thick and humid. The stream began to sound distant. We climbed a little higher and came to a steep cliff where the path was only about a foot and a half wide—we were lucky we had a handrail! From this point we could see "The Eye of the Needle" which is a rocky mountain with a hole all the way through the top of it.

We kept hiking up, up, up! We kept seeing signs of where bears had been along the trail but we still hadn't seen any bears!

We finally reached the top and went to the lodge office. It was about 12:30 then. We bought some candy bars and checked where we were and how far we had to go.

We then began walking down the rocky path. We were glad that the path going down was a shorter route than the path going up. In another half an hour we decided to stop for lunch. We sat on a log a little ways off the path where we had a beautiful view of the other mountains around us.

They were a dark green color with a few patches here and there of houses. They became a more grayish-green toward the top where the clouds made them look as if they could just fade away. It was really a beautiful sight!

We soon finished and were on our way down the mountain again when we began to see many marks on the trees from where bears had been so we kept watching for them the rest of the hike.

The trail began to get very narrow because we were walking along a ridge. We still had a long ways to go when it started to rain. At first it was just sprinkling but soon it began to pour. We were all uncomfortably wet and muddy by the time it finally stopped. The trail soon began to widen as we got closer to the end. We got out of the thick fog and it began to get very hot and sunny. By this time we could finally hear the soft roar of the stream again.

My feet were beginning to hurt and the trail was just getting steeper and rockier. The roar of the stream continuously but gradually kept getting louder. Soon the trail got a lot better and we began to be able to see the stream.

When we finally got down to the stream the trail turned away from it and got a lot wider. There was absolutely no breeze what-so-ever but overhead I heard some rustling in the trees. All of a sudden I saw a mother bear with two cubs!

"Hey, Dad! Look at the bears!" I shouted as I pointed to where they were.

"All right, Katrina! You found some bears! That really makes the whole hike!" he exclaimed. We stood there just watching them for a while. They were eating leaves and climbing around. Pretty soon one of the cubs started to climb down and we could hear it's mother scolding him. It was so cute!

It was getting pretty late so we left the bears behind as we walked on. In about 15 minutes we came to the end, got in the car and drove home.

When we got back I took off my shoes, flopped on my bed and just thought about the whole hike. I knew right away that it was the best hike that I'd ever taken.

(By the seventh grade Katrina had already published a short story in *Stone Soup*, a literary magazine for children. I encouraged her to tap her own experience for some nonfiction stories. The sighting of the bears provides a perfect climax to a richly detailed and descriptive narrative.)

• • •

Newfound Companions •
By Kristin Klinkenberg (eighth grade)

Mr. and Mrs. Barts sit in the lobby, waiting for us. When they see Alison and me, they quickly call out, "Here come our rays of sunshine!"

Outside there's a fountain with crystal clear water flowing from it. There are flowers, beautiful ones, arranged neatly in rows. The one-story modern building is the home of some very special friends.

Sunny Shores is a nursing home, a place where senior citizens live when they need constant care. I work there as a volunteer. I walk with them, talk with them, laugh with them, and cry with them.

As I walk in, Kim pushes "play" on a tape recorder. It fills the room with peppy music and a woman's voice filled with energy, explaining how to exercise properly. The residents have crowded into the lobby of the health center to exercise.

I pass the exercisers and head straight for Florence's room with my friend Alison, the other volunteer, with me. Florence is one of my favorite persons there. I remember the first time Alison and I walked into her room. She said, "Wanna talk about boys?" Florence is a very sweet 93-year-old woman. She is very funny, too.

A little while later we find ourselves walking down the halls with Nora, who's holding her walker up to her chest. Quickly she puts it down when a nurse passes. "Nora," I ask, "why do you use a walker when you walk fine?"

"Well," she answered, "the nurses make me. See, I carry it, but when the nurses come, I put it down so they think I'm using it." We both laugh.

Mertyl sees us then, and calls us over. We go. She begins to sing, "Take me out to the ball game. ..."

Thinking back, I can recall when I got the job. My mom suggested I call Sunny Shores, the nursing home where *Cocoon* was filmed. But I couldn't. I was too embarrassed to call and see if I could be a volunteer worker. So Mom ended up calling. The answer she passed to me was negative. Kim, the activity director was to check with the administrators. The next day Kim called and said to be there at 10:00 A.M. Monday morning. I got the job!

Monday morning I was a wreck! I was nervous and scared. I kept thinking, "What if they die when I'm there?" But now I'm not scared, because I love these people. They're my friends, and I'm theirs!

(Writing teaches values, to both the writer and the reader. Here Kristin shares with readers her experiences as a volunteer in a nursing home. Through description and anecdote she invites us to meet the interesting characters who populate Sunny Shores. More important, Kristin is willing to share her anxieties—about undertaking a new experience and about confronting death, sadness, and regret. One result of this story was that other students in the class became interested in the possibility of doing volunteer work in nursing homes.)

• • •

Bruce •
By Alison Clark (eighth grade)

I just couldn't believe it! It was fabulous. A six-hour drive in a little yellow Datsun, but it was worth it. I finally got to see Bruce Springsteen in concert.

The drive up to Tallahassee was not bad at all. The time went by surprisingly fast. I drove up with my dad and his friend. When we got to the hotel, Kristin and her parents had already arrived. We checked into the Holiday Inn and I got changed in our room.

There were about fifteen people in our group that were going to see Bruce with us. We were all hungry so we decided to grab a bite before the concert. We went to a Chinese restaurant that was around the corner from the hotel. I was a little too excited to eat fortune cookies and wonton but I got it down okay.

After everyone was done eating, we started to walk to the Tallahassee Civic Center. It was only a one-mile walk, but it seemed more like a one-hundred mile walk.

We finally reached the civic center, gave the man our tickets, and found our seats. I was absolutely astonished at how close I was to the stage. The fifth row! It was out-rageous. The concert was supposed to start at 7:30 but you know how all rock stars are. They love to keep their fans in suspense.

Finally, at 8:30, all of the lights went out and everyone started to yell Bruce. It sounded something like this: Bru-u-u-u-ce! I loved it. Then out of nowhere I heard 1-2-3-4! Everyone jumped on their chairs and bright lights came on. I was totally dumbfounded. Bruce was wearing a white T-shirt, a denim vest jacket, and blue jeans. He was dancing on the amplifiers and I could have sworn he winked at me. The concert had started. I was so excited. It was tremendously loud but I enjoyed it.

He sang and sang. He finally sang my favorite song, "Thunder Road." That was the last song of the first set. Right before the break or intermission he said something that made the audience anxious for the second half to start. He said, "We have not yet begun to rock." It made me melt.

About twenty minutes later, he came back on and played until about 12:30. The smell of the air was unusual but I finally figured it out. It was a mixture of pot and beer. Whew! What a smell. Try putting up with that for four hours straight.

When the concert was over I wasn't sure whether I was happy or sad. Happy that I finally got to see Bruce or sad that it was all over. Well, figuring out my feelings wasn't half as bad as figuring out our way home. Kristin, my dad, my dad's friend and I went in one direction and the others in our group went another. But luckily, we had my dad and his keen sense of direction. Walking around at 1:15 A.M., in a strange city not knowing where you are in 55 degree weather is not what I call a great ending to a great day. Luckily there was a Domino's Pizza place open and he gave us the correct directions on how to get back to the hotel. At 2:30 in the morning, we spotted the Holiday Inn. I was so glad.

All of the adults wanted to go out and party so I slept in Kristin's hotel room. We were a little nervous about being left alone in a hotel room but we were okay.

I was woken up at 8:00 in the morning by Kristin's mom. Thinking I was at Kristin's house, I sat up slowly, opened my eyes slowly, got out of bed slowly, and realized I was still in Tallahassee, and the night before I had actually seen Bruce Springsteen.

(Alison captures the fun and excitement of her trip to see rock star Bruce Springsteen. It might be instructive for readers to compare this story with the one Alison wrote about her trip to New York City (page 223). Alison was nine years old when she wrote about New York, and almost thirteen when she wrote about Springsteen, so it should not surprise anyone to see her mature in her writing style. Her story on Springsteen is superior in its use of detail, its coherent structure, and its narrative development. Transitions are tighter and more logical. And yet I can hear Alison's voice in both stories. Alison is a different child at thirteen than she was at nine. Yet both stories sound like Alison, at least to me, her father.)

● ● ●

My Mother ●
By Nedra Williams (eighth grade)

My mother and I share alot of things. We share our secrets, feelings, clothes and just about everything. We go shopping, together, (for clothes) to the movies together, to the park. (on usually picnics) and to the grocery store too. She is a very warm-hearted person, always thinking of others first. She would rather miss her dentists appointment than miss her children's school play. And on hot days she would have some nice cold lemonade, or sometimes tea made. When me and my sister walked through the door after coming from a long day at school. On weekends she would ask me do I a couple of friends that would like to come over and have some take out pizza or someone who could stayed the night or weekend. She is also very brave, like when the doctor told her she would have to come into the hospital to take some test because the first one showed that she had lukemia. Yes, she had lukemia and took it very well. And when it got to a point that she had to stay in the hospitol, not one tear fell from her eyes. She was a brave woman. A woman who had big dreams for her children, and only wished good things to other people. And now she is gone. But she will always be in my heart. Always.

(The use of the present tense through most of this story helps Nedra create a sense of her mother's spiritual presence. The story shifts to the past tense in the sentence where we learn that her mother "had lukemia." From that point on, as the reader comes to realize that Nedra has lost her mother, the story becomes poignant. Nedra's experiment with time continues in the final two sentences, written in the future tense, symbolic of the eternal nature of the relationship between mother and daughter. Nedra has crafted, unselfconsciously, a narrative on spiritual love. The mechanical problems in this draft do not detract significantly from the power of the narrative, but they should be solved in subsequent drafts so that readers can appreciate this moving story without distraction.)

Chapter Seventeen

Teachers at Work

You can learn a certain amount about tennis or cooking or romance from reading books, but the key to expertise is in three simple words: practice, practice, practice. So it is with the teaching of writing. Teacher Lynn Holloway remembers that her reading of Donald Graves's *Writing* had little direct effect on her teaching until she had the opportunity to observe teachers practicing the techniques and then struggled herself to put them into practice. Graves's book, or this book, or any book is only a window to the world of teaching writing. True reform comes through being brave, rolling up the sleeves, and working with students.

I read Donald Murray's work but only came to understand the conference technique when I watched Murray in action. Murray addressed a group of journalists and asked them to spend a few minutes writing on a topic of their choice. He went around the table systematically, asking the writers questions that helped them make important decisions about their work. Over and over he would ask: "What do you think about that? Anything there surprise you? What will you do next?" I carefully timed him and was shocked to realize that in no case did he spend more than ninety seconds with any writer.

In the following weeks, with both professionals and students, I tried the technique myself. I would read the work of the writer, ask questions, try to take advantage of the writer's knowledge, and make useful observations. By watching other teachers and by reading, I grew in confidence. I also became more efficient as a teacher and my students became more proficient in their writing.

Any effort at reform within a school or school system must involve programs to retrain teachers. Administrators can change textbooks, develop innovative curricula, and mandate new systems of teaching for teachers at every level, but change that begins at the top and filters down to students risks being resented, misunderstood, or ignored by teachers in the inner sanctum of their classrooms. For reform to be both pervasive and effective, it must be generated from where the action is: in classrooms directed by talented teachers who are dedicated to the teaching of writing and hungry for new ideas on how to do the job better.

Good teachers lead by example. They create an enthusiastic atmosphere that carries beyond their own classroom and infects the entire school. Their students exceed what is expected of them. Parents become curious about "what is going on in that classroom." Other teachers visit to learn some new tricks. Good teachers form the core of teaching excellence around which can rally all those who want to improve.

In an era when the public seems so collectively depressed about the state of education in America, it is encouraging to hear a different kind of testimony from outstanding teachers who are accomplishing wonderful things in their classrooms.

- Mary Osborne (fifth grade): "It's really working. I had an LD [Learning Disabled] student who was writing well. We asked the LD teacher if she could write during her LD class. I've since looked at her folder, and she has ten stories which she typed herself. I let the LD teacher work in my class so she could learn how to confer with the student. . . . When my principal saw the improved scores of my students on the standardized tests he came to me and said, 'Keep doing that writing stuff.' "
- Mary Ann Adams (sixth grade): "I took all the stories the students had written about themselves and put them in the back of the classroom. Each period, children from another class would go back there and read them. . . . Even the basic skills kids enjoy the conferences. One boy comes to me and wants to write; one girl has written a story and wants to send it to *Guideposts.*"
- Peg Brown (seventh grade): "I feel good about what's happening. The parents are responding well. Our stories are posted in the media center, and all the kids are running to read them. . . . One girl writes a paper that was

the snobbiest thing I'd ever read, about how leaving Connecticut and coming to Florida was the worst thing that could happen to her. She read her paper to the class and said 'I don't like that paragraph. I sound like such a snob.' I felt so relieved."

- Nancy Lombardi (seventh grade): "Everything I've done has been successful. I teach two regular, three basic, and one advanced class. I'm doing exactly the same things with all my classes. My regular classes were whispering in the hallways that they were asked to do something very important."

- Sue Doerr (eighth grade): "A high school English teacher was at a teacher training workshop we conducted. He was so turned on by our enthusiasm for the program that he has tried the techniques successfully with his own students."

- Ruth Harris (seventh grade): "The basic students usually are hard to discipline, but they really enjoy the writing. They want to write. They spend the period working and find that the time has gotten away from them."

- Pam Powell (eighth grade): "The school newsletter is starting a new page to publish student writing. . . . Children are communicating enthusiasm to other teachers, who are showing interest in the techniques. Some teachers who used to accept one-word answers on tests and homework are now encouraging students to respond in complete sentences."

- Mardi Weiskopf (elementary reading specialist): "Each class published a book. They took their books around to other classes to read from them. The children just loved it."

- Pat Stanton (fifth grade): "Joey was a writer who would vacillate between two and three sentences. A series of conferences led to some breakthroughs. The first good story he wrote was about his beer can collection. He had one beer can that was fifty years old. . . . Joey came up with a story about seven paragraphs long on Halloween. It was indented. It had transitions. "Joey, this is so fantastic," I said. He said, "Don't take any of the credit, I had my conference with Philip [another student]." That was an important moment. I knew it doesn't have to be me. Now our fifth-grade students are having conferences with the kindergarten kids. And we just received a grant to get a computer. Kids can type stories into the computer and we'll be able to generate five copies from the printer."

- Bob Drafahl (fourth grade): "We had some people in the school come in and talk to the kids. The guidance counselor came in with all her equipment and talked about her experiences. The children listened and took notes and asked her questions. When she left they gave her a great ovation. It was an ego-building experience for her. I've already talked to the head custodian. I think kids should learn an appreciation for people on the school staff. My students, who read on the second-grade level, who never wrote one sentence, are now writing lengthy stories."

What these teachers share, along with their enthusiasm for teaching, is the experience of a program in St. Petersburg called "Writers' Camp." The camp is a collaborative learning experience for young students, public school teachers, and professional writers and editors.

Training programs such as the Bay Area Writing Project out of Berkeley, California, and The New Hampshire Writing Program have helped thousands of teachers across the country learn and share new techniques in the teaching of writing. Such programs begin with the premise that teachers should write to understand what a writer feels and how a writer works. These feelings and techniques can then be communicated to the student. Teachers trained this way can make their own classrooms a learning laboratory for any other teacher who wants to learn the process.

The idea is a noble one. It has what James Gray of the Bay Area project would describe as a "bottom up" philosophy. It assumes that good teachers want to improve their skills and that they can become leaders in their craft. The system grows from within, building achievement upon achievement.

Writers' Camp takes that concept and moves it one step further. In the summer of 1983, The Poynter Institute and the Pinellas County School System brought together eleven teachers, who worked together every day for a month to learn from each other. The teachers wrote every day, conferred with each other, discussed the writing process in all its parts, read their stories aloud, received more criticism, and rewrote and revised their work. By the end of the month, the teachers, once afraid of writing, felt much more comfortable and confident. Writing was no longer a mystery to them, since they were performing every day. At the beginning they would say things like, "Do we really have to do this?" or "Would someone please pass the Maalox?" Behind their nervous laughter was a special teacherly anxiety and fear of failure.

Four weeks of writing changed the nature of their conversation. Suddenly one could overhear talk about finding story ideas, strategies for collecting information, rehearsing stories in one's head, finding a focus, developing and organizing stories, editing and revising. During the month, teacher Sue Doerr became a hero by getting her story published on the op-ed page of the *St. Petersburg Times.*

That writing time together was special time, but it represented only a third of our six-hour day. For it is one thing to understand the writing process, and it is another to teach it. The key ingredient to the success of the program was the addition of thirty interesting young writers, ages nine to thirteen.

If you are a fifth grader, live on the west coast of Florida, and happen to be interested in dance, theater, computers, or art, there have been places you could go to cultivate your skills. If you happened to be hooked on writing, there was no place—until Writers' Camp. Each year now, the camp attracts scores of applications from talented young writers in the community. These are children who can write without teachers but who also appreciate the nurturing help of supportive adults.

Each teacher works in a group with three or four students. For three hours in the morning, they write together, conduct individual and group conferences, read each other's work, and share their writing with the whole class.

In this intensive, intimate environment, teachers come to understand what motivates students to excellent work and how the young writer develops, or fails to develop. The teacher considers each draft and each revision, reads it carefully and critically with the student, and asks questions that will inspire the student to perfect the work.

The teacher also confronts her own challenging questions. How can I identify the major problem in this story? How can I help this student generate good story ideas? What questions and observations are most helpful to this writer? These tiny clusters of writers at Writers' Camp became laboratories for students and teachers alike.

The successes of Writers' Camp grow out of its safe, supportive environment, which allows teachers to study young writers and try some new tricks, and provides opportunities that may

Writers' Camp teams writing teachers with small groups of students. In these clusters teachers can observe and study the work and behavior of young writers. Teachers write with students and confer with them. In such a special atmosphere teachers can practice new techniques of writing and teaching. They can learn how young writers work and, with the support of other teachers, they gain the confidence to try new strategies with regular classes during the school year.

be impossible in a regular classroom setting. Sitting in a small circle of desks with rotating groups of three or four children, teachers gain a special perspective on how students write and learn. The teachers:

- Observe children when they write and when they do not write.
- Watch them revise or resist revision.
- Observe how children organize their desks and materials.
- Watch how they develop in the learning of new skills, such as interviewing and notetaking.
- Write with students.
- Confer with them on their stories.
- Confer with them on the teacher's own stories.
- Encourage them to confer with each other.

- Study their behavior as they share each other's work.
- Experiment with a variety of conferring techniques. Make good mistakes that lead to new insights in a safe environment.
- Analyze how students grow through daily writing.
- Confront difficult problems that can be solved with help from other teachers.
- Compare and contrast a student's performance and behavior with that of others in the group.
- Analyze body language and other signs of students' attitudes.
- Help students discover story ideas.
- Analyze how students read their own work.
- Learn whether mistakes are made out of ignorance or carelessness.
- Learn to what extent students can find and correct their own mistakes.
- Teach mini-lessons on style, grammar, and spelling.
- Help students select and prepare their work for publication.
- Consider the classroom environment and configurations of furniture that help writers do their best work.
- Learn which teacher responses give writers confidence, and which do not.
- Get to know the students as persons.
- Rehearse how these new strategies and insights can be applied to daily teaching.

When the students leave at noon, the teachers begin making sense of the morning session. They share problems and triumphs and consider applications of the camp experience to the practice of daily teaching in the public schools. They have specific and important questions:

- How much writing should students do every day?
- How many brief conferences can a teacher conduct in a single class?
- How often should a teacher confer with a single student?
- How often should teachers attempt to publish the work of students in one form or another?
- When should students find their own topics and when should they receive assignments?

- How do you build writing instruction into a fairly rigid middle school curriculum?
- How do you teach writing to 160 students in six sections?
- How do you motivate good students to rewrite when they are convinced their work is finished and perfect?
- How do you get a shy or insecure writer to share her work with the class?
- What if a student is unwilling to rewrite?
- What if other teachers in your school are giving writing as punishment?

I try to answer these questions as thoughtfully as I can, but better answers usually come from the collective consideration of the teachers themselves. It gets easier in the second year of the program, for then we let new teachers in the program mix with a team of teachers who have spent a year applying the principles of Writers' Camp to daily teaching. The more experienced teachers bring their enthusiasm, tempered with realism, into the discussion. They testify that most of the problems are solved in the simple act of freeing students to write regularly, asking questions and making observations that help them improve, and turning control of the writing back to students. They have also cultivated a canny political sensibility that makes them good advocates for their students and lobbyists for resources.

Both students and teachers benefit from sharing another perspective, that of the professional writer and editor. Jeff Klinkenberg, a writer with the *St. Petersburg Times,* visited the camp with his editor Bob Silver. They described for the group the secrets of interviewing, notetaking, lead writing, organizing, and revising.

Jeff displayed a series of computer printouts revealing the evolution and revision of one of his stories. He showed students where he had crossed out a word, made additions, and drawn arrows and asterisks in the margin for emphasis. Through such contact with professionals, students and teachers come to understand that they are part of a larger communion of writers. "I thought I was the only one who did that," said a teacher, of one particular writing quirk. "How comforting to learn that it is a 'professional technique.' "

Contact with journalists inspires students to move away from superimaginative stories in which writers take little responsibility for information. Students come to camp writing about spaceships or Dungeons and Dragons and leave writing about their experiences and observations. If they do write fiction, it springs from research or reporting. On the first day Lydia writes about unicorns, but after a month she is writing about her hearing aids and her father, who is an audiologist. Dalia begins writing about leprechauns and winds up writing about how her father became a rabbi.

The editors bring another skill to the camp: the process of critical reading. They inspire writers and teachers to read stories with great care, to diagnose problems, and to build on strengths. Students learn to read their own writing well and to ask the tough questions that make good revisions possible: Should I change this word for emphasis? Is this sentence repetitious? Is my meaning clear? Through writing, students become better readers in a single month.

● ● ●

It is one o'clock on a hot July afternoon in St. Petersburg. The temperature and humidity both transcend 90, but the Writers' Camp teachers are cool in room 207 of Bayboro Hall at the University of South Florida. The students have left for the day, and the teachers are doing some troubleshooting, trying to figure out ways to help students in their work.

Wendy will not finish a story. She is not selective enough in her choice of materials, so good and bad material comes bleeding out. She is frustrated by her inability to finish. It's as if she were running a marathon instead of a mile race. (Strategy: Wendy's teacher will help her focus on a single short piece and not allow her to drift from story to story. The goal is to let Wendy feel a sense of completion from having finished and published a story.)

The good news about Maria is that she is willing to work hard to improve her stories. She is also a daring writer, eager to try out new techniques and open to criticism and suggestions. The bad news is that she gabs a lot, wants lots of attention, and seeks out dozens of conferences in a given week. (Strategy: Separate Maria from a friend she likes to gab with. Try to engage her energies in stories and projects that go beyond the ordinary. Praise her during any sustained period of quiet work.)

Martha is a strong student who wants a lot of praise all the time, who declares that every story is perfect and "absolutely finished," and who resists efforts to get her to rewrite. (Strategy: It is obvious that Martha has been praised in the past for good work but not challenged to exceed it. Her teacher will be persistent, and will praise any effort at revision that Martha tries. Publication of her very best work will be the goal set before her.)

Robby has a short attention span, is not dutiful on most stories, and in teachers' lingo is difficult to keep "on task." He brings books and games with him to the class and finds ways to play with them. He has an engaging personality that makes it possible for him to develop complicated schemes for avoiding work. (Strategy: To match his attention span, Robby will be given one small task at a time to accomplish. The writing of the story will be broken up into concrete, specific, manageable jobs. The teacher will recruit older students to oversee Robby's work and to keep him on the job.)

Dwayne keeps his hand raised for ten minutes seeking a conference. He is a frustrating child to work with. He writes long narratives and is unwilling to make any decisions on his own about what to rewrite. He wants you to tell him what to do, and when you do, he complains and rejects your requests. I had dozens of fruitless conferences with him. (Strategy: Because he writes at such length, he may resist efforts to get him to rewrite because he fears the consequences of having to "write it over again." For him Writers' Camp has become writer's cramp. So his teacher will help him brainstorm ideas for short poems and stories, small units of writing that he can better revise and manage.)

We teachers observe students' work habits and notice other quirks: Willie likes to sit over in a corner, away from the crowd, to do his best work; unwilling to share her work, Heidi hides it when anyone approaches her desk; Doreen has beautiful hand-writing and is unwilling to "ruin" her neat page by crossing out, but will only erase.

Even though the teachers of Writers' Camp work with what most people would describe as "good students," nothing ever goes smoothly. In fact, most teachers find work with such students the most challenging kind of writing instruction. With weaker students the goal of instruction may be obvious: to get a student who writes nothing to write a sentence, or to get the student who writes a sentence to write a paragraph.

A much more complicated transaction takes place when the teacher seeks to take a good paper by a skilled child, with a stronger ego, and help raise it to a new level of excellence. Too often, the work of our best students is ignored, just as the work of top reporters in American newsrooms does not get the editorial attention it deserves. At Writers' Camp, teachers demand that students strive for the best.

The teachers themselves gain confidence from adversity. They want their students to write well every time, but they know that is impossible. They know it because when they themselves write, they have good days and bad. All failures lead to revisions that lead to more failures that lead to revisions that result in publication. The process ends more often in redemption than in perfection.

● ● ●

Veteran eighth-grade teacher Bette Reddick prepared to read her story "The Poem" to the other teachers of Writers' Camp. Bette had more confidence than many teachers when it came to sharing her writing. She knew she had something important to say, and she read her story in a clear voice:

The Poem
I saw her today, stooped and bent with time. She looked up as I passed, gave a nod, then turned and went inside. There was no sign of recognition, and she had, no doubt, long since put the incident aside. But I once more remembered, and once more tried to forgive, wondering how it might have been if only she had been kind—if only she had said, "This is nice, my dear." If she had, I might have taken my precious sheet of paper with its carefully sought-out words and returned to my desk proud and happy, never to think of it again.

"You are to write a poem," she had said. "What? Oh, on anything that comes to mind."

I was thoughtful for awhile, then slowly—ever so slowly I began to see the crowd, the waiting, the anticipation. "It's coming!" someone shouted. "I hear it!" cried another. "It's coming! And listen—they're playing Stars and Stripes Forever!"

There was no doubt, my poem had to be about a parade. I could see the people as they stretched their necks to catch a glimpse as it made its way down Main Street. At last, it would come into view and at its head would be the Flag, the American Flag, with its colors of red and white and blue waving to and fro. Then I pictured a man, one man among the crowd, who felt the stirrings of pride and patriotism at the sight and carefully and reverently removed his hat and held it in his hands until the strains of the music lessened and the Colors disappeared from view.

It was not unusual to select such a theme, for in those days we were taught patriotism and love for one's country. Nor was it unusual to have a parade. In a town of that size there were always parades. A parade on Labor Day, a parade on Memorial Day, on Arbor Day, the Fourth of July and on any day that was deemed appropriate. So I worked diligently. No one must know its contents until that day when I placed it in her hands. The words came easily as I wrote, and at last it was ready. I decided then and there that if writing poems were as easy as this, I would write hundreds of them, for this was bliss for me—sheer bliss.

"All right, children," she said one day. Her look was stern and cold as always. She seldom smiled, and sometimes I wondered why. "You will each bring your poem to me when I call your name." She hoped we had done well and was certain she would enjoy them very much. "But continue with your work," she said, "while I take you one at a time."

I was excited, of course. I knew without a doubt that never had such a poem been written. It was difficult to add my numbers, and the letters in my reader were merely blurs. I was waiting for the sound of my name whence I would walk proudly to her desk and place the beloved poem in her hands. Surely she would smile and declare to all that this was the most marvelous poem she had ever read.

At last it came: my turn. I lifted the paper from my desk. Even the title was pure magic, "The Man with a Hat in His Hands." Oh, would that she saw him as I saw him, standing proud and firm. Would that she too could hear the strains of music and see the Flag in all its glory. Would that she could feel what the man and the crowd could feel as the band marched past and then disappeared from view.

When the final words were read, she looked at me. Her eyes were hard and cold. I can still remember standing there beside her desk wondering what must I have done wrong, wondering why she didn't like my poem. Then at last she said, *"You* could never have written *this* poem," and I watched as the pieces of the paper, torn and ragged, fluttered to the basket below.

Yes, I saw her today—that teacher of so long ago—bent and stooped with age. She had long since forgotten, but I, will I forget? Someday, perhaps. Yes, perhaps I will—someday.

The room was hushed as Bette neared the climax of her story, but when it came, Bette's voice cracked with emotion and she said, "I always cry when I come to that line." The line, of course, was *"You* could never have written *this* poem." Another teacher picked up the paper and finished the reading as Bette composed herself. After a moment of awkward silence, I finally blurted out what I was thinking: "Can't we find this woman and break her legs?!" Everyone agreed that would be a fit punishment for the torment she had inflicted on a little child trying to write a poem. The tears turned to laughter.

I keep a collection of newspaper stories, a genre called "outrage" stories, about educators who cannot write. Some of the stories reveal that experienced teachers have problems with spelling and simple grammar. I wish the writers and readers of these stories could have sat around our circle of teachers and listened to the wonderful, touching, funny stories composed by the teachers of Writers' Camp. Through the writing we became emotional and intellectual allies, revealing our fears, experiences, tragedies, and triumphs in the same way we would ask our students to do.

Jean Rutan wrote about her son's brush with death after he ran into a sliding glass door: "His hair was matted and his beautiful face covered with blood. His deepest injury was a four-inch gash which started just below his eyebrow and gaped ominously across his forehead and up beyond his hairline. He also had numerous cuts on his nose, lips, and ears."

Becky Reynolds told the story of how a field day turned into a tornado scare: "Above me, the clouds had turned into an array of grays, blues, and dark green in color. Looking up, I could see a thin, tail-like strand of cloud trailing beneath the mass of other clouds. That's when I began to panic."

Sue Doerr wrote about her divorce and traumatic move to a new city: "Twelve hundred miles later, I saw the same monstrous van in front of our new house. I looked again at the van and I cried. The girls, too young to understand Mommy's tears, helped me to hang the gold four-leaf clover over the front door. This time things will be better—won't they?"

Adrienne Mizia paid tribute to her old Italian grandmother: "Her ebony hair had turned silver, but her cheeks were always pink. Somehow, the rivers of age had nestled gently on her countenance, and served only to accent her beauty. Her hands revealed a deftness which paralleled her demeanor. I watched frequently and with great curiosity as her fingers prepared pasta al forno, rollatini of veal, and arancini with rice, some of my favorite dishes."

Kate Fullerton shared her affection for a fourth-grade punk rocker named Sara: "She taught all of us about jewelry and spikes, how to make hair stand on end, about Boy George and Duran Duran. But she also told and wrote mature, feeling, exciting and mysterious stories that kept all of us 'tuned-in' to what was Sara. But more than that, we all learned that what she wore or how she wore it made no difference. Sara had become an important part of every child's life, and mine. What could have been ongoing fear and ultimate disaster turned out to be daily joy: Sara."

The stories went on and on: about sick children, spoiled vacations, class reunions, about parents and students and teaching. All of us wanted to put our best work forward. We were writing teachers, after all, and were supposed to be good at this. But because we were writing teachers, we shared a peculiar vulnerability and anxiety. We wondered if the writing that our students might enjoy and learn from would pass muster with adults. No one ripped into anyone else's story. Instead, the conferences we had with each other were supportive and positive, and many helpful questions and ideas were passed along. These often inspired rethinking and revision. Out of fear, insecurity, and old-fashioned peer pressure, we unconsciously developed a system of mutual support and encouragement that became our best model for how we should treat our students.

● ● ●

The teachers of Writers' Camp have a series of meetings through the school year. They come together for dinners and discussions; they attend additional workshops on writing; they run workshops so that other teachers can share their successes; other teachers visit their classrooms; they train additional teachers in subsequent camps; they become the center of excellence within their schools; principals brag about them, students embrace them, parents fight to have children put in their classes; they work miracles with their worst students; they get grants and attract resources; they become the center of curriculum reform; the test scores of their students show dramatic increases.

The children of Writers' Camp return to their schools ablaze with writing enthusiasm. They become classroom leaders and lobby for opportunities to write; they get their schools interested in writing instruction; through leadership and example they help other students who want to write; they win writing awards and publish stories in the newspaper and become ambassadors of excellence for their schools.

The professional journalists who work with students and teachers do so for different reasons. They recognize a spiritual connection between the camp and their own values and experiences. They believe that newspapers have a vested interest in public literacy. They want to help teachers educate a new generation of newspaper readers, young citizens concerned about their world and their future. They also want to help create a new generation of writers, students who will want to grow into journalists and become the people who, through their courage and insight, lead this democracy into the next century.

Suggested Reading

I. On teaching children to write

Applegate, Mauree. *Easy in English: An Imaginative Approach to the Teaching of the Language Arts.* New York: Harper & Row, 1960. This book represents the best traditional thinking on how to teach writing to children. Applegate assumes that children are creative and imaginative and want to write. Each chapter is followed by a "cupboard of ideas" for teachers on how to motivate students.

Calkins, Lucy McCormick. *The Art of Teaching Writing.* Portsmouth, N.H.: Heinemann Educational Books, 1986. This work contains invaluable insights on teaching writing effectively, conferring with students, and teaching different forms of writing. Calkins shows how children change as writers through different grade levels.

————. *Lessons from a Child: On the Teaching and Learning of Writing.* Portsmouth, N.H.: Heinemann Educational Books, 1983. Calkins creates a microcosm of effective writing instruction by following a single child through her development as a writer. This book is especially valuable for its sharp focus.

Graves, Donald H. *Writing: Teachers and Children at Work.* Portsmouth, N.H.: Heinemann Educational Books, 1983. This is the one indispensable text on teaching writing to children. Teachers will find helpful advice on what to do the first day, how to respond to the work of children, how to confer, and how to publish the writing of students. Graves confronts the toughest questions teachers have about the teaching of writing.

Koch, Kenneth. *Wishes, Lies, and Dreams: Teaching Children to Write Poetry.* New York: Perennial Library, 1970. Koch offers teachers advice on getting children to think and write like poets. An introductory chapter describes technique, and the rest of the book exhibits some excellent work by children. Koch presents many useful ideas and forms for poems. A weakness of the book is that it does not involve teachers enough in the full process of conceiving and revising the work.

Neill, Shirley Boes. *Teaching Writing: Problems and Solutions.* Arlington, Va.: Education News Service for the American Association of School Administrators, 1982. Reading this report provides a rich overview of writing instruction in American schools, K–12. Neill offers numerous case studies of innovative school systems trying to teach writing more effectively. Teachers and administrators will find useful ideas on how to develop successful writing programs, on in-service training, on the evaluation of student work, and on the writing process. Neill conducts revealing interviews with Donald Graves, Donald Murray, and James Gray.

Newkirk, Thomas, and Atwell, Nancie, eds. *Understanding Writing: Ways of Observing, Learning & Teaching K–8.* Portsmouth, N.H.: Heinemann Educational Books, 1986. This collection contains helpful essays on the teaching of writing by experienced teachers in the New England area. Topics include prewriting activities, conference strategies, and connections between reading and writing. A good bibliography on writing and teaching concludes the work.

Temple, Charles A.; Nathan, Ruth G.; and Burris, Nancy A. *The Beginnings of Writing.* Boston: Allyn and Bacon, 1982. Teachers interested in how children can use invented spellings will find this text of particular interest.

II. On the writing process

Brande, Dorothea. *Becoming a Writer.* Los Angeles: J. P. Tarcher, Inc. Distributed by Houghton Mifflin. Reprint of 1934 edition published by Harcourt, Brace, New York. This rediscovered classic offers advice on how to think and work like a writer. Brande deals not with questions of technique, but with the problem of confidence. Written primarily for students of "creative writing," this book will help any teacher who wants to work with young writers. The late John Gardner has written an interesting foreword.

Elbow, Peter. *Writing Without Teachers.* New York: Oxford University Press, 1973. Elbow is the leading proponent of free writing as a way to let a story "cook" and "grow." Despite the title, this book offers teachers good advice on how to help students through the writing process. Elbow emphasizes how students learn from each other in small, collaborative groups.

Hall, Donald. *Writing Well.* 4th ed. Boston: Little, Brown, 1982. This college composition text stands out from the rest. Most important, it is splendidly written and filled with good advice for writers of all ages. Its author happens to be one of America's most versatile and prolific writers, a man who begins his writing day at 4 A.M. and who regularly produces fine poetry, criticism, children's literature, and journalism.

Macrorie, Ken. *Uptaught.* Rochelle Park, N.J.: Hayden Book Company, 1970. Macrorie's work inspired many teachers looking for new, more effective ways to teach writing. Macrorie describes his personal journey toward being a good teacher. Along the way he discovers many strategies for helping students become better writers.

Murray, Donald M. *Learning by Teaching: Selected Articles on Writing and Teaching.* Montclair, N.J.: Boynton/Cook, 1982. Murray has been a leading figure in the writing process movement since the 1960s. This book collects some of his most important essays on how writers work and how teachers help writers. Perhaps the most useful essay is "The Listening Eye: Reflections on the Writing Conference."

———. *Write to Learn.* New York: Holt, Rinehart and Winston, 1984. Designed for college students, this text takes the reader through the stages of the writing process: conceiving, collecting, focusing, ordering, drafting, and clarifying. Most interesting is the way in which Murray reveals his own writing process through the various stages of a story about his grandmother.

———. *A Writer Teaches Writing.* 2d ed. Boston: Houghton Mifflin, 1985. This book is a new version of a work Murray first published in 1968. Murray describes his growing awareness of how writers write and how successful teachers teach. Murray inspires both writers and teachers by his faith in them. Readers will enjoy Murray's willingness to be surprised by what he produces at his desk and what his students produce in the classroom.

Strunk, William, and White, E. B. *The Elements of Style.* 3d ed. New York: Macmillan, 1979. This short, inexpensive text is a standard of style and usage. It offers writers and students specific prescriptive advice on questions of writing and syntax. The book is more helpful for advanced students or professional writers than for beginners.

Taylor, Robert H., and Liebert, Herman W. *Authors at Work.* New York: The Grolier Club, 1957. Teachers can use this book to demystify writing for students. The book contains photographs of manuscript pages of famous writers, from John Locke to Dylan Thomas. The pages reveal the writers at work, showing the splendid dissatisfaction that leads to useful revision. When students see the messiness of these pages, they respond with approval and delight.

White, E. B. *Essays of E. B. White.* New York: Harper & Row, 1977. Teachers will enjoy the work of one of the great prose stylists of this century. Of particular interest is "The St. Nicholas League," written in December 1934. In this essay White describes the benefits of publication for children. He reveals how many famous American writers got their start on the children's pages of *St. Nicholas* magazine.

Zinsser, William. *On Writing Well.* Rev. ed. New York: Harper & Row, 1985. This popular guide to writing nonfiction is a narrative Strunk and White. An experienced writer and teacher, Zinsser reveals the secrets of a clean and clear prose style. Most helpful are two pages in which Zinsser shows how he removed "clutter" from his own writing.

III. On the craft of journalism

Clark, Roy Peter, and Fry, Donald, eds. *Best Newspaper Writing 1985.* St. Petersburg, Fla.: The Poynter Institute for Media Studies, 1985. This is the latest volume in an annual series that goes back to 1979. Each volume contains prize-winning newspaper stories. The editors comment critically on the stories and interview the writers.

Mencher, Melvin. *News Reporting and Writing.* 3d ed. Dubuque, Iowa: Wm. C. Brown Publishers, 1984. Mencher has written the best introductory text on how journalists think and work. Important advice on reporting, writing, and editing. Designed for college journalism students, the book will help anyone interested in writing and journalism.

Murray, Donald M. *Writing for Your Readers.* Chester, Conn.: The Globe Pequot Press, 1983. Murray is one of the few teachers whose influence extends from college classrooms into the nation's newsrooms. Here Murray describes what he learned from working with writers and editors at *The Boston Globe.* This book contains the best advice on how professional reporters and editors can use the writing process to their advantage.

Scanlan, Christopher, ed. *How I Wrote the Story.* Providence, R.I.: The Providence Journal Company, 1983. This collection of stories from the *Providence Journal-Bulletin* contains narrative accounts of how reporters conceived and executed their stories. These accounts reveal much about how talented journalists write. The second edition contains important insights on how good editors help writers do their best work.

IV. On children and literacy

Bettelheim, Bruno, and Zelan, Karen. *On Learning to Read: The Child's Fascination with Meaning.* New York: Vintage Books, 1981. This book reports on research about how children create meaning when they read. The authors pay particular attention to the "errors" that children make during reading and how these are often fraught with meaning. There are some provocative implications in this research for teachers of writing.

Friere, Paulo. *Pedagogy of the Oppressed.* New York: Continuum, 1970. Translated from the original Portuguese manuscript in 1968. This is a powerful, politically charged work by a Brazilian educator and philosopher. Freire's pedagogy grows out of his concern for the impoverished people of Brazil. He sees literacy as the essential liberating skill of every culture, a skill that allows people to inspect their world with a critical eye.

Postman, Neil. *The Disappearance of Childhood.* New York: Delacorte Press, 1982. This is the most provocative study on the contemporary plight of children. Postman analyzes advertising, the media, and popular culture and concludes that the electronic media have contributed to the disappearance of childhood as we know it. Postman's thesis, heavily influenced by the works of Marshall McLuhan, is a challenge to all teachers who believe in the careful nurturing of children.

Acknowledgments

Special thanks to teachers Joan Collins, Karen Kisten, Pearl Driver, and all the good people at Bay Point Elementary School and Bay Point Middle School who let me come and go as I pleased. Thanks to Margaret Howell and all the school administrators in Pinellas County for their support. Thanks to Pat Stanton, Janie Guilbault, Mary Osborne, and all the teachers of Writers' Camp.

Thanks to my colleagues and helpers at The Poynter Institute, a wonderful place to work. Adelaide Sullivan typed the manuscript and was the first person to declare it "good." Joyce Olson and Billie Keirstead provided great support in the preparation of the final versions of the manuscript. Mario Garcia offered expert advice on design. Jo Cates helped with the bibliography. Don Fry marked up pages, helped with revisions, and gave me much encouragement. The directors of the institute, first Don Baldwin and now Bob Haiman, applauded my efforts to work with young writers.

Thanks to the journalists at the *St. Petersburg Times,* the newspaper that published my first stories about teaching. Peter Gallagher gave me the idea to work with children. Ricardo Ferro took excellent photographs, and George Sweers gave good advice about their use. Tom French and Chip Scanlan were good friends and good listeners throughout the process. Jeff Klinkenberg offered his friendship, his time, and his excellent writing.

Thanks to my friends from New Hampshire. Donald Murray, the pope of good writing, gave me his blessing and, more important, helped me get the book in print. Donald Graves gave me crucial advice at key moments. Minnie Mae Murray gave me shelter from the storm.

Thanks to James Slevin of Georgetown University. Jim read the manuscript and convinced me to move things around. Thanks to Peter Meinke for sharing the early drafts of his poetry and fiction.

Thanks to the editors of Heinemann Educational Books. They believed in this book and made my job easier. Philippa Stratton gave me confidence and helped me make important decisions related to focus and emphasis. Donna Bouvier led me through the production process, listened to my ideas, and offered detailed criticism and advice, always helpful. Linda Howe copy-edited the manuscript and fixed hundreds of sentences. Maria Szmauz created an excellent design.

Thanks to my family, especially my parents, who have been trying to sell copies of the book months ahead of publication. Thanks to my wife, Karen, for everything.

Index

General Index

(An index of student writers is provided on pages 280–81.)

Index of Student Writers

Readers may want to use this index of student writers in various ways: to look up useful examples; to compare or contrast writers at the same grade level; to examine the work of different students writing on the same topic; or to track the development of individual writers (such as Bonnie Harris or Alison Clark) over a period of time.